Including Whistler & the Gulf Islands

Vancouver

The Ultimate Guide

Completely Revised and Updated • 5th Edition

Terri Wershler & Judi Lees

CHRONICLE BOOKS
SAN FRANCISCO

Fourth Chronicle Books edition published in the United States in 1996.

Published in Canada by Douglas & McIntyre, Vancouver

ISBN 0-8118-1095-X

Library of Congress Cataloging-in-Publication Data available.

Editing by Maja Grip and Nancy Flight
Cover design by Jill Jacobson
Front Cover photo by Bill Staley/Tony Stone Images
Text design by George Vaitkunas
Maps by David Gay and Barbara Hodgson
Map assistance by Brenda Code and Fiona MacGregor
Typeset by Vancouver Desktop Publishing Centre
Printed in Canada by D. W. Friesen and Sons Ltd.
Printed on acid-free paper

10 9 8 7 6 5 4 3 2 1

Chronicle Books
275 Fifth Street
San Francisco, CA 94103

Contents

List of Maps v

About Vancouver 1
The Look of the City, Getting Oriented, History,
Population, Weather, Major Industries

Essential Information 11
Emergency Phone Numbers, Major Hospitals, Motor Vehicles,
Travel Information, Public Holidays, Lost and Found,
Foreign Visitors, Banking, Churches and Synagogues, Sales Taxes,
Post Office, Late-Night Services, Babysitting, Liquor/Beer/Wine,
Radio, Television, Newspapers and Periodicals

Where to Stay 19
Hotels, Alternative Accommodation, Bed and Breakfast,
Trailer Parks/Campgrounds

Restaurants 39
Breakfast/Brunch, Bakery Cafés, Lunch, Seafood, Pizza, Vegetarian,
Late Night, Outdoors, With a View, Espresso Bars, By Nationality,
By Location

Getting Around 65
Public Transit, Coach Lines, Cars, Taxis, Limousine Service, Trains,
Ferries, Vancouver International Airport, Flights to Victoria

Sightseeing 81
The Sights, Granville Island, Royal Hudson/MV *Britannia* Excursion,
Chinatown, Touring Vancouver, Special Interest Tours,
Calendar of Events

Parks/Beaches/Gardens 101
In the City: Dr Sun Yat-sen Classical Chinese Garden, Jericho Beach to
Spanish Banks, Queen Elizabeth Park/Bloedel Conservatory,
Stanley Park, VanDusen Botanical Garden
At the University of British Columbia: Nitobe Memorial Garden,
UBC Botanical Garden, Pacific Spirit Regional Park
(University Endowment Lands)
On the North Shore: Capilano River Regional Park, Grouse Mountain,
Lynn Canyon Park, Lighthouse Park, Mount Seymour Provincial Park,
Seymour Demonstration Forest
Other: George C. Reifel Migratory Bird Sanctuary

Museums/Art Galleries 123
First Thursday, Major Museums, Other Museums, Public Art Galleries, Major Private Galleries, Artist-Run Galleries, Photo Galleries, Indian or Inuit (Eskimo) Galleries, Craft Galleries

Entertainment/Culture 135
Theatre, Classical Music, Dance

Nightlife 143
Jazz, Rhythm and Blues, Comedy, Nice Quiet Bars, Lively Pubs and Bars, Nightclubs, Gay Clubs

Sports/Recreation 149
Auto Racing, Camping, Canoeing/Kayaking/Rowing, Cruising, Cycling, Fishing, Golf, Hiking/Mountaineering/Indoor Climbing Walls, Horse Racing, In-Line Skating, Jogging, Professional Sports, Rafting, Sailing, Scuba Diving, Skating, Skiing, Swimming, Tennis, Windsurfing

Shopping 175
Shopping Areas, Accessories and Extras, Art Supplies, Auctions/Antiques/Oriental Rugs, Books and Magazines, Books (Used), Clothing, Home Furnishings, Kitchenware, Outdoors Equipment, Photo Supplies/Film Processing, Recorded Music, Shoes (Men's and Women's), Souvenirs, Specialty Food Stores

With the Kids 195
Kids and Animals, Day Trips, Other Outings, Museums, Babysitting, Entertainment, Restaurants, Shopping

Excursions from Vancouver 207
Gulf Islands, Galiano Island, Mayne Island, Saltspring Island, Whistler

Index 229

List of Maps

Southwestern British Columbia 2
Greater Vancouver 4
Restaurant Locations 63
Downtown Vancouver 66
West End: Hotels and Sights 68
SkyTrain/SeaBus Routes 70
Ferry Routes 75
Granville Island Area 82
Granville Island 84
Chinatown/Gastown/Japantown 90–91
Vancouver Harbour 98
Stanley Park 106–7
Vanier Park/Kitsilano Beach 125
Howe Sound 152
Ski Areas 167
Gulf Islands 208
Whistler Valley 222

About Vancouver

The Look of the City 2

Getting Oriented 3

History 5
Native People, Exploration, Settlement, Vancouver As a City, Later Landmark Years

Population 8

Weather 9

Major Industries 10

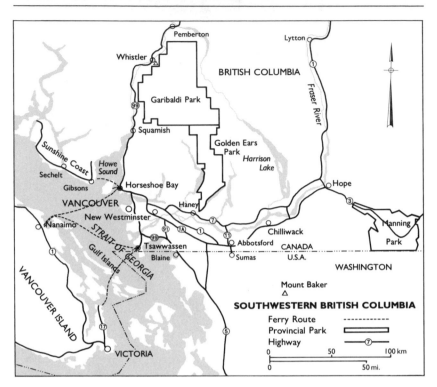

The Look of the City

Vancouver is known throughout the world for its magnificent setting. And it's true, the towering Coast Mountains and the shimmering Pacific Ocean provide an unbeatable urban setting. In addition, the city's close-to-the-wilderness location means that outdoor activities like hiking, skiing and water sports are mere minutes from residential areas.

Many of these neighbourhoods are right in—or close to—the downtown core. The city's West End, which wraps around English Bay, is one of Canada's most densely populated areas. From here, business-suited people don walking shoes and are at work in 15 minutes. From nearby Kitsilano, they strut briskly over Burrard St Bridge to start the work day in the towers of city centre.

These neighbourhoods give the city a vitality both during the day and at night. Suburbanites come into the city for a cappuccino on Robson, a stroll through the Gastown shops, a sunset on English Bay or a visit to the market and galleries of Granville Island.

In contrast to its eastern counterparts, Vancouver has the look and feel of a young city—in fact, it is just over a century old. Although Vancouverites laugh at the description of "Lotus Land," this West Coast city does resemble cities in California more than those in Ontario, both in architecture and in its laid-back lifestyle.

The 1990s have seen an explosion of construction in the heart of the city. Although Vancouver is located on a peninsula and thus has limited room to grow, the city's new—and often spectacular—architecture is no longer focussed on the few blocks around Granville and Georgia. The look of Vancouver has changed immensely in this decade as the city centre has stretched out to meet the harbourfront.

A mini-city encompassing residential and commercial properties is being developed on the former Expo 86 site on False Creek. In 1995 a controversial but impressive building (resembling the Roman Coliseum) was built on Hamilton to house the Vancouver Public Library. Right across the street the 1824-seat Ford Centre for the Performing Arts opened, allowing Vancouver audiences to enjoy large-stage productions for extended runs for the first time in the city's theatrical history.

Also in 1995, the Vancouver Canucks hockey team moved to General Motors Place, another eye-catching dome close to B.C. Place Stadium. They share this home with the Vancouver Grizzlies basketball team, a new addition to the city's sports scene in 1995.

On Burrard Inlet, Coal Harbour is an ambitious, three-phase project that began in 1992 and will add a variety of residential units and green spaces to the harbour setting. Among other amenities, there will be a 3 ha (8-acre) park with a waterfront walkway linking Stanley Park to downtown.

Even to new arrivals, it's evident that this city is on the move. And it is this sense of progress that makes Vancouver an exciting place to live and to explore.

Getting Oriented

Because the city centre is encompassed by water on three sides, newcomers should become familiar with the many bridges that connect the city to its environs. Burrard Inlet, which separates the North Shore communities of North and West Vancouver from the city proper, is spanned by two bridges. The Lions Gate Bridge links downtown with the North Shore; one end is in Stanley Park and the other between West and North Vancouver. The Second Narrows Bridge runs between the East End of Vancouver and North Vancouver.

False Creek juts into the heart of the city and is crossed by three bridges connecting the West End and downtown to the rest of Vancouver. From east to west, these are the Cambie St Bridge by the stadium at B.C. Place, the Granville St Bridge and the Burrard St Bridge. The Fraser River, which marks the southern limit of the city, is spanned (from west to east) by the Arthur Laing Bridge, the Oak St Bridge, the Knight St Bridge, the Alex Fraser Bridge, the Pattullo Bridge and the Port Mann Bridge.

South of the city is Vancouver International Airport, located on Sea Island at the mouth of the Fraser River.

Most of Vancouver's streets form a grid, laid out by surveyors who had only utility in mind, and this makes simple work of finding your way around. The area south of False Creek is especially easy, since east-west roads are numbered avenues. The dividing line between east and west is roughly Main St To avoid confusion, be sure to check whether avenues are preceded by a "W" for West or "E" for East.

Hwy 1, the Trans-Canada, goes through east Vancouver, crosses the Second Narrows Bridge to the North Shore and ends at Horseshoe Bay. From there, ferries run to Nanaimo on Vancouver Island, Langdale on the Sechelt Peninsula and Bowen Island.

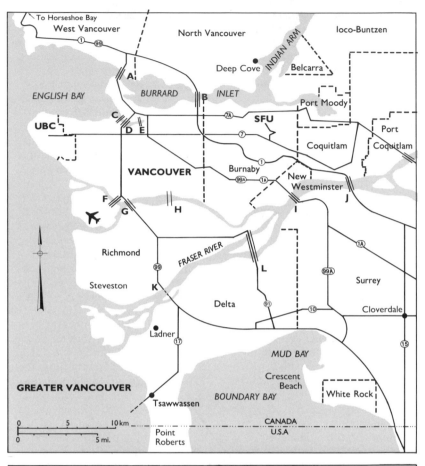

A Lions Gate Bridge	**I** Pattullo Bridge
B Second Narrows Bridge	**J** Port Mann Bridge
C Burrard St. Bridge	**K** George Massey Tunnel
D Granville St. Bridge	**L** Alex Fraser Bridge
E Cambie St. Bridge	**UBC** University of British Columbia
F Arthur Laing Bridge	**SFU** Simon Fraser University
G Oak St. Bridge	✈ Vancouver International Airport
H Knight St. Bridge	—⑨①— Highway

Hwy 99 runs south and goes under the south arm of the Fraser River via the George Massey Tunnel. Past the tunnel, Hwy 17 branches off for Tsawwassen and the terminal for ferries sailing to Victoria, Nanaimo and the Gulf Islands. Hwy 99 itself continues on to the U.S. border, about an hour's drive from downtown.

Hwy 99 also runs northward to the ferry terminal at Horseshoe Bay, then on to Whistler and points beyond.

Towering Douglas firs on Granville St in the 1880s. (Vancouver Public Library, Historical Photos)

Hwy 91 runs from the border to the eastern municipalities of Burnaby, New Westminster and Port Coquitlam.

Greater Vancouver consists of the city of Vancouver and a number of communities. Across Burrard Inlet are Lions Bay, West Vancouver and North Vancouver. South of the city, across the Fraser River, are Richmond, Delta, Surrey and White Rock. To the east are Burnaby, New Westminster, Port Moody, Port Coquitlam, Coquitlam, Ioco-Buntzen and Belcarra. In many of these communities, avenues run east-west and streets run north-south. Often the names of both avenues and streets are numbers, so take careful note of addresses.

History

Native People

The Coast Salish have had villages on the shores of Burrard Inlet and the Fraser River delta for more than 5000 years. The three principal villages in the late 1700s were at Locarno Beach, at Stanley Park and on the North Shore east of the Capilano River. Their ancient culture was highly developed, and they were master carpenters and canoemakers and exquisite craftsmen.

Exploration

1791 A Spanish navigator, José María Narváez, was the first European to arrive in the immediate area. He sailed into Burrard Inlet but did not explore the inner harbour.

1792 Capt George Vancouver arrived and claimed the land for Britain while searching for a northwest passage to Asia. He spent only one day on the site of the city named after him 100 years later. After chart-

After the Great Fire of 1886, the first City Hall was in a tent. (Vancouver Public Library, Historical Photos)

ing Burrard Inlet, he had an amicable meeting with a Spanish explorer, Dionisio Alcalá Galiano.

Although the Spanish did not play a large part in the history of this area, they left their mark with place names: Alberni, Galiano, Cordova, Langara, San Juan, Saturna and Juan de Fuca.

1808 Explorer and fur trader Simon Fraser of the North West Company reached Georgia Strait overland by a river he thought was the Columbia. It was not, and the river was later named after him. He did not reach Burrard Inlet.

Settlement

"By all accounts, from the present Granville Street to the tip of Point Grey grew one of the most magnifi-

cent stands of virgin timber the world has ever seen." Alan Morley, *Vancouver: From Milltown to Metropolis*

1827 The Hudson's Bay Company set up a fur-trading post, Fort Langley, 48 km (30 miles) east of Vancouver on the Fraser River. It was the first settlement in the Lower Mainland, but homesteaders were not encouraged since land clearing would drive away fur-bearing animals.

1858 Gold was discovered up the Fraser River, and the valley was flooded with 30,000 prospectors, mostly from the depleted gold mines of California. To provide law and order among the gold seekers and to secure the land from encroachment by the United States, the area was declared the Crown colony of British Columbia.

1859 New Westminster, a town on the Fraser River, was named the capital of British Columbia.

A British survey ship discovered coal on the shores of Burrard Inlet. (This bay at the entrance to Stanley Park is still called Coal Harbour.)

1862 Unable to find gold, three British prospectors acquired 200 ha (500 acres) of land on the south shore of Burrard Inlet to start a brickworks. It failed—who wanted bricks with all that wood? (This land, now the entire West End, is one of the most expensive pieces of real estate in Canada, but it was then valued at $1.01 per acre.)

1867 John Deighton, called "Gassy Jack" because he was so talkative, opened a saloon near Hastings Mill on Burrard Inlet. Since liquor was prohibited on company land, business boomed for Jack; he was so successful that a community known as Gastown grew around his saloon.

1869 Gastown was officially incorporated as the town of Granville.

1884 The Canadian Pacific Railway (CPR) decided on Coal Harbour, at the mouth of Burrard Inlet, as its transcontinental terminus. This decision was pivotal to the subsequent rapid development of Vancouver.

For a time the CPR controlled the town. It was, in fact, the general manager of the CPR who chose the name Vancouver.

Vancouver As a City

1886 The town of Granville, population 1000, became the City of Vancouver. On 13 June the entire city was wiped out in less than an hour by a clearing fire gone wild. Fewer than half a dozen buildings remained.

Despite the chaos of rebuilding, the inaugural city council showed remarkable foresight by turning the First Narrows Military Reserve into a park. It was named Stanley Park after Governor General Lord Stanley. (The Stanley Cup is also named after him.)

After the fire, the city grew at a rapid rate. By the end of the year there were 800 buildings.

Later Landmark Years

1887 The first CPR train chugged into Vancouver. The transcontinental railway was complete!

1889 The original Granville St Bridge was built, the first to span False Creek.

1893 The Hudson's Bay Company opened its first department store at Granville and Georgia, the same site as the present store.

1908 The University of British Columbia was founded.

1925 The original Second Narrows Bridge opened, connecting Vancouver with the North Shore.

1936 Vancouver's city hall was completed in the popular art deco style of the time.

1938 The Lions Gate Bridge opened.

1939 The Hotel Vancouver (the third and existing one) was completed. Construction was suspended during the depression, so the hotel was 11 years in the making.

1950 Park Royal, Canada's second shopping centre, was built in West Vancouver.

1964 The B.C. Lions football team won the Grey Cup.

1965 Simon Fraser University, designed by architect Arthur Erickson, opened for classes.

1970 The Vancouver Canucks hockey team made its NHL debut.

1977 The SeaBus began a regular commuter ferry service between North Vancouver and downtown.

1979 The Vancouver Whitecaps won the North American Soccer League championship.

1983 B.C. Place Stadium, the state of the art in inflated domes, opened.

1986 Vancouver's centennial. The city hosted Expo 86, a world transportation exhibition. Canada Place, Vancouver's cruise ship terminal and trade and convention centre, officially opened. A rapid transit service called SkyTrain began operation from downtown to New Westminster.

1992 The 200th anniversary of Capt George Vancouver's voyage into Burrard Inlet was celebrated.

1993 Vancouver hosted the Peace Summit between U.S. president Bill Clinton and Russian president Boris Yeltsin.

1994 Vancouver was awarded an NBA franchise and the Vancouver Grizzlies were formed.

The B.C. Lions football team defeated Baltimore in the last few minutes of the game to win the Grey Cup. This was the first time a U.S. team participated in Grey Cup play-offs.

1995 The Vancouver Public Library moved into a new, distinctively designed building; General Motors Place opened to host Vancouver Canucks and Vancouver Grizzlies games; and the Ford Centre for Performing Arts opened.

Population

In just over 100 years Vancouver has grown to be the third-largest city in Canada, after Toronto and Montreal. According to the most recent Statis-tics Canada estimates, the population of the City of Vancouver is 509,000, and Greater Vancouver is home to 1.8 million.

The main ethnic groups in Greater Vancouver are:

British	392,000
Chinese	150,000
German	60,000
Indo-Pakistani	46,000
French	29,000
Italian	29,000
Dutch	25,000
Scandinavian	24,000
Ukrainian	23,000
Filipino	14,000
Japanese	12,000
Native Indian	11,000
Jewish	11,000
Greek	6,000

Chinese. There have been three major waves of immigration: from San Francisco in 1858 for the Fraser Valley gold rush, from southern Guangdong province in the 1880s to construct the Canadian Pacific Railway and, most recently, from Hong Kong because of uncertainty about its political future. Today the Chinese community in Vancouver is the second largest in North America, after the one in San Francisco.

German, Dutch, Jewish, Scandinavian and Ukrainian. Although these are sizable groups, they have integrated into Vancouver life and are not highly visible ethnic communities.

Indo-Pakistani. Many of the early immigrants came from the Punjab because of their logging skills. The Indo-Canadian shopping area is concentrated on Main between 49th and 51st Ave.

French. The French in Vancouver have their own church, newspaper, and radio and television stations. There is a French community called Maillardville in Coquitlam.

Italian. The Italians also publish their own newspaper, available in "Little Italy" on Commercial north of Broadway. Many Italians arrived at the turn of the century, and a second wave arrived after World War II.

Filipino. Many Filipinos are women who came to Vancouver in the 1960s because of a severe shortage of nurses. More recently many women immigrated because of a demand for nannies.

Japanese. Many immigrated at the turn of the century to fish, farm, work in sawmills or build the railway. Japantown, along Powell east of Main, was much larger before World War II. Steveston, south of Richmond, still shows evidence of its heritage as a Japanese fishing village.

Native Indian. The Coast Salish originally inhabited this area.

Three Salish bands (Burrard, Squamish and Musqueam) now live on two large reserves in Greater Vancouver, but most of the Native people here are originally from elsewhere in British Columbia.

Greek. Most Greeks arrived after World War II, opening restaurants and shops or working in construction. Their community is centred on Broadway west of Macdonald.

Weather

When people talk about Vancouver, the subject of weather invariably arises. Vancouverites are either pitied because of the rain or envied because of the balmy climate. A myth abounds that Vancouver is the wettest city in Canada. It's just not true. In fact, every major city east of Montreal gets more precipitation than this western one. So there.

Summers in Vancouver are warm and winters are mild, with little snow, whereas the rest of Canada experiences hot, humid summers and cold, snowy winters. Temperatures below −18°C (0°F) have been recorded only once in Vancouver.

One reason for the balmy climate is that weather systems move from west to east. So when the rest of Canada is submerged in cold air from the

Weather Chart

	Average minimum temperature °C	°F	Average maximum temperature °C	°F	Days with precipitation	Total precipitation cm	in.	Hours of sunshine
Jan	2	36	5	41	20	21.8	8.6	55
Feb	4	40	7	44	15	14.7	5.8	93
Mar	6	43	10	50	16	12.7	5	129
Apr	9	48	14	58	13	8.4	3.3	180
May	12	54	18	64	10	7.1	2.8	253
June	15	59	21	69	10	6.4	2.5	243
July	17	63	23	74	6	3.1	1.2	305
Aug	17	63	23	73	8	4.3	1.7	255
Sept	14	58	18	65	9	9.1	3.6	188
Oct	10	50	14	57	16	14.7	5.8	116
Nov	6	43	9	48	18	21.1	8.3	70
Dec	4	39	6	43	20	22.4	8.8	44

mountains and the prairies, Vancouver basks in warm Pacific airstreams.

Although Vancouver is blessed with mild temperatures, the many microclimates of the region mean that the weather varies drastically from one area to the other. While it can be pouring on the North Shore—the picturesque mountains protect the city from wind but also latch onto rain clouds—it will be sunny to the south in Tsawwassen. The closer people live to the mountains, the more they get rained on. For example, the annual level of precipitation on Grouse Mountain is 3500 mm (140 inches), whereas downtown Vancouver receives 1400 mm (55 inches) and sunny Richmond only 1000 mm (40 inches). Rain does have its advantages: the grass stays green, and the air is usually fresh and clear.

If you visit between May and Sept, bring a sweater, a light raincoat and an umbrella. In winter months, you'll need a warm raincoat, an umbrella and waterproof boots.

For a recorded weather forecast, phone 664-9010. For an air-quality report, call 436-6767.

Major Industries

Industry has developed in Vancouver largely because of two factors: the province's wealth of natural resources and the city's great natural harbour.

Throughout the province, industry is based on mining, fishing and forestry, and Vancouver is active in the processing and shipping of raw materials. Mills, canneries and oil refineries are common on the outskirts of the city, and commercial fish boats dock along city waterways, unloading their catches of salmon, shrimp, herring, sole and halibut.

Burrard Inlet is one of the world's largest natural harbours; it is deep, sheltered and ice-free all year. Vancouver is a major North American port because of its harbour and because it is the Canadian gateway for all cargo coming from and going to Asia. In 1995 the old Ballantyne Terminal, which had been closed for years, was reopened to assist with increased cargo and cruise ship traffic. Along with the nearby coal superport of Roberts Bank, the Port of Vancouver handles more tonnage than any other port on the West Coast and is second only to New York in the Western Hemisphere.

Outgoing cargoes include grain, forest products, coal, potash, sulfur, fish, asbestos, iron ore and copper.

Freighters anchored in English Bay are as much a part of the city's panorama as the North Shore mountains. In the summer they are joined by an ever-increasing fleet of sleek Alaska-bound cruise ships gliding under Lions Gate Bridge. These elegant liners symbolize the newest star on the city's economic scene: tourism. Growth has been steady in this industry since Expo 86, when Vancouver was "discovered" by the world. Tourism, the world's fastest-growing industry, is alive and well in this city, where it generates over $2 billion in visitors' spending annually.

Essential Information

Emergency Phone Numbers 12

Major Hospitals 12

Motor Vehicles 12

Travel Information 13
In Vancouver, Travel Infocentres

Public Holidays 14

Lost and Found 14

Foreign Visitors 14

Banking 14
Currency Exchanges

Churches and Synagogues 15

Sales Taxes 15

Post Office 15

Late-Night Services 16
Pharmacies, Restaurants

Babysitting 16

Liquor/Beer/Wine 16

Radio 17
AM Radio Stations, FM Radio Stations

Television 17
Network and Cable TV, Additional Cable Channels, Pay TV

Newspapers and Periodicals 18

Emergency Phone Numbers

Police, Fire, Ambulance
Call 911 in Greater Vancouver.

Doctors and Dentists
Side by side on the lower level of the Bentall Centre at Dunsmuir and Burrard are drop-in medical and dental clinics: Medicentre (683-8138) and Dentacentre (669-6700). Medicentre is open Mon to Fri; Dentacentre is open Mon to Thurs.

Rape Relief and Women's Shelter
Call 872-8212.

Alcoholics Anonymous
Call 434-3933.

Veterinarian
The Animal Emergency Clinic (734-5104) at 4th and Fir is open 24 hours every day.

Legal Services
For a referral, phone 687-3221; for free general legal information, phone 687-4680. These services are offered by the B.C. branch of the Canadian Bar Association.

Marine and Aircraft Emergencies
Call the Canadian Coast Guard at 1-800-567-5111.

RCMP Tourist Alert
The RCMP attempts to contact travellers with urgent messages via radio, TV, newspapers, B.C. Travel Info-centres and provincial campgrounds. Call 264-3111 and your call will be transferred to the correct local for assistance.

Major Hospitals

Vancouver General Hospital
855 W 12th near Oak
875-4111

Area Codes in B.C.

The area codes in B.C. will change in mid-October 1996. There will be a seven-month changeover period. The area code in Vancouver and east to Hope and north to D'Arcy, as well as all of the Sunshine Coast, will remain 604. The area code for the rest of the province, including Vancouver Island, will become 250.

St Paul's Hospital
1081 Burrard near Davie
682-2344

B.C. Women's Hospital (Obstetrics)
4490 Oak at 29th
875-2424

B.C.'s Children's Hospital
4480 Oak at 29th
875-2345

University Hospital: UBC
2211 Wesbrook Mall, off University Blvd
822-7121

Lions Gate Hospital
231 E 15th at St Georges, North Van
988-3131

Burnaby Hospital
3935 Kincaid at Sunset
434-4211

Motor Vehicles

Seatbelts are compulsory in B.C.; motorcyclists must wear helmets. Children under 5 must be secured in infant restraint systems.

Right turns on red lights are allowed after you have come to a complete stop. Speed limits and road distances are posted in kilometres, and gas is sold in litres.

Emergency Road Service

The BCAA offers 24-hour emergency road service to its members and members of other auto clubs. Call 293-2222. (Be patient, since it is often difficult to get through.)

Towing

If you've been towed from the street, call Unitow at 688-5484.

The Unitow lot at 1410 Granville at Pacific is open 24 hours. Pay the towing charge ($23.49) with cash, Visa or MasterCard.

If you were towed from a private lot, call Busters at 685-8181. Busters' lot, at 104 E 1st near Quebec, is open 24 hours. The $70 charge can be paid with cash, Visa or MasterCard.

Road Conditions

Call the Ministry of Transportation and Highways at 1-900-451-4997 for a recorded announcement.

Travel Information

In Vancouver

Vancouver TouristInfo Centre

Waterfront Centre
Plaza Level, 200 Burrard at Cordova
683-2000
Will book accommodation, tour reservations, car rentals and restaurant reservations. Souvenirs, maps, brochures and B.C. Transit tickets, schedules and passes are available here. Hours: June to Aug, 8–6 daily; Sept to May, Mon to Fri, 8:30–5; Sat, 9–5.

Discover British Columbia is an information and reservation service; call 663-6000. From out of the city, including the U.S., call 1-800-663-6000.

A Vancouver TouristInfo Centre kiosk is in the plaza outside the main entrance to Pacific Centre at Granville and Georgia. In the summer,

hours are Tues to Fri, 10–6; in winter, Tues to Fri, 10–5. This TouristInfo Centre is fine for general directions or quick information, but for brochures and details visit the one at Waterfront Centre.

Information about Vancouver can be accessed through Internet's World Wide Web Home Page at http://www.city.vancouver.bc.ca/

Travel Infocentres

Burnaby Travel Infocentre

Metrotown on Kingsway
(in the pedestrian concourse between Metrotown and Eaton Centre)
430-9260 (summer)
294-7944 (year-round)
Open daily during the summer 10–6.

New Westminster Travel Infocentre

New Westminster Quay Public Market
810 Front at 8th St
526-1905
Open daily.

North Vancouver Travel Infocentre

Capilano at Marine
980-5332
Open daily from Victoria Day to Labour Day.

White Rock Travel Infocentre

1554 Foster at North Bluff
536-6844
Open seven days a week in July and Aug, Mon to Fri the rest of the year.

U.S. Border Travel Infocentre

Hwy 99, just inside the Canadian border
Open daily.

Metric Conversion

Unit	Approximate equivalent
Length	
1 kilometre	0.6 mile
1 mile	1.6 kilometres
1 metre	1.1 yards
1 yard	0.9 metre
1 centimetre	0.4 inch
1 inch	2.54 centimetres
Capacity	
1 litre	1.06 U.S. quarts
1 U.S. quart	0.95 litre
Weight	
1 kilogram	2.2 pounds
1 pound	0.45 kilogram
1 ounce	28 grams
1 gram	0.04 ounce
Temperature	
0°C	32°F
10°C	50°F
20°C	68°F
30°C	86°F

Public Holidays

New Year's Day, Jan 1
Good Friday, date varies
Easter Monday, date varies
Victoria Day, third Mon in May
Canada Day, July 1
B.C. Day, first Mon in Aug
Labour Day, first Mon in Sept
Thanksgiving, second Mon in Oct
Remembrance Day, Nov 11
Christmas, Dec 25
Boxing Day, Dec 26

Traffic at border crossings and on the ferries is extremely heavy around a holiday weekend; avoid both if possible.

Lost and Found

B.C. Transit
682-7887

Police (Property Room)
665-2232

Foreign Visitors

There are about 45 consulates in Vancouver but no embassies. Check the *Yellow Pages*.

After a 48-hour visit, U.S. citizens can take home $400 (U.S.) worth of goods every 30 days. This may include one litre of alcohol, 200 cigarettes and 100 cigars (not Cuban). After a visit of less than 48 hours, $200 worth of goods is allowed. Call 278-1825 for more information.

Banking

There are more than 25 foreign banks in Vancouver.

Check the *Yellow Pages*.

Currency Exchanges

American Express
1040 W Georgia near Burrard
669-2813
Open Mon to Sat.

Thomas Cook Foreign Exchange
1016 W Georgia near Burrard
687-6111
Open Mon to Fri.

Royal Bank
Vancouver International Airport
665-0855
Open daily 5:30 AM–10 PM. Also, 24-hour currency-exchange machines, dispensing 15 foreign currencies, are scattered throughout the airport. Each machine has a different selection of currencies.

Many banks in Vancouver are open

on Sat but generally not the downtown branches. The main downtown branches all have foreign exchange departments.

Churches and Synagogues

Some centrally located churches are:

Christ Church Cathedral (Anglican)
690 Burrard at Georgia
682-3848

First Baptist Church
969 Burrard at Nelson
683-8441

Holy Rosary Cathedral (Catholic)
646 Richards at Seymour
682-6774

Redeemer Lutheran Church
1499 Laurier at Granville
737-9821

Vancouver Mennonite Brethren Church
5887 Prince Edward near 43rd
325-3313

Pentecostal Assemblies of Canada
2700 E Broadway near Slocan
253-2700

Presbyterian Church in Canada
1155 Thurlow near Davie
683-1913

Unitarian Church of Vancouver
949 W 49th Ave at Oak
261-7204

St Andrew's Wesley United Church
1012 Nelson at Burrard
683-4574

Beth Israel Synagogue
4350 Oak at 49th
731-4161

Sales Taxes

A provincial sales tax of 7 per cent is applied to most purchases, with the exception of groceries, books and magazines. Goods shipped out of the province directly by the vendor are also exempt.

The 7 per cent federal Goods and Services Tax is also added to virtually everything you purchase except groceries. Non-residents can apply for a rebate of the tax on accommodation and consumer goods taken out of the country if the tax totals at least $7 (but not for such items as restaurant meals, gas and tobacco). Rebate application forms, available at most hotels, must be accompanied by original receipts and mailed to Revenue Canada. (Receipts are not returned.)

If you are driving to the U.S., you have the alternative of taking the original receipts and proof of residence (identification with a picture) to a participating duty-free shop at the border for an immediate cash rebate. At the main border crossing, on Hwy 99 south of Vancouver, this is the Heritage Duty-Free Shop. The last exit, Beach Rd, will take you directly there. The shop is open daily, 5 AM–midnight. Phone the shop at 541-1244 if you need more information.

Post Office

The main post office at Georgia and Homer is open Mon to Fri, 8–5:30. A substation is at 757 W Hastings at Granville and is open Mon to Fri, 8:30–5. The Hallmark Card Shop at 1014 Robson near Burrard is open seven days a week: Mon to Fri, 9–7; Sat, 10–5; and Sun, 11–4. There is also a centrally located post office in the basement of Eaton's, 701 Granville at Georgia, which is open Mon to Fri, 9:30–5:30, and Sat, 9:30–4:30.

Basic postal services are available at designated drugstores and convenience stores Mon to Sat or Sun. Look for the Canada Post sign in the front window.

Late-Night Services

Pharmacies

Shopper's Drug Mart
1125 Davie at Thurlow
685-6445
Open 24 hours.

Safeway
2733 W Broadway at Trafalgar
732-5030
The pharmacy in the supermarket is open 8 AM–midnight every day.

Restaurants

The Bread Garden
812 Bute at Robson
688-3213
1880 W 1st at Cypress
738-6684
1040 Denman at Comox
685-2996
2996 Granville at 14th Ave
736-6465
Healthy soups, sandwiches, salads and muffins, as well as decadent desserts. Open 24 hours daily.

Benny's Bagels
2503 W Broadway at Larch
731-9730
1095 Hamilton at Helmcken
Funky place serving bagels, of course, plus desserts and salads. Open 24 hours. See Restaurants (Late Night).

The Naam
2724 W 4th near Stephens
738-7151
A 24-hour vegetarian restaurant with beer, wine and espresso. See Restaurants (Vegetarian).

Hamburger Mary's
1202 Davie at Bute
687-1293

Open daily until 4 AM except Sunday night, when it is open until 2 AM.

Babysitting

Most major hotels can arrange for babysitters if notified in advance.

A Babysitter Every Time
737-2248
Same-day booking. Adult sitter comes to you for $10/hour. MasterCard and Visa accepted.

Moppet Minders Child and Home Care Services
942-8167
Same-day booking. Adult sitters; charge is $8/hour for one or two children for a minimum of four hours. An additional charge of 50¢ an hour for each additional child. Maximum four children. Payments in cash.

Liquor/Beer/Wine

In B.C. you must be at least 19 to purchase or consume alcohol. Spirits are sold only in government liquor stores, which are also the main outlet for beer and wine.

Private beer and wine stores sell their products at slightly higher prices than government stores but are convenient because they are generally open seven days a week and sell chilled wine and beer.

Pubs have "off-licence sales" whereby they are allowed to sell cold beer to be consumed off the premises.

Centrally located government liquor stores are at the following locations:

1120 Alberni near Thurlow
Mon to Sat, 9:30–9. Includes a specialty store.

1716 Robson near Denman
Mon to Sat, 10–6.

1155 Bute near Davie
Mon to Sat, 9:30–6; Fri, 9:30–9.

2020 W Broadway at Maple
Mon to Sat, 9 AM–11 PM.

5555 Cambie at 39th
Mon to Sat, 9:30–9. The largest liquor store in the province; wine consultants on staff.

Only private stores sell chilled wines. Some private stores are:

Granville Island Brewing Co
1441 Cartwright, Granville Island
687-2739
Open Sun to Thurs, 9–7; Fri and Sat, 9–9. This company brews and sells B.C.'s best beer and offers a small selection of international wines.

Marquis Wine Cellar
1034 Davie off Burrard
685-2446
Open Mon to Wed, noon–8; Thurs to Sun, noon–9. Wine only. Carries labels not found in the government stores.

Broadway International Wine Shop
2752 W Broadway near Macdonald
734-8543
11–9 daily. Good selection of wines from around the world.

Radio

Cable stations are in parentheses.

AM Radio Stations

600 CKBD, contemporary Christian music (90.9)
650 CISL, '50s to '70s hits (91.3)
690 CBU-CBC, news, talk, music, no commercials (93.1)
730 CKLG, top 40 (94.7)
980 CKNW, news, talk, MOR music, sports (96.3)
1040 CKST, talk, varied music (88.5)
1130 CKWX, country (97.1)

1320 CHMB, Cantonese news, talk, music (97.5)
1410 CFUN, soft rock (100.1)
1470 CJVB, Cantonese news, talk, music (103.3)

FM Radio Stations

93.7 CJJR, country (92.5)
96.9 KISS, soft rock (103.9)
97.7 CBUF-CBC, French (102.3)
99.3 CFOX, adult rock (99.7)
101.1 CFMI, light rock (105.3)
101.9 CITR, UBC station, alternative music (101.9)
102.7 CFRO, community radio (102.9)
103.5 CHQM, easy listening (106.1)
105.7 CBU-CBC, classical music, talk, no commercials (107.1)

Television

The following is a list of TV cable channels for Vancouver, Richmond and parts of Burnaby. For other areas of the Lower Mainland, check the local TV listings for cable networks.

Network and Cable TV

2 TV Guide.
3 CBUT Vancouver CBC
4 Community TV Vancouver
5 Knowledge Network Vancouver
6 CHEK Victoria CTV
7 CBUFT Vancouver CBC, French
8 Information Network, news highlights
9 KCTS Seattle PBS
10 KOMO Seattle ABC
11 BCTV Vancouver CTV
12 KVOS Bellingham
13 UTV Vancouver
14 KSTW Seattle
15 KIRO Seattle CBS
16 KING Seattle NBC
17 CHSC Shopping
18 Pay Per View Preview Channel
19 CPAC Parliament
20 Multicultural

21 **Transportation/Weather/ B.C. Legislature,** includes airline departure and arrival information
22 **Value Plus Network**
23 **Weather Network**
24 **Vision,** multireligious
25 **YTV,** youth programming
26 **CBC Newsworld,** 24-hour news
27 **WTN, Women's Television Network**
28 **KCPQ (FOX)** 13
50 **Stocks/Voice Print**
59 **Homes Plus**
70 **RDI,** 24-hour French news

Additional Cable Channels

29 **MuchMusic**
30 **TSN,** sports
31 **Arts and Entertainment**
32 **Nashville Network**
33 **CNN News Network**
34 **TLC, The Learning Channel**
35 **MusiquePlus,** French
36 **TV5,** French mixed programming
37 **Headline News**
38 **NCN, New Country Network**
39 **Showcase Television**
40 **Bravo!** 24-hour arts and culture
41 **Life Network**
42 **The Discovery Channel**
43 **WTVS,** Detroit Public Television

Pay TV

44 **CNBC,** Business and Financial coverage
45 **WSBK** Boston, Eastern Superchannel; includes sports
46 **KTLA** Los Angeles
47 **TBS** Atlanta
48 **WGN** Chicago
49 **WPIX** New York, Eastern Superchannel; includes sports
51 **Family Channel**
52 **Superchannel**
53 **MovieMax!**
54 **Fairchild Television**
55 **Talentvision**

Newspapers and Periodicals

Vancouver Sun
Published every morning except Sun. Complete entertainment listings on Thurs, weekly *TV Times* on Fri.

Province
Published every morning except Sat. Entertainment and TV listings on Fri.

Georgia Straight
An excellent free weekly that focusses on entertainment and current issues. Published on Thurs, available at newsstands, corner stores and theatres.

Business in Vancouver
Excellent weekly in tabloid format, published on Fri.

Vancouver Magazine
General-interest city magazine published eight times a year. Available at newsstands.

CityFood
A free tabloid published 10 times a year that focusses on food and includes restaurant reviews.

Coast
Free outdoor recreation tabloid published eight times annually. Available from outdoor stores, community centres, libraries and some coffee shops.

Westcoast Families
Family-oriented articles and an excellent calendar of fun and family activities. Published 10 times a year and available free from community centres, libraries, children's stores, family attractions and all McDonald's outlets in the Lower Mainland.

Out-of-town Newspapers
The best selection is at Mayfair News, 1535 W Broadway off Granville, which is open daily 8 AM–10:30 PM. There is a smaller store in Royal Centre, Burrard at Georgia.

Where to Stay

Hotels 20

Downtown, Robson Street, West End, Kitsilano, Near the Airport, Kingsway, North Shore

Alternative Accommodation 31

Bed and Breakfast 32

In Vancouver, Near Vancouver

Trailer Parks/Campgrounds 36

In and Near Vancouver, Near Tsawwassen, White Rock, Surrey, Coquitlam/Port Moody

Like many grand cities, Vancouver has grand hotels, including two five-diamond AAA/CAA-rated hotels: the Four Seasons, and the Sutton Place Hotel. Only recommended hotels are listed. Comments may seem overly enthusiastic, but these are a few chosen from many. The hotels are grouped by location and then listed by price in each section.

After the hotels are listings for Alternative Accommodation, Bed and Breakfast, and Trailer Parks/Campgrounds.

Prices quoted are *starting* prices ("rack rates," as the hotels call them) for a standard double in high season, but always ask about special rates: weekend, weekly, seniors', off season, corporate and so on.

If you are planning an extended stay, you may want to book through **Executive Accommodations** (875-6674), which can find you an apartment, townhouse or family home. Accommodation can include a fully equipped kitchen, maid service, a fireplace, plants—whatever makes you feel at home. Children are welcome. Accommodation for pets is limited, so it is best to book well ahead. For a long-term stay, this type of accommodation represents a substantial savings over a hotel stay. There are daily, weekly and monthly rates. Daily rates start at $90/night.

Hotels

Downtown

Pan Pacific Vancouver
999 Canada Place, foot of Howe
662-8111
1-800-663-1515 toll free (Canada)
1-800-937-1515 toll free (U.S.)
Fax 685-8690
A deluxe convention hotel on the Canada Place cruise ship pier. An eight-storey atrium with totem poles draws you into the spacious lobby, where the lounge and café have 12 m (40-foot) glass walls and a panorama of the harbour. Japanese influence is present everywhere in the decor, including the grasscloth wall coverings, subdued earth tones and graceful rattan furniture. All rooms have views (so do the bathrooms in rooms 10 and 20 on each floor) and every convenience for travellers.

A heated outdoor pool is open all year. There's an extra charge for the health club, but you'll see why immediately; state-of-the-art exercise equipment and weights, a low-impact running track, trainers on duty, racquetball and squash courts, a video aerobics room and the Sports Lounge, with a wide-screen TV, all make it the best hotel health club in Canada.

The Pan Pacific has three restaurants: the Five Sails offers spectacular waterfront views, the Café Pacifica features a Friday night Italian Opera Buffet complete with singing chef, and Misaki serves fine Japanese cuisine. Located in the business district, the hotel is minutes away from Gastown and about a 10-minute walk from the shops on Robson. It is the city's most expensive hotel, and many people think that it's worth the price. Doubles $345.

Metropolitan Hotel
645 Howe near Georgia
687-1122
1-800-667-2300 toll free
Fax 689-7044
Originally part of the Mandarin chain, this ultra-deluxe hotel then became Delta Place and now it is the Metropolitan. (There is also a Metropolitan Hotel in Toronto.)

The luxurious surroundings and the location are still the major attractions. The elegance is quiet but pervasive: marble everywhere, hand-carved oak desks and silk-covered coat hangers. One floor is set aside for a health centre (including racquet and squash courts, lap pool, sun deck, exercise room, whirlpool, massage and, believe it or not, saunas with TV) and a business services centre. Excellent location. Doubles $310.

Wall Centre Garden Hotel
1088 Burrard at Helmcken
331-1000
1-800-223-5652 toll free
Fax 331-1001
Your first hint that this is a high-end hotel comes from the driveway, which is a mosaic of shiny tiles, giving the effect of a vast, sweeping work of art. Then there's the lobby, with fragrant, fresh flowers, soft lighting and discreet furnishings. The two dark-glassed towers added 391 luxurious rooms and suites to the Vancouver hotel scene in September 1994. (The "apartment" tower provides for long-term as well as short-term stays.)

The furnishings in the rooms are not elaborate and the closets are on the small size, but there are many amenities; each room has several phone lines, voice mail, dataport, a hair dryer, a make-up mirror, an in-room safe, duvets and air conditioning. All the works of art in the hotel are originals. One wonders what conveniences the hotel world will dream up next to impress guests—here it's a succinct "weather report," such as "sunny" or "cloudy," that is highlighted on the wall-size mirrors located at the elevators.

The Indigo restaurant has a colourful, West Coast look. There is also a café, a bistro and a fully equipped health club—you can enjoy a snack at the juice bar after doing laps in the 15 m (50-foot) pool or lifting weights. Doubles $300.

Four Seasons Hotel
791 W Georgia at Howe
689-9333
1-800-268-6282 toll free (Canada)
1-800-332-3442 toll free (U.S.)
Fax 684-4555
Stay at the Four Seasons if you want to be pampered. Some of the niceties are bathrobes, hair dryers, VCRs, free shoeshine (just leave your shoes outside the door overnight), 24-hour valet service, a year-round indoor-outdoor pool and a rooftop garden. The hotel is connected to Pacific Centre shopping mall, making it a handy location but unfortunately turning the lobby into a thoroughfare. Above the lobby level the Four Seasons regains that tranquil feeling of a luxurious hotel.

Children and pets are also pampered here. The younger set receives complimentary milk and cookies on arrival, terry robes, movie videos, aerobic videos in the health club, infant equipment, toys and a children's menu. Fido gets the "silver bowl" service—bottled water and dinner served from sterling silver!

Chartwell is one of the best dining rooms in the city (see Restaurants, Lunch). The Garden Terrace is a great place to relax after shopping or a business meeting, and the lush greenery gives it an outdoor feeling. The hotel was originally planned for a location near Stanley Park, but when that didn't work out some of the park was transplanted to this lovely setting. It has a five-diamond AAA/CAA rating. Location handy to everything. Doubles $285.

The Sutton Place Hotel
845 Burrard near Robson
682-5511
1-800-810-6888 toll free
Fax 682-2926
Formerly Le Meridien and part of the Air France chain, this fine hotel

became part of the Sutton Place Grande Hotels Group in January 1995. The name was all that changed, however; the hotel remains under the same ownership and management and is committed to the same high standard of service.

The ambience is that of a luxurious European hotel. The lobby exudes elegance, with its extravagant floral arrangements, French provincial furniture and an air of tranquillity. The exquisite fittings continue in the rooms, which have detailed mouldings, flowered bedspreads and marble bathrooms—this is the place for a romantic getaway.

Although large, Sutton Place is not a convention hotel and it maintains an intimate feeling. Amenities include a business centre, a private dining room, downtown limousine service, pool, sun deck and Le Spa Health, Beauty and Fitness Centre.

Le Club is a formal dining room with a continental menu; the Table d'Hôte (Chef's Specialty) is an extravagant meal, but it features "toned-down" sauces to suit today's health-conscious diner. Café Fleuri's chocolate dessert buffet will satisfy the most insatiable chocoholic (Thurs to Sat evenings), and it is also noted for the best Sunday brunch in town (see Restaurants, Breakfast/Brunch). The Gerard Lounge, with its deep-toned wood, fireplace and soft leather, is so popular that happy hour patrons sometimes spill out into Café Fleuri and then have a choice of libations or the afternoon tea, which is served Mon to Sat, 2–5. The hotel is in a good location for business meetings, shopping and restaurants. Another five-diamond AAA/CAA rating. Doubles $215.

Waterfront Centre

900 Canada Place, foot of Howe
691-1991
1-800-441-1414 (Canada and U.S.)
Fax 691-1999

The Waterfront is across from Canada Place cruise ship terminal. Entering this CP hotel is a pleasant surprise, since the exterior (which is overshadowed by the grandeur of the Five Sails and the magnificent harbour setting right across the street) does not do justice to the interior, where the traditional and the contemporary are beautifully melded with such touches as fossilized limestone frames around lobby doorways, oxidized iron finishes and weathered wood. It is one of the few hotels (along with Sutton Place and the Four Seasons) where guest room furnishings appear to have come from a home rather than a hotel supply house. Warm shades of sand, butterscotch and terra cotta are welcoming and relaxing.

It's worth strolling the hotel to enjoy the original artwork from Canadian and Pacific Northwest artists.

Sunday brunches (11:30–3) are a musical treat here as members of the Vancouver Symphony entertain with a repertoire that ranges from Bach to pop. Soon after it opened, the Waterfront Centre was awarded a four-diamond rating from AAA/CAA. Although it may qualify in other respects, it will never achieve the coveted fifth diamond because it has an informal restaurant rather than a formal dining room. But the restaurant and bar off the lobby please patrons with the floor-to-ceiling windows looking out on Coal Harbour and the lively corner the hotel shares with Canada Place. An open kitchen, a rare thing in a hotel, makes you feel that you really will get that three-minute egg or extra-rare steak.

Canadian Pacific hotels offer special service and extra amenities in their Entree Gold class (see Hotel Vancouver listing for details) that are truly deluxe.

The landscaped deck, with a heated outdoor pool, is so large that it can handle both energetic children and sleepy sun-bathers. Doubles $209.

Wedgewood Hotel
845 Hornby near Robson
689-7777
1-800-663-0666 toll free
Fax 688-3074

The Wedgewood is one of the best places to stay in Vancouver. The place exudes elegance and charm, and the staff really seem to care. This is probably because the manager of the hotel, Eleni Skalbania, is also the owner. It is a small and intimate hotel containing only 93 rooms, each with a large balcony, and you won't find huge tours or conventions here. Some of the extras are blackout drapes, flowers growing on the balconies, afternoon ice delivery, a daily sheet of menu specials, turn-down service and 24-hour room service.

The restaurants and bar are outstanding. The Bacchus Ristorante and Lounge resembles a marvellous Tuscan inn (terra cotta, faux marble), and the food is excellent. This is a favourite with the before- and after-theatre crowd and a great place to relax after a shopping spree.

It's a five-minute walk to the business district. Doubles $190.

Hotel Vancouver
900 W Georgia at Burrard
684-3131
1-800-441-1414 toll free (Canada and U.S.)
Fax 662-1929

This 1939 Vancouver landmark is one of the château-style hotels built by the Canadian National and Canadian Pacific railways. These French châteaux, with gargoyles, ornate chimneys and steep copper roofs, were built as a romantic enticement to visitors across Canada.

The decor of the rooms is traditional. Complimentary morning coffee and newspapers on each floor are nice touches.

Treat yourself to Hotel Vancouver's Entree Gold, where an entire floor of premium rooms and exceptional service includes a reception desk and concierge on that floor, a continental breakfast and afternoon canapés served in a lovely private lounge, and an adjoining board room at the disposal of Entree Gold guests. Other perks include secretarial services and computer hookups along with fresh flowers, plants and crystal glasses in your room. This is what the stately Hotel Vancouver was meant for, and it's worth every penny.

Another treat at the Hotel Vancouver is a visit to the Lobby Lounge, where comfy, high-backed chairs welcome you to Afternoon Tea every day at 2:30. This is the traditional "crustless sandwiches and scones with clotted cream" tea that is the epitome of relaxation for sightseers and businesspeople. (For a time in 1996, while the hotel lobby is going through restoration, the Lobby Lounge will be located on the 15th floor in the the Roof Restaurant. As well as making the hotel lobby more elegant, this refurbishment will add a a new San Francisco–style restaurant.)

The health club provides a skylit lap pool, Jacuzzi and exercise room. Recently, an outdoor patio complete with gazebo and garden was added.

Staying at a grand old hotel is a special experience and offers a brush with history. The location is excellent for business and shopping. Doubles $185.

Hotel Georgia
801 W Georgia at Howe
682-5566
1-800-663-1111 toll free
Fax 682-8192

Other cities have several of these

Hotel GeorgiA

distinguished stone high-rises, built in the 1930s, that are now good, medium-priced hotels. In Vancouver the Georgia is one of a kind.

The small lobby has oak panelling and ornate brass elevators. The rooms are larger than in modern hotels and have retained some of their old-fashioned charm, although furnishings are contemporary. Rooms on the south side have a view of the art gallery gardens.

There's no health club and the hotel restaurant is nothing to get excited about, but because of the Georgia's great location (for both business and shopping) there's no shortage of restaurants close by. The hotel has two bars; George V, the English pub downstairs, is a popular after-work stop. Doubles $140.

Executive Inn
1379 Howe at Pacific
688-7678
1-800-570-3932 toll free
Fax 688-7679
Because this hotel is only a few years old—it opened in June 1994—and has an eager, cheerful staff it is a bar-

gain. Although it's a little off the beaten track, there is a regular shuttle to several downtown locations. And despite its location right beside the Granville St Bridge, there is no problem with traffic noise. It is tastefully furnished, and the lobby is bright and welcoming, with floor-to-ceiling windows.

Although the closet and bathroom are both on the small size in the standard room (there seems to be a trend in hotels to pint-size closets), there are amenities such as coffeemakers, in-room safes, individual air conditioners, clock radios, hair dryers and magnifying mirrors in the bathrooms. Many of the upper floors have spectacular views of the mountains and the sea. There are 22 suites for short- or long-term stays. Café Angles, on the second floor, specializes in Pacific Northwest dishes. The exercise room has a superb view.

This hotel is part of a B.C. chain (there are two others in the suburbs), and you may find that the staff here simply tries a bit harder. It's walking distance to English Bay and the Granville Island ferry. There is secured underground parking and valet parking. Doubles $139.

YWCA Hotel
733 Beatty at Georgia
895-5830
1-800-663-1424 toll free (B.C. and Alberta)
Fax 681-2550
After close to 100 years on Burrard, this co-ed Y hotel moved to a new, modern building in the fall of 1995. The 155 rooms on 12 floors are bright and cozy. All rooms have telephones and mini-refrigerators, and there are kitchens, TV lounges and laundry facilities to be shared. Rooms vary in size; they can accommodate single travellers or families of five. There are both private and shared bathrooms.

Guests have the use of the Health and Wellness Centre at the YWCA co-ed facility at Hornby near Dunsmuir. The indoor pool, steam room, classes in aerobics and aqua fitness, and full exercise facilities are free to Y hotel guests, but massage and other treatments cost extra.

Although the new hotel is not as close to the business district as the old Y, this location is a short walk to sports facilities at B.C. Place Stadium and General Motors Place and is in the same neighbourhood as Library Place, the Ford Centre for the Performing Arts and the Queen Elizabeth Theatre. And it is mere minutes from a SkyTrain station. No other central location with modern facilities is this cheap. Credit cards accepted. Weekly and monthly rates available. Doubles $59.

Kingston Hotel
757 Richards near Robson
684-9024
Fax 684-9917
Approaching the Kingston, you realize immediately that it is not a typical cheap hotel. Cheap, yes; typical, no. Care has been taken to give this small hotel a warm atmosphere—it's more like a European hotel, complete with continental breakfast. Rooms are small but clean. Prices are reasonable because extras such as room service, TVs and private baths have been eliminated. (Of the 60 rooms, 7 have private baths.) All rooms have telephones, and local calls are free. The Kingston is four storeys high and has no elevator. Laundry, sauna and parking are available. A real bargain near the centre of the city. It's popular with backpackers and others who wish to be close to the action but are on a budget. Weekly and monthly rates available. Doubles $45.

Robson Street

Robson St is the perfect location—it's close to downtown, Stanley Park and the beaches. It is always lively—some of the city's classiest shops are here, and the many restaurants provide an eclectic array of alternatives to hotel food.

Here are some of the best bets.

Pacific Palisades Hotel
1277 Robson at Jervis
688-0461
1-800-663-1815 toll free
Fax 688-4374
The only North American property of the prestigious Shangri-La International Hotel, the Palisades is known for its excellent service.

It is an all-suite hotel. The twin 21-floor towers were built in the '60s as apartments, and so every unit has a small kitchenette. The Executive Suites, all with balconies, are very large and are worth the extra dollars. The deluxe rooms are above the tenth floor and have excellent views and a few extras such as fresh flowers, three phones and two TV sets. There are excellent business facilities. The Monterey Lounge and Grill is a dining and entertainment favourite, with its West Coast cuisine, award-winning wine list, grand piano and dining area that opens to Robson St—great for people-watching on a sunny day. The health club is huge and has a lap pool, exercise machines, a juice bar, tanning rooms, an outdoor patio and mountain bike rentals. (It's a five-minute ride to Stanley Park.)

There are weekly and monthly rates available. Doubles $195.

O'Doul's Hotel
1300 Robson at Jervis
684-8461
1-800-663-5491 toll free
Fax 684-8326
O'Doul's is a small, modern hotel that

has the amenities associated with the big chains: room service, voice mail, valet parking, in-room movies, an indoor pool and exercise room, sophisticated security systems and secretarial services. Each room has three telephones, remote-control TV, a hair dryer, a mini-bar, individual temperature control, air conditioning and windows that open. The decor in the rooms and public areas is very West Coast—bright and airy in blues and greens with lots of plants. The electronic locks (reprogrammed for each guest), valet parking and an elevator with an additional security system make it popular with women travellers. And its Robson St location is convenient for shopping, eating and getting to English Bay and Stanley Park. Doubles $170.

Riviera Motor Inn

1431 Robson at Broughton
685-1301
A converted 11-storey 1960s apartment building with 13 large studios and 27 one-bedrooms. All have balconies and well-equipped kitchens. A 1994 renovation added new furnishings and appliances—there's free coffee and a coffeemaker in each unit—and the Riviera is clean (unlike some hotels nearby). The view of the harbour and the North Shore mountains from the back of the building is terrific. There's free parking. The location is very good for tourists—it's about a 10-minute walk to the park and the same to shopping and restaurants—but a little out of the way for business travellers. Doubles $128.

Blue Horizon

1225 Robson at Bute
688-1411
1-800-663-1333 toll free
Fax 688-4461
The best things about the Blue Horizon are the large rooms, the views and the location. The building has 31

floors and is shaped like a cross, so all rooms have corner windows. Add in the balconies and you have a panorama of the harbour and English Bay that can't be beat. Unless you're here on business, the location is about as good as it gets, right in the heart of the shops and restaurants on Robson. For years the dowdy Blue Horizon lagged behind the glitz of Robson, but the '60s building has now had a complete face-lift.

This is not a luxury hotel; there's no concierge or room service, but all the basics are there, plus those million-dollar views. A small gym includes a lap pool and a few exercise machines, but ask about free access to the fitness centre around the corner. Doubles $125.

West End

Westin Bayshore Hotel

1601 W Georgia at Cardero
682-3377
1-800-228-3000 toll free
Fax 687-3102
Overlooking the scenic harbour and sitting next door to Stanley Park, the Bayshore is a city hotel with all the amenities of a resort. The trademark of this hotel is the friendly doormen in decorative Beefeater outfits.

Rooms are available in a tower and a low-rise built around a large outdoor pool and garden, with a marina and the ocean at your feet.

There are magnificent views of the North Shore mountains on the north or west side of the tower. Rooms in the original lower-level section have recently been refurnished; the tower rooms are larger and have views and balconies.

Stay at the Bayshore if you want the advantage of a short walk to the Stanley Park seawall; it's definitely more relaxing than staying downtown. A shuttle bus takes you to the heart of downtown in five minutes. Years ago, Trader Vic's, the dining room, was one of the "in" restaurants, but it closed at the end of 1995. Doubles $219.

Sunset Inn
1111 Burnaby (near Davie and Thurlow)
1-800-786-1997 toll free
The Sunset Inn is the best of several West End apartment buildings that have been converted into hotels. All the units—studios and one-bedrooms—were refurnished in spring 1994 and have kitchens and balconies. The one-bedrooms have sofa beds and sleep four. The hotel is fairly well maintained and has laundry facilities and underground parking.

Located in a residential area close to shops and buses, the hotel is a 10-minute walk from downtown. Particularly recommended for families and/or long stays. Weekly and monthly rates available except in July and Aug. Doubles $138.

Rosellen Suites
2030 Barclay at Guildford
689-4807
Fax 684-3327
The plain exterior of this three-storey apartment hotel makes the black, beige and peach designer furniture inside seem even more striking. The Rosellen caters to the film industry and executive travellers and their families. Minimum stay is three nights, and prices go down the longer you stay. Amenities in the large one- and two-bedroom units include microwaves, remote-control TV, tape decks, twice-weekly maid service, washers and dryers, and fully equipped kitchens with juice, tea and coffee to get you started. Each unit is individually decorated and has a private telephone line; local calls are free. Some two-bedrooms have fireplaces and dishwashers. Free health club facili-

ties are in the neighbourhood. Limited parking.

The Rosellen is a quiet residential spot right beside Stanley Park, a 20-minute walk from downtown and near lots of restaurants. In short, a home away from home. Doubles $130.

English Bay Inn
1968 Comox at Chilco
683-8002
A Vancouver treasure, this five-room inn is in a 1930s house that has been smartly renovated in a British private club style. It occupies a quiet corner a block from the beach and Stanley Park. All rooms have private baths, and all but one have a sleigh bed or an 18th-century four-poster.

Breakfast is served in a formal dining room complete with Gothic dining suite, fireplace and grandfather clock. The parlour is elegant and comfortable with high wingbacked armchairs, thick British-India rugs and exquisite antiques. Touches like sherry and port in the parlour each afternoon or, if you prefer, tea or coffee served in your room, make a stay here a memorable one. A small private garden can be enjoyed by guests.

Unless you prefer the anonymity of a large hotel, the English Bay Inn is undoubtedly the best place to stay in Vancouver. As at all small inns, getting a reservation on short notice can be difficult.

But English Bay Inn is so special it may be worth planning a trip to Vancouver a few months down the road just to stay here. Doubles $130.

West End Guest House
1362 Haro near Jervis
681-2889
Fax 688-8812
Although it is only one block from the action and glitz of Robson St, this small 1906 guest house suggests the comforts and pace of another era. It is

The Sylvia Hotel on English Bay is a landmark heritage building. (Rosamond Norbury)

a carefully restored Victorian house with period furniture. The original owners had a photography business, and so the early years of the West Coast are chronicled throughout the house in dozens of wonderful old photographs. The cozy parlour has a gas fireplace and overstuffed furniture; breakfast is served in an exquisitely furnished dining room. (Or breakfast can be served in bed!)

The seven guest rooms are beautifully furnished, and there are extras like the terry bathrobes and knitted

slippers. You're guaranteed a good sleep on feather mattress pads. Each room has a private bathroom, telephone and TV.

In the afternoon, guests gather for sherry in the parlour or iced tea under the shade of the canopy on the sun deck. Smoking in outdoor areas only. Doubles $130.

Buchan Hotel
1906 Haro (near Robson and Denman)
685-5354
Fax 685-5367
A small, inexpensive hotel, the Buchan is located in one of the quietest residential sections of the West End. Rooms are spotless though small; those on the east side are brighter and overlook a mini-park. No smoking is allowed in the hotel.

The staff is friendly, but at these prices there are none of the usual hotel services. Underground parking is available nearby but not right at the hotel. There is a laundry room.

Stanley Park is at your doorstep, and so are the shops and restaurants on Robson and Denman. English Bay beach is 5 minutes away, and downtown is a 15-minute walk. Weekly rates available. Doubles $85.

Sylvia Hotel
1154 Gilford at Beach
681-9321
The eight-storey Sylvia Hotel has long been a Vancouver landmark—it is popular because of the English Bay view and the reasonable prices. Built in 1912, the ivy-covered brick structure was declared a heritage building in 1975. A new low-rise wing was added to the hotel in 1986. All 119 rooms have bathrooms, and 23 have kitchens. Rooms on the south side overlook English Bay and the beach across the street. The Sylvia Restaurant in the addition has outdoor dining in the summer, one of the city's best places to people-watch and catch

the sunset. And, although the decor in the lobby lounge is uninspiring, it also has a view and is a popular bar.

The rooms are plain, and some could use a little sprucing up, but it's hard to complain when you consider the price. It's a 20-minute walk through the lovely residential West End to downtown. Because of the low prices, it is necessary to book well in advance for a summer stay. Doubles $55.

Kitsilano

Kenya Court Guest House
2230 Cornwall near Yew
738-7085
Only a 10-minute drive from the heart of the city, this small apartment building facing Kitsilano Beach is a great alternative to staying downtown. This lovely 1920s guest house has four units: large one- and two-bedroom apartments that sleep up to six, with tasteful period furnishings and gleaming hardwood floors. ("Immaculate" is taken to new heights at Kenya Court.) All the units have kitchens for preparing snacks but not for full meal preparation. A complimentary breakfast is served in a cheery rooftop solarium that has a breathtaking view of English Bay and the North Shore mountains. No smoking in the building. Run by a friendly couple who speak Italian, French and German. On-street parking. Book well in advance for the summer. No credit cards. Doubles $120.

Near the Airport

Radisson President Hotel & Suites
8181 Cambie Rd at No. 3 Rd,
Richmond
276-8181
1-800-333-3333 (worldwide)
The Radisson, with a four-diamond AAA/CAA rating, has a modernistic sweeping glass exterior and a lobby highlighted by an open staircase and an impressive two-storey-high glass chandelier.

The 184 guest rooms (39 are suites) are smart and sensible rather than elegant in decor but have many amenities. Each room has a coffeemaker, hair dryer, iron, ironing board and refrigerator, as well as two telephones, voice mail and dataport. Opened in May 1994, this hotel, with its first-class business centre and close-to-the-the-airport location, is already a favourite with the business set.

The Radisson has an Asian feel to it, and no wonder—there is a Chinese supermarket next door and a Buddhist temple on the roof, the lobby art gallery features Asian art, and the President Chinese Restaurant has quickly became known for its authentic Cantonese delicacies. The Gallery Restaurant specializes in Pacific Northwest cuisine. There is a fitness centre complete with pool, whirlpool and exercise area. The hotel is five minutes from the airport via the free shuttle service. It's also within walking distance of several large shopping malls and a short drive to golf courses. Doubles $190.

Delta Vancouver Airport Hotel & Marina
3500 Cessna, Richmond
278-1241
1-800-268-1133 toll free
Fax 276-1975
This 418-room hotel in a quiet location on the Fraser River is geared to business travellers. All rooms have views—the south side is best—and some have balconies. In 1995 all the rooms were refurbished and a small weight room was added on the top floor. The marina offers boat charters. There is an outdoor pool and a jogging route along the river and guests have full use of the exceptional facilities at the nearby Delta Pacific Resort & Conference Centre. A shuttle is

available to and from the two hotels, to the airport and to and from Lansdowne Shopping Centre. Most convenient hotel to the airport. Doubles $155.

Delta Pacific Resort & Conference Centre

10251 St Edwards, Richmond
278-9611
1-800-268-1133 toll free
Fax 276-1121

Two towers and a low-rise on 6 ha (15 acres) make up this 458-room convention hotel/resort. The rooms in the low-rise open onto a grassy area and outdoor pool, perfect for families. The large rooms have all been recently refurnished, but it is the facilities that are the main drawing card: indoor tennis courts with instructors (and partners if you wish), squash courts, two outdoor pools and one indoor, volleyball court, golf practice range, equipment rentals, outdoor exercise circuit, aqua-fit classes, poolside bar and grill and a complete business centre. An addition in 1995 was the 69 m (225-foot) indoor tubular water slide.

Children are catered to here—as well as the water fun, there is a playground and activities centre, where they can be left for up to two hours to play. Transportation to the airport ($2.00 for hotel guests) and free transportation to the local mall. Doubles $155.

Kingsway

2400 Motel

2400 Kingsway at Nanaimo
434-2464
Fax 430-1045

The 2400 has an old-fashioned but appealing look with a dozen little white bungalows and a two-storey building of connected units. The bungalows are the best, just like smaller versions of home, with kitchens and front and back doors. The grounds are landscaped, and pets are allowed. A playground, a park and good Chinese restaurants are nearby. If you have a choice, get a unit at the rear of the complex. Two-diamond AAA/CAA rating. Doubles $59.

North Shore

Although the North Shore, particularly West Vancouver, is a delightful place, it is difficult to recommend staying there because of the horrendous rush-hour traffic around Lions Gate Bridge. If you choose to stay on the North Shore, plan your day to avoid the bridge at rush hours.

Lonsdale Quay Hotel

123 Carrie Cates Court, North Van
986-6111
1-800-836-6111 toll free (U.S.)
Fax 986-8782

Right beside the SeaBus (a 13-minute ferry trip to downtown Vancouver; see Getting Around, Public Transit), this is the North Shore's most convenient hotel. Most of the rooms take advantage of the waterfront location and the fabulous view, with either a full balcony or French doors. The rooms are modern and were all re-decorated in the summer of 1994; facilities include a restaurant, lounge (with a dance floor) and fitness centre. Parking is available. An added bonus is that the hotel is perched directly on top of Lonsdale Quay Market, where you can spend hours browsing through the fresh food stalls and various boutiques and eateries. Doubles $155.

Park Royal Hotel

540 Clyde off Taylor, West Van
926-5511
Fax 926-6082

Call to check, but don't count on the Park Royal unless you have made a reservation months in advance. The ivy-covered building is Tudor in style,

The hotel and public market at Lonsdale Quay are a short SeaBus ride from downtown.

and the atmosphere is British country inn, with exposed beams, stone fireplaces and a pub.

The 30-room hotel is tucked back on the bank of the Capilano River. Rooms are small and cozy, and the ones on the garden side are favourites. From the patio and gardens you can enjoy the view of the river (great for salmon and steelhead fly-fishing) and the surrounding woods, or you can go for a stroll along the riverbank.

It's hard to believe that Park Royal Shopping Centre is just minutes away. The hotel is difficult to find; go over Lions Gate Bridge, head into West Vancouver and take the first right onto Taylor Way; then turn right immediately at Clyde Ave. Doubles $115.

There is a small string of motels on Capilano Rd just above Marine. The best are:

Lions Gate Travelodge
2060 Marine near Capilano
985-5311
1-800-578-7878 toll free
Fax 985-5311
Doubles $110

Holiday Inn Express Vancouver, North Shore
1800 Capilano off Marine
987-4461
1-800-663-4055
Fax 984-4244
Doubles $95.

Canyon Court Motel
1748 Capilano off Marine
988-3181
Fax 988-3181, local 391
Doubles $85.

Alternative Accommodation

La Grande Résidence
845 Burrard at Smithe
682-5511
1-800-961-7555 toll free
Fax 682-5513
La Grand Résidence is a luxury apartment building connected to and run by the Sutton Place Hotel. It has maid service, 24-hour switchboard, front desk, concierge and all of the other services of the five-diamond hotel. A home away from home where staff will change a flat tire, sew on a button, organize a party or buy groceries. This 18-storey building has 162 completely equipped one- and two-bedroom apartments. An outstanding feature is the

exceptional quality and good taste shown in the furnishings. All units have dishwashers, microwaves and balconies with patio furniture, and there is storage available for bicycles or skis. VCRs are available, and there are also free bicycles for guest use. Views are best on the quiet west side. Spa facilities are shared with Sutton Place Hotel, where the indoor pool opens onto a sunny deck. Minimum stay is 30 days; rates start at $3750 a month.

Walter Gage Residence
Student Union Blvd at Wesbrook Mall
University of British Columbia
822-1010
Fax 822-1001
The residence, open to the public May, June, July and Aug, consists of three towers, each with 1200 rooms. Six single bedrooms are clustered around a kitchen (with limited cooking facilities), bathroom and living room to form self-contained units.

Single accommodation is provided in these rooms for $32 a person. Self-contained studios and one-bedroom suites are available for single or double accommodation at $56–74 for the room. Larger suites at $95, usually reserved for families, are the only units available all year.

Free visitor parking is next to the residence, and meals are available at the Student Union Building across the street (the food is not bad). In 1995 the Gage Bistro was added in the lobby of the residence; it is open weekdays 5–9 PM and weekends and holidays 7 AM–9 PM. Dinner is served daily.

UBC is a 20-minute drive from downtown.

Vancouver Hostel
1515 Discovery near 4th
224-3208
Fax 224-4852
Despite its origin as an air force bar-

racks, the renovated hostel building is far from bleak. Beside Jericho Park, it is also adjacent to tennis courts, a sailing club and one of the finest beaches in the city. Although the setting is perfect, the location is not, since it's a 30-minute bus ride from downtown.

Food at the hostel is good and cheap. Breakfast and dinner are served during the summer, or you can cook meals in the fully equipped kitchen. Separate sleeping accommodation for men and women is dormitory style. There are also private rooms, and some are suitable for families. (These must be booked ahead.) Bring a sleeping bag or rent sheets and blankets. No pets. The hostel has a coin-op laundry, storage facilities, satellite TV and mountain bike rentals. Parking is available.

Although the capacity is 285, you may need a reservation (including one night's deposit) from May to Sept. An adult Canadian Hostelling Association membership is $27 a year. Members stay for $15 a day, and nonmembers for $18.50. MasterCard or Visa accepted. Unlike some, this hostel is not closed during the day.

Bed and Breakfast

In Vancouver

Bed and breakfast agencies represent homes throughout the city (or the province), with accommodation ranging from a basic room to a gorgeous suite with a view. The B&B concept is not as developed in Vancouver as it is in the Gulf Islands, the western U.S. or even Victoria, partly because Vancouver does not have an abundance of lovely old houses that could easily be converted to bed and breakfast inns. Here B&Bs tend to be three or four rooms in someone's house.

Johnson House is one of Vancouver's best bed and breakfasts.

If you're new to this, don't worry about privacy. The hosts are usually friendly but professional and seem to know just how much interaction guests want. They will make every effort to ensure that your stay is as private and comfortable as you would like. Registries encourage guests to call if they have a complaint, but it doesn't often happen.

The advantages of B&Bs are price, which is generally less than half what downtown hotels charge; variety; and more contact with the locals, who'll give you information on everything from local politics to real estate.

Some B&Bs accept children, some have facilities for people with disabilities, and some take pets. Discounts may be available for long stays or for off season. MasterCard and Visa are generally, but not always, accepted.

The average price for a double with a shared bath is about $65; with a private bath, $85. Listed below are two registries with descriptions of some

of their more special houses. These usually fill up early, so book well in advance.

Town and Country Bed and Breakfast Registry
731-5942

The location of **Johnson House** is perfect: a graceful tree-lined street (with lots of parking) that is a quick drive from downtown and a short walk from the shops on 41st Ave.

The owners, former antique dealers, have spent seven years restoring the large 1915 house. Intricate period mouldings and pressed-tin ceilings embellish the rooms, but what is most remarkable are the numerous antiques—all painstakingly refurbished. Gramophones, coffeegrinders and wooden carousel animals are the favourites, and fortunately the house is large enough to accommodate them without appearing cluttered. The whole main floor is devoted to guests and includes a large living room with TV and fireplace, a breakfast room and a huge open kitchen. Johnson House is non-smoking and for adults only.

One of the guest rooms is enormous ($120), with a curtained four-poster bed, a sitting area and a bathroom as large as the dining room. Two smaller rooms ($70 and $75), also furnished exclusively with antiques, share a bathroom with a claw-foot tub and lovely old pedestal sink. A sunny back deck and peaceful front porch are well used by guests.

Berries and rhubarb from the garden are often included in the full breakfast.

Locarno Beach Bed and Breakfast is altogether different. It is much more like a European B&B, where you are part of the household (including teenagers and dogs). Sigred makes frequent trips to Asia and the Middle East to collect folk art, jewellery and furniture, which she imports to Canada. The breakfast area is chock-a-block with these objets d'art, which compete for your attention with the other out-of-the-ordinary feature of the house— Locarno Beach, right outside the window. This may be the only B&B in Vancouver so close to a beach. Also within a short walk is one of the best public golf courses, a driving range, tennis courts and windsurfing rentals.

There are three rooms; the room with the best view of English Bay and the North Shore mountains is $85. The two others share a bathroom and are $75 each. The furnishings in the guest rooms lean towards Canadiana, with quilts and big pine beds. Wingbacked armchairs and footstools add to the comfort. Breakfast follows the northern European tradition, with boiled eggs, cheese and cold cuts served alongside fruit, cereal, croissants and muffins. Families with children 10 years and older are welcome.

Old English Bed and Breakfast Registry

986-5069
Fax 986-8810

A stay at the **Lynn Canyon Bed and Breakfast** is a true West Coast experience, since this B&B is located up the North Shore mountains. A block away is the entrance to Lynn Canyon Park and Lynn Headwaters Regional Park and their 100 km (60 miles) of trails. Guests are often outdoors people, taking full advantage of the hiking, jogging and skiing possibilities.

The house is tucked into a forest of cedar, fir and hemlock towering above lush ferns and rhododendrons on a vast lot. It is a familiar coastal version of a spacious 1950s rancher, with wood panelling, a loft and a fireplace. One guest room, tucked off to the side, has a private bath with a Jacuzzi tub for two. One of the upstairs rooms is average size but has its own deck; the other is huge and has a separate sitting room and private deck. Native baskets, snowshoes, a spinning wheel and horseshoes from the horses that used to live on the property give this large room a rustic Canadiana feel. Both share a bathroom.

Giselle, the proprietor, speaks Dutch and German and prepares a full, healthy breakfast, including eggs from her own chickens (but there is no obnoxious early-rising rooster), which are on a special diet to produce low-cholesterol eggs. Breakfast can be served on the delightful backyard patio—it's remarkable how sunny the yard and decks are, considering the big trees—where a panorama of nature unfolds with woodpeckers tapping, chipmunks brazenly grabbing peanuts from the feeder and raccoons inspecting the pond.

Despite its location, well away from the centre of things, the house is easily accessible by public transit. Even if you are in Vancouver without a car, there is no reason not to enjoy this woodsy retreat. Doubles $85.

The **Lighthouse Park Bed and Breakfast** is another example of West Coast architecture. This house, perched on a treed cliff above Lighthouse Park, was designed by Arthur Erickson in his celebrated style of strong horizontal beams of rough wood and walls of glass to maximize views and to both integrate with and counterpoint the setting. The house is stepped down the cliff, and there are expansive decks on the roofs of the storeys below. Bowen Island, the Strait of Georgia, Vancouver Island, ferries coming and going out of Horseshoe Bay and eagles in neighbouring treetops are all part of the

River Run Cottages is a floating bed and breakfast where ducks, loons, bald eagles and seals are right next door. (River Run)

view. It seems odd to call this a B&B, simply because of its elegance. The furnishings are a tasteful mix of oriental, French provincial and contemporary. Three enveloping wine- coloured leather sofas face the fireplace adjacent to the bright white open kitchen. A French provincial armoire of Belgian walnut houses the TV. Silver, crystal and fine china are laid out for breakfast. The formal elegance of the house belies the warmth and friendliness of Elizabeth, the hostess.

The guest rooms are huge, each about the size of a small one-bedroom apartment, and both have seating areas, decks and private baths with Jacuzzi tubs. The beds are king- or queen-size and made up with white embroidered linen.

A car is necessary to get to the house, but after you arrive, you may feel that you don't want to leave, even to hike at Lighthouse Park, golf at Gleneagles or play tennis at the nearby public courts. It's only 30 minutes from downtown, but the elegance, the view and the setting make you feel kilometres from the city. Doubles $115 and $125. No children. Don't miss this one, unless you're on a sneakers and T-shirt kind of holiday.

The homey **Kitsilano B&B** is just a few blocks away from the lively commercial district of W Broadway. Three guest rooms are decorated in blue and white with quilts, white wicker and some early-Canadian maple and pine pieces. Walls are accented by the hostess's collection of Afro-Asian textiles. The guest room on the main floor, which has its own bathroom next door, opens out onto a beautiful terraced backyard and a sunny patio. One of the upstairs rooms takes advantage of the hilltop location with an expansive view. The small room next door would be perfect for a child. Doubles $95.

Near Vancouver

If you prefer a quiet country ambience or an island retreat, here are two B&Bs where you can't go wrong and you are still close enough to sightsee in the city.

Ladner

River Run Cottages
4551 River Road W Ladner
946-7778
Wake up to river breezes and a gentle floating sensation in *Waterlily*, a homey houseboat, one of three cottages nestled along the Fraser River. Located in the sleepy fishing and farming community of Ladner, River Run Cottages are the stuff of picture postcards. Large decks overlook the Fraser, in summer hanging baskets explode with colour and fresh herbs, and you're in your own private community—just you and the river view, shared with ducks, swans, loons, eagles and seals.

Although small, *Waterlily* is a favourite, with its queen-size loft bed, claw-foot tub, potbelly stove and private deck. *Farmer's Cottage* and *Net Loft* both jut out onto the shoreline, are more spacious and are beautifully furnished. Each cottage has a separate telephone line and a CD player.

A kayak, a row boat and bicycles are available. The location is ideal—you can walk the dyke into Ladner, cycle to the George C. Reifel Migratory Bird Sanctuary (see Parks/Beaches/Gardens) or catch a ferry to one of the Gulf Islands for the day (see Excursions from Vancouver). It's a 30-minute drive to city centre. Doubles $125.

Bowen Island

Seaside Reflections
365 Cardena Dr, Bowen Island
1-604-947-0937
Tucked above Snug Cove, the expansive decks and full-length windows give an outdoor feeling to Seaside Reflections. Your private deck overlooks the cove, the mountains and Howe Sound. Seaside Reflections is geared to adults; proprietors Bev Lindsay and Brian Hotel understand that people want to get away from it all. They left

the busy corporate world and city for this retreat, and they enjoy sharing it. The guest room is lovely, with flowered chintz drapes and spread, and the Snuggler's Den is a cozy haven where you can spend hours with a book after walking the nearby wooded trails. A couple on their own can use both rooms, but it also works for two couples since the den has a comfortable, queen-size pull-out bed. The two rooms and bathroom are on a lower level and are very private.

Breakfast on the deck (guests are encouraged to make this their home and to wander and lounge wearing the cozy robes provided), or in the large living room and dining room, is your choice of continental or buffet. Freshly squeezed juices, artistically designed fruit trays, and specials like basil/tomato scones make a great combination with the sea air. The days may end with candlelight and wine on your private deck. This place is peaceful and made for romance.

There are express West Vancouver buses (#257) from bus stops along Georgia in Vancouver (call 985-7777 for schedule). Ferries depart Horseshoe Bay between 6:05 AM and 9:25 PM daily. It's a 15-minute ride. Bowen has wonderful walks and a delightful small town to be explored. Prices vary, depending on breakfast choice. Doubles $75–$100.

Trailer Parks/ Campgrounds

Prices listed here are for a trailer and two people in high season, with a full hookup if available.

In and Near Vancouver

Capilano Mobile Park
295 Tomahawk, West Van
987-4722

Underneath the north foot of the Lions Gate Bridge, beside the Capilano River. Trailers, tents and RVs on 208 sites. Newly renovated facilities include showers, Jacuzzi, games room, pool, laundry room and supervised playground. Sani-station, propane. Reservations for June, July and Aug must be accompanied by a deposit. Surprisingly quiet, considering the proximity to the bridge. Adjacent to shopping centre, beach and park. Five minutes from downtown. $30.

Burnaby Cariboo RV Park

8765 Cariboo Place
Cariboo exit from Hwy 1, Burnaby
420-1722
This highly rated RV park offers a heated indoor pool, Jacuzzi, store, sani-station, telephone jacks, laundry, free showers, cablevision and RV wash. Trailers, RVs and tents; 217 sites. Adjacent to Burnaby Lake Regional Park and pickup stop for Grayline Tours. $29.

Richmond RV Park

Hollybridge at River Rd, Richmond
270-7878
Open Apr 1 to Oct 31. Free showers, laundry, sani-station, propane, games room and mobile septic service. Tents, trailers, RVs; 200 sites. Central location. $22.

Near Tsawwassen

ParkCanada Recreational Vehicle Inn

4799 Hwy 17 (exit north on 52nd St), Delta
943-5811
Near the ferry terminal. Tents, RVs and trailers; 150 sites. Laundry, free showers, sani-station, heated outdoor pool, store. Near golf course and water park. $22.

White Rock

Sea Crest Motel and RV Park

864–160th St
531-4720
For RVs only; 31 sites. Showers, laundry; close to beach and golf course. $20.

Parklander Motor and Trailer Court

16311–8th Ave
531-3711
"Adult oriented"; tents, trailers and RVs; 45 sites in a parklike setting. Showers. $20.

Hazelmere RV Park and Campground

18843–8th Ave at 188th St
538-1167
In a forest setting on the Campbell River. Tents, RVs and trailers; 154 sites. Showers, laundry, propane, sani-station, store. $22.

Surrey

Dogwood Campgrounds

15151–112th Ave
583-5585
Take the 160th Ave exit from the Trans-Canada Hwy. Tents, RVs and trailers; 350 sites. Showers, laundry, store, propane, heated outdoor pool, Jacuzzi, playground, salmon bakes and bus tours. Natural treed setting. $26.

Tynehead RV Camp

16275–102nd Ave
589-1161
Tents, trailers and RVs; 117 sites. Heated outdoor pool, showers, laundry, lounge, store, games room, minigolf. Adjacent to forest and near shopping centre. $25.

Fraser River RV Park

11940 Old Yale Rd
580-1841
Beside the Fraser River. Tents, trailers

and RVs; 135 sites. Showers, laundry, sani-station, dock, boat ramp and pub. $21.

Peace Arch RV Park
14601–40th Ave
594-7009
From Hwy 99 north, take the North Delta exit and follow signs. Tents, RVs and trailers on 300 sites. Heated pool, mini-golf, telephone jacks, satellite TV, horseshoe pitch, playground, laundry, free showers. $27.

Coquitlam/Port Moody

Four Acres Trailer Court
675 Lougheed Hwy, Coquitlam
936-3273
Close to Lougheed Mall. Trailers, RVs and tents; 30 sites. Showers, laundry, sani-station. $15.

Anmore Camplands
3230 Sunnyside, Port Moody
469-2311
Located at the entrance to beautifully forested Buntzen Lake, with its beaches and hiking trails. Tents, RVs and trailers; 150 sites. Free showers, security gate, laundry, sani-station, store, heated outdoor pool, covered barbecue area, fire pits, canoe rentals, playground, sports court. Horse rentals and guided trips available next door at Alpine Riding Academy. This is not an easy place to find, but if you want a country stay with lots of outdoor activity, it's worth the effort. Call first for directions. $23.

Restaurants

Breakfast/Brunch 40

Bakery Cafés 43

Lunch 44

Seafood 45

Pizza 46

Vegetarian 46

Late Night 47

Outdoors 47

With a View 48

Espresso Bars 49

By Nationality 50
Chinese, Dim Sum, Contemporary, Continental, East Indian,
Ethiopian, French, Greek, Italian, Japanese, Jewish, Mexican, Spanish,
Thai, Vietnamese/Cambodian, West Coast

By Location 63
Broadway (between Main and Granville), Chinatown, Downtown,
East Side, Granville Island, Kitsilano/West Side, North Shore,
South of 33rd Avenue, West End

Cooks quit, restaurants close, menus change, and so do hours: restaurant guides are written on sand. In addition, Vancouver has approximately 3000 restaurants. Here we attempt to focus on the tried and true as well as on those newcomers that just can't be ignored.

Today's diners are a discriminating lot. They consider the freshness of the greenery and the fat content of the dressing as routinely as they peruse the choices on the wine list. For this reason, we've included a guide to healthy eating in Vancouver—a selection of restaurants that participate in the Heart and Stroke Foundation of B.C. & Yukon's "Heart Smart Restaurant Program." We've also included a section on B.C. estate wineries.

If you're on a budget, you'll find the best value in some of the many Asian restaurants—Cantonese, Mandarin, Japanese, Vietnamese, Cambodian, Thai and Korean are all here.

There's also French dining, a plethora of Greek and Italian favourites, some intriguing Indian—even Ethiopian—ones, and, of course, a fine selection of restaurants that serve up West Coast fare. In addition, some of the world's best seafood is found here.

The restaurants listed here are all recommended, some more highly than others. Each one has been chosen because whatever its price range, it reliably gives good value.

A standard tip is 12 to 20 per cent. Provincial sales tax of 10 per cent is levied on alcohol served in restaurants. The federal Goods and Services Tax of 7 per cent is applied to restaurant meals.

Restaurants marked with one $ are inexpensive; a generous dinner for one, excluding alcohol and tip, costs $20 or less. In a moderate restaurant ($$), expect to pay between $20 and $35; in an expensive restaurant ($$$), more than $35.

Breakfast/Brunch

Café Fleuri $$$
The Sutton Place Hotel
845 Burrard near Robson
682-5511
Any morning you need a gentle entry to the day and don't mind spending money to get it, eat breakfast at Café Fleuri. Classical music, muted browns, soft surfaces to absorb any discordant sounds, coffee and orange juice poured just before the menu is presented—it's a cocoon of discreet service. You can order the usual run of pancakes and eggs, wake up over crêpes, or venture into a Japanese breakfast: miso soup, raw egg, rice and broiled salmon. Café Fleuri is also known for having the best Sunday brunch in the city, which includes all the usual breakfast fare plus chef-prepared omelets while you watch, seafood specials and a mind-boggling array of desserts. This meal will keep you going the whole day. Open breakfast, lunch and dinner daily. Brunch is on Sun and holidays, 11–2.

Capers $$
2496 Marine Dr at 25th, West Van
925-3316
2285 W 4th at Vine
739-6685
1675 Robson near Bidwell
687-5288
Hidden in the back of a lavishly handsome health food store, Capers in West Vancouver serves traditional breakfasts made from free-run eggs and nitrate-free bacon, along with yogurt, müsli and fruit.

All three Capers restaurants have a laid-back atmosphere, with lots of plants; service can be slow and occasionally forgetful. The West Vancouver Capers is open at 8 daily for breakfast, lunch and dinner (no dinner Sun). The 4th Ave restaurant serves brunch Sat, Sun and holidays,

9–4; open daily for lunch and dinner.

The most recently opened Capers, on Robson, is a deli-style café with about a dozen tables inside and on a patio; best for snacks, sandwiches and fresh juices. Open daily, 8 AM–11 PM.

Gladys $
2278 W 4th near Vine
738-0828

Sometimes when visiting a city, it's fun to breakfast with the locals. In Kitsilano, that means going to Gladys.

You want down-home, the way Mom used to cook? Then start your day with corned beef hash—bacon, mushrooms, onions, potatoes, spices and the best corned beef. This dish is famous; people travel across the city for it.

For a more refined breakfast, there's smoked salmon Benedict on a bagel or omelets, French toast, hot cakes . . . All the jams and sauces at Gladys are made by owner Renee Thomas, who has owned the place since 1984. Before that, it did belong to Gladys, and when Renee bought it, she kept the name because that was her mother's name.

Renee, who is usually there, runs a welcoming restaurant that is popular with all age groups. Breakfast is served daily from 8 AM to 3 PM. Gladys is also open for dinner, and it's comfort food—beef stew, barbecued ribs, liver and onions, pastas and seasonal greens. For breakfast, arrive early, since there's often a lineup by 10.

Open daily; closes at 4 on Mon.

Isadora's Co-operative
Restaurant $$
1540 Old Bridge, Granville Island
681-8816

Isadora's is the best place in Vancouver to take children for breakfast. Windows on one side overlook the Granville Island water park. There's an indoor play corner, children's servings and change tables in both washrooms. Isadora's has good cappuccino, well-done versions of brunch classics and a sunny, glad-to-greet-the-day atmosphere.

The rest of the day's menu is modern eclectic: samosas, stuffed croissants, salads and burgers (including a nutburger).

Open at 7:30 weekdays and 9 on weekends. Very popular for weekend brunches; go before 10 if you don't want to wait in line. Reservations for six or more. Breakfast, lunch and dinner daily (no dinner Mon, Sept to May).

The Tomahawk $
1550 Philip near Marine, North Van
988-2612

The Tomahawk serves gigantic breakfasts at good prices. It started out as a hamburger stand 65 years ago, when North Vancouver was mostly trees, and is now run by the son of the original owner.

The decor is kitsch museum, with portraits of royalty, Native baskets and carvings, settlers' tools and placemats with a '50s-style tourist map of the province. The Yukon breakfast is five slices of back bacon, two eggs, hash browns and toast; muffins are gigantic. Or go for the pancakes. No reservations, no alcohol. Most of the breakfasts are served throughout the day. Breakfast, lunch, dinner daily; opens at 8.

Also
Bacchus, see Lunch
Benny's Bagels, see Late Night
The Naam, see Vegetarian
Teahouse, see Outdoors
Dim sum, see Chinese
See Bakery Cafés, below.

Ten Healthy Eats in Vancouver

Gone are the days when healthy eating meant raw carrots and celery sticks. Today's chefs pride themselves on low-fat, high-fibre culinary treats that entice the palate and please the eye. The Heart and Stroke Foundation of B.C. & Yukon produces a booklet, "The Heart Smart Restaurant Program," listing over 350 restaurants throughout the province that adhere to the Heart Foundation's mandate for healthy eating. Healthy menu items are identified, often by a check mark. Although many of today's eateries do have healthy menu items, here's 10 in the city that are on the Heart Smart Program.

1. **Fish House at Stanley Park $$**
2099 Beach in Stanley Park
681-7275
Fresh seafood menu changes daily; lovely setting.

2. **Fogg n Suds** $
1323 Robson near Jervis
683-2337
500 W Broadway at Cambie
872-3377
3293 W 4th at Blenheim
732-3377
Casual, fun restaurants; besides offering healthy items, thay have a selection of over 200 beers from around the world.

3. **Griffin's Restaurant** $$
900 W Georgia at Burrard
662-1900
One of Vancouver Hotel's three restaurants that offer healthy menu items (as does room service), Griffin's is bright and cheerful, and you can order à la carte or choose from a full buffet.

4. **Joe Fortes Seafood House $$**
777 Thurlow near Robson
669-1940
A lively, San Francisco–style restaurant and bar with 18 daily selections of fresh seafood.

5. **Mongolie Grill** $
467 W Broadway near Cambie
874-6121
Choose fresh veggies, meat or sea-

food, and a chef cooks on a large grill in front of you.

6. **Pastels** $
1101 Robson at Thurlow
685-8963
Over a dozen Vancouver locations, including two in Pacific Centre and one in the Kids Only Market. Pastel's counter service is fast, and the food is fresh.

7. **Rubina Tandoori** $$
1962 Kingsway near Victoria
874-3621
One of the city's favourite East Indian restaurants. See Restaurants (East Indian).

8. **Seasons in the Park** $$
Queen Elizabeth Park
874-8008
The view and the setting are as good as the food. See Restaurants (With a View).

9. **Surat Sweet Restaurant** $
1938 W 4th Ave
733-7363
Vegetarian food with a flare.

10. **The Cannery** $$$
2205 Commissioner near north end of Victoria
254-9606
One of the city's best for seafood. See Restaurants (With a View).

Bakery Cafés

Ecco Il Pane $
238 W 5th near Alberta
873-6888
2563 W Broadway near Trafalgar
739-1314
Pamela Gaudreault and Christopher Brown started out baking healthy bread (no additives, sugar, oil or dairy products) in the back of a food store. A year later they opened Ecco Il Pane—which means "here is the bread"—a Tuscan country-style bakery on a quiet street. They put in a few chairs and tables, in case customers picking up their hand-shaped, stone-hearth-baked breads cared to relax with a coffee. Next they expanded their seating area to hold a cozy 32, and then they opened a second location on W Broadway. This one is three times larger and more elegant than casual. A special feature is the Italian-made, wood-burning stove, where you can observe hot loaves coming out of the oven. (This location also serves light dinners.)

Both locations specialize in *pane* (bread), *biscotti* (cookies) and *dolci* (sweet bread). What time you come for bread depends on what tempts you. In the morning, there's freshly squeezed orange juice and a breakfast *panino* (fritatta on grilled asiago focaccia with roasted tomatoes). Drop by around noon to munch on a thick sandwich like the Mortadella—tomatoes and provolone cheese on rosemary focaccia.

Don't forget to buy your bread—there's a dozen varieties. You may come in with multigrain on your mind but leave with a loaf packed with green and black olives. For a special treat, don't miss the sour cherry chocolate. Open daily, Mon to Fri, 8–5; Sat, 8:30–5; Sun, 9–4.

Savary Island Pie Company $
1533 Marine Dr near 15th, West Van
926-4021
If your idea of a heavenly breakfast is a latte and a little something sweet, it's worth travelling across the bridge and standing in line at the Savary Island Pie Company. There's a selection of delicious baked goods, including muffins, cinnamon buns, seasonal pies (the lemon buttermilk pie is fabulous) and the best blueberry scones in town. But this is more than a coffee and sweet stop—take time to wander into the back and watch the bakers work in the large, open kitchen. You'll be tempted to stock up on goodies to take home. On weekends, in particular, it's busy all day and evening, since wine and beer on tap are now served. The restaurant has a neighbourhood atmosphere—if you're enjoying pie and coffee, they won't rush you out at closing time. Open daily; 7 AM–11 PM.

Terra Breads $
2380 W 4th near Balsam
736-1838
Start the day with Terra Breads' famous grape bread laced with pine nuts and walnuts. Like all Terra's breads, it's healthy (no fat, eggs, dairy products or preservatives) and crusty, since it's baked directly on the oven's stone hearth (no pans or tins used). Homemade granola, fruit scones, cinnamon buns and other hearty breads served hot with jam are all perfect starters to the day.

There's a warm, pink-toned slate floor and gleaming Douglas fir counter with eight seats. For a quick breakfast, there are juices, teas, coffees and cappuccino along with some 18 varieties of bread including fig and anise, Italian cheese, challah (braided egg bread) and a tasty pumpkin seed loaf. For lunch you can choose from focaccia sandwiches, soups and salads.

Terra Breads has a bakery only at Granville Island Public Market. Both locations are open daily; hours at Kitsilano bakery are Mon to Thurs and Sat, 8–6; Fri, 8–6:30; Sun and holidays, 8–5.

Lunch

Bacchus $$$
Wedgewood Hotel
845 Hornby near Robson
689-7777

Bacchus, the lounge and informal restaurant in the Wedgewood Hotel, is for days when lunch is the main event. You need time to loll about in one of those deep armchairs—near the gas fireplace if it's a rainy day—and soak up the relaxed charm. There's an excellent antipasto plate, plenty of pasta choices, grilled fish and a very pleasant prosciutto, Roma tomatoes, vegetables and grilled mozzarella frittata. Bacchus serves breakfast until 11:30 on weekdays —hazelnut waffles and French-toasted brioche, along with the more standard offerings. On weekends brunch is 11–3.

Open daily for breakfast, lunch and dinner.

Chartwell $$$
Four Seasons Hotel
791 W Georgia at Howe
689-9333

Serious power lunchers choose Chartwell, named for Winston Churchill's country estate and modelled after an upper-class British men's club: dark floor-to-ceiling wood panelling, deep leather armchairs, barons of beef under brass domes. Try Chef Marc Miron's Fraser Valley vegetable pie with pine nuts, feta cheese and eggplant caviar.

Dessert lovers will revel in the offerings here; port and Stilton available, of course.

Lunch Mon to Fri; dinner daily; special theatre menu offered daily, 5:30–6:30.

Gallery Café $
Vancouver Art Gallery
Robson at Howe
688-2233

A sharp, clean, modern restaurant in the sharp, clean, modern Arthur Erickson re-design of the Vancouver Art Gallery, the Gallery Café is an upscale cafeteria. The fare is light meals, lots of salads, a limited selection of wine and beer, and killer desserts. Sit on the terrace overlooking Robson Square on sunny days. It's packed at lunchtime, but the line-up moves quickly. Open daily 9–6 except Thurs and Fri, 9–9, and Sun, 12–6.

Japanese Deli House $
381 Powell near Jackson
681-6484

The best place for an early lunch if you're browsing the remains of Vancouver's pre-war Japantown is also one of the city's least expensive sushi outlets. Sushi is made in advance for the 11:30 AM opening; eat close to noon and you'll have it at its freshest. The appetizer menu is worth exploring—for example, the squid tempura.

Truck stop–meets–Japanese restaurant decor, made restful by the graceful, high-ceilinged room, the main floor of a turn-of-the-century commercial building. No credit cards. Lunch daily; no dinner on Mon. Tues to Sat closes at 8; Sun closes at 6.

Tony's Neighbourhood Deli $
1046 Commercial at Napier
253-7422

Commercial Dr is one of the best neighbourhoods to wander. Originally dubbed Little Italy, today the East Side street melds a rich ethnic mosaic and young professionals who are prettying up old houses. Organic food outlets, used book stores, world music record shops, eateries of every origin—they're all here.

For a cheap and hearty lunch, you can't beat Tony's. Originally a market that was once owned by a Tony, today's deli has Mediterranean fare with rusticca breads and grilled focaccia sandwiches. Tony's counter service offers the best sandwiches in town. There's a super selection of salamis, cheeses and vegetarian specials. Sandwiches are Tuscany-style *paninis* (which means "little bread," but it doesn't seem little). There's about a dozen varieties on the menuboard, which changes weekly depending on what's fresh in the markets.

On a street where cappuccino is the password for a good time, Tony's is becoming known for its brevé (a latte made with heavy cream). In summer try an iced brevé, or for a heavy-duty drink go for the brevé negro (cream, chocolate, vanilla, honey and whipping cream). Not for calorie counters.

Creaky wooden floors, small round tables—it ain't fancy, but it's cheap and the food is delicious and filling. Open Mon to Sat, 7:30 AM–10:30 PM.

Water St Café $$
300 Water at Cambie, Gastown
689-2832
If you are sightseeing in Gastown, this is the place for lunch. You'll find large windows, cheerful service and a dependable menu, especially if you're a pasta and salad fan. The helpings are on the large size—a prawn and papaya salad in a tangy, oriental dressing will satisfy most appetites. But if you want more, there's lots to choose from, and the focaccia bread arrives warm.

On a sunny day, reserve early for a table outside or by the windows. Do specify, since there are several tables

here where you are really in the midst of waiter and customer traffic. Dining outside, you'll have a seat to observe the half-hourly blasts of steam from the steam clock across the street and the throng of onlookers gathered at this corner.

There are two upstairs rooms for private events; one has a fireplace. Lunch and dinner daily.

Also
Benny's Bagels, see Late Night
Bridges, see Outdoors
Le Crocodile, see French
Le Grec, see Greek
Isadora's, see Breakfast/Brunch
Kaplan's, see Jewish
Kirin, see Chinese
Marineview Coffeeshop, see Seafood
Pink Pearl, see Chinese
RainCity Grill, see Contemporary
Raintree, see West Coast
Settebello, see Outdoors
Teahouse, see Outdoors
Topanga, see Mexican
See Chinese (*Dim Sum*)

Seafood

Marineview Coffeeshop $
611 Alexander at Princess
253-0616
The Marineview used to be a fishermen and dock workers' café, perched above the Campbell Ave docks, with a great view of fish boats and mountains and a legendary reputation for its crab sandwiches. When the building was demolished, the Marineview moved. The new building—actually the old American Can Building, renovated and filled with architects' offices—doesn't have a view. The counter is from the old restaurant, but the fishermen and dockworkers are gone. The crab sandwich (and the shrimp, for that matter) is still one of the great examples of its kind. Don't order anything else on the menu, and

get there before noon if you don't want to wait. Open Mon to Fri until 4 PM.

The Cannery $$$
2205 Commissioner near north end of Victoria
254-9606

This refitted cannery with its industrial view of the Burrard Inlet waterfront may be the perfect marriage of great seafood and an absorbing view. Tugs hustle by against a backdrop of the North Shore mountains, the grain elevators and, to the west, Lions Gate Bridge. The menu has clam chowder and Caesar salad for people who want to concentrate on the view, and live lobster, a good choice of East Coast oysters, a shopping list of fish to grill and a strong wine list for those who want to eat well.

Choose the upstairs for cozy, cluttered romance, the downstairs if you like a more spacious seaside dalliance. To find the restaurant, travel east on Hastings to Victoria, turn left on Victoria, then right on Commissioner. Lunch Mon to Fri; dinner daily.

Also
Pink Pearl, see Chinese
Salmon House on the Hill, see With a View
Shijo, see Japanese
Tojo's, see Japanese

Pizza

Flying Wedge $
1937 Cornwall near Cypress
732-8840
1175 Robson near Bute
681-1233

On some days, pizza by the slice is the perfect hearty snack. Flying Wedge has two well-placed locations: one on Robson, one close to Kits Beach. The pizza here has a whole-wheat herb crust and trendy toppings—Broken

Hearts is artichoke hearts, onions, tomatoes, mushrooms; Deep Purple is marinated eggplant, onions, mushrooms, asiago cheese. Hot Licks (pepperoni, mushrooms, green peppers, spicy sauce) is hot enough to bring tears to your eyes. $3.25 for a big slice. Open daily to midnight, Fri and Sat to 1 AM.

Also
Settebello, see Outdoors
Simpatico, see Greek

Vegetarian

The Naam $
2724 W 4th near Stephens
738-7151

A landmark of counterculture history, the Naam has been serving vegetarian food in the same location since the 1970s. Now the herbal tea has been joined by cappuccino, and there are some killer chocolate desserts on the menu, but the Naam is still a safe place for people who don't eat animals. Best bets are ethnic specialties, particularly if you get scary flashbacks at the sight of a plate of stewed vegetables. Although the young staff are always cheerful, the service is no great shakes. Decor is homey, with wooden tables, kitchen chairs and, in the back, an outdoor courtyard that's a fine, leafy place to be on a warm day. No reservations. Open 24 hours daily.

Also
Capers, see Breakfast/Brunch
Isadora's, see Breakfast/Brunch

Late Night

The Accord $$
4298 Main at 28th
876-6110

Behind the Accord's formidable white venetian blinds is a haven for anyone with a late-night need for good Chinese food. Tanks full of live lobster, crab, shrimp and rock cod ensure freshness. Less opulent than the most expensive of the new Cantonese pleasure palaces, more comfortable than the old Chinese-Canadian greasy spoons, the Accord has a minimally decorated but comfortable dining room. Try prawns steamed in their shells, to be peeled and dipped in a brown vinegar, soy and hot-pepper sauce, or beef tenderloin *teppan* with peppercorn sauce. Dinner daily; open Sun to Thurs until 2 AM; Fri and Sat until 3 AM.

Benny's Bagels $
2503 W Broadway at Larch
736-4686

Benny's Bagels is a place to chat over espresso and apple crisp until late, with a candle flickering amid a soothing hubbub of voices. The food is basic and wholesome (and available 24 hours a day): bagels, salads, desserts and coffees. The scene is young and unpretentious—the comfortable feel of the place is the main reason to come—a place to people-watch or just sit and read. You won't be alone. In fact, in the evening, come early or late or you won't get in at all. It's a great breakfast spot too, but we'd sooner drink coffee by candlelight or by moonlight on the patio.
Open 24 hours.

Also
Bread Garden, see Essential
   Information (Late-Night Services)
Hamburger Mary's, see Essential
   Information (Late-Night Services)

The Naam, see Vegetarian
Simpatico, see Greek

Outdoors

Bridges Restaurant $
1696 Duranleau, Granville Island
687-4400

For a summertime lunch or an early dinner, Bridges' bistro is the place where Vancouverites like to take visiting easterners. You overlook a busy harbour scene of fishing boats coming into harbour, kayaks, sailboats and tiny ferries; seagulls call; the sun glistens off the cityscape across the water; and you feel that all is well with the world. It's so Vancouver.

Bridges also has a lively pub and a dining room upstairs, but the main floor bistro's huge outdoor deck is the main reason for a stop here. It's always busy, yet you always get seated. Cheerful young servers arrive with heaping platefuls of seafood, salads, pizza, and pasta. The menu is pretty standard fare, but the fish is fresh and it's all good. No reservations.

Open daily; bistro, 11–11; dining room, 5:30–10.

Dundarave Concession $
Dundarave Pier, West Van
Foot of 25th St

The aroma hits you when you round the corner of the little wooden concession building: equal parts hamburger and nostalgia. Vera Hochstader doesn't make the city's biggest burger, but it may be the best: good meat, fresh iceberg lettuce, a fresh bun—heaven in one handful. Walk your burger to the beach and find a log to sit on. No French fries, no alcohol, no credit cards, no side issues.

Open May to Oct, 10 AM to dusk.

Settebello $$

1131 Robson near Thurlow, upstairs
681-7377
Settebello is a great place to relax after heavy shopping. The large patio is one of the prettiest in the city, and if the food isn't superb, it's at least adequate. The menu is pasta, salads and brick-oven pizzas, washed down with wine and, if all goes well, sunshine. Lunch and dinner daily.

The Teahouse Restaurant at Ferguson Point $$

Stanley Park
669-3281
Patio tables under the trees on the front lawn are a civilized addition to what was already the best place to eat in Stanley Park. The glassed-in conservatory wing is pleasant on colder days and is stuffed to the gills on Mother's Day and Easter. Carrot soup with chive chantilly, perfectly grilled fish, brunches with the usual variations on eggs in hollandaise and, for giddy desserts, there's a choux pastry swan filled with rum-flavoured custard, whipped cream and chocolate sauce. Drive through the park to Ferguson Point, breathe country air, see squirrels, enjoy all the benefits of eating at a country inn without having to brave a freeway. Reservations required for brunch and weekend dinners. Lunch Mon to Fri; brunch Sat and Sun; dinner daily.

Also
Gallery Café, see Lunch
Isadora's, see Breakfast/Brunch
The Naam, see Vegetarian
Seasons in the Park, see With a View
Water St Café, see Lunch

With a View

Salmon House on the Hill $$$

2229 Folkestone Way, West Van
926-3212

This well-established and well-located West Vancouver dining room is a must on most travellers' lists. It is well worth the drive up the mountainside to see the best view of the city, and on a clear day or evening you also see Vancouver Island and Mount Baker. When the harbour is dotted with white sails and you catch a cruise ship passing under Lions Gate Bridge, it's an unforgettable scene. The West Coast Native artifacts adorning the entrance hall and dining room walls are also to be admired.

The salmon here is alder-grilled, meaning that it has a distinctive, slightly smoky and succulent flavour. Chef Dan Atkinson is known for his innovative creations, such as the alder-grilled salmon marinated in single malt Scotch whiskey, lemon grass and golden sugar with lemon and ginger butter. The grilled oysters here have always been a winner; when jalapeño and bacon vinaigrette was added to the dish, it became even more enticing.

A good wine list with an excellent Northwest representation. Salmon House on the Hill is not known for its "extras"; some find the salads and entrées on the small side. Nevertheless, this is a popular restaurant, so reserve early.

Lunch and dinner daily; brunch on Sun, 11:30–2:30.

Seasons in the Park $$

Queen Elizabeth Park
874-8008
A big, comfortable restaurant with light wood and deep carpeting, Seasons in the Park has an unmatchable view of city and mountains from the highest point inside city limits. The parklike feeling expands into the dining room as, in one section, you dine beneath a a broad-leafed fig tree. President Clinton admired the panorama and dined on grilled salmon with dill and rosemary during the Vancouver

Summit. A favourite with regulars is the seared fresh prawns and scallops. Pacific Northwest wines are featured, and the double chocolate truffle cake is as decadent as desserts get. Seasons is owned and managed by Brent Davies of the successful Teahouse at Ferguson Point (see Outdoors); both restaurants have incredibly beautiful settings as well as excellent food.

Outdoor seating on the patio.

Brunch Sat and Sun; lunch Mon to Fri; dinner daily.

Also
Bridges Restaurant, see Outdoors
The Cannery, see Seafood
Raintree, see West Coast
Tojo's, see Japanese

Espresso Bars

Delany's on Denman Coffee House
1105 Denman near Comox
662-3344
A favourite with West Enders, this coffee house opened in October 1993 and instantly gathered a following. Owner Robin Delany wanted to create an atmosphere where "anyone could drop in and instantly feel comfortable." He's achieved this—regulars write letters in a quiet corner, curl up on a padded bench with a book or one of the many magazines or newspapers that are stocked, or people-watch from the window bar. In summer, the dozen outdoor tables are full from dawn to past dusk.

Delany's is known for its baked goods. You can go decadent with dynamite cheesecake or cinammon buns or go healthy with low-fat muffins or cake. Fresh baked goods are brought in daily from six bakeries; Delany's own creations include baked-daily cookies with white and dark Callebaut chocolate. There's coffee, teas, freshly squeezed juices and fruit shakes.

Delany's, says one regular, is "bustling without being crowded, you don't rush in and out, you want to stay here."

Daily 6 AM–midnight; Fri and Sat until 1 AM.

Starbucks $
1100 Robson at Thurlow
1099 Robson at Thurlow
811 Hornby near Robson
1116 Denman near Pendrell
102–700 W Pender at Granville, etc.
Love 'em or hate 'em, Starbucks is everywhere in this city—even across the street from each other on Robson—and there are dozens of other locations. Wherever you are, you can walk to a Starbucks.

The mood is designer Italian: pop in for a quick jolt of coffee and drink it standing up, leaning against the bar—there are never enough seats to go around. The menu is sandwiches and pastries, including *biscotti* to soften in your latte, and you can buy Starbucks' excellent coffees by the pound. It's a continuing debate as to which Starbucks blend is best.

At 1100 Robson, Sun to Thurs, 5:30 AM–midnight; Fri and Sat until 1 AM. At 1116 Denman, Mon to Sun, 5:30 AM–10 PM. At 700 W Pender, Mon to Fri, 5:30 AM–6 PM; closed Sat, Sun and holidays. At 811 Hornby, Mon to Fri, 6 AM–6:30 PM; weekends, 7:30 AM–6.

Also
Ecco Il Pane, see Bakery Cafés
Savary Island Pie Company, see Bakery Cafés
Terra Breads, see Bakery Cafés

One of the two Starbucks espresso bars at Robson and Thurlow. (Rosamond Norbury)

By Nationality

Chinese

Keeping up with Chinese restaurants in Vancouver is a challenge. New ones open every week, each more opulent than the last. People who felt relatively sure of themselves while ordering crab with ginger and green onion in some homely family restaurant on E Hastings now have to consider whether or not a soup with bird's nest and shark's fin is actually worth $32 a person and what effect a tastefully appointed dining room and waiters in uniforms whisking away plates as soon as they collect a single crab shell may have on the enjoyment of dinner.

Furthermore, the old signs that marked a good Chinese restaurant are no longer reliable. It used to be that a truck stop decor, the absence of the phrase "Chinese and Canadian cuisine" and a location outside of Chinatown were solid indicators. Anything that looked as if money had been spent on the interior was a hint that sweet and sour spareribs in neon hues awaited inside.

The new signs? Well, you can find wonderful food in some of the new, glossy Hong Kong–style palaces, often at prices that aren't all that much higher than the ones charged in more modest surroundings.

One style to look for: the self-effacing Chinese restaurant that turns a blank face of vertical venetian blinds to the street. If you poke your head in and the place has live fish tanks and is reverberating with the Cantonese wall of sound, it's worth trying.

Pink Pearl $$
1132 E Hastings near Glen
253-4316
The Pink Pearl is an old Vancouver-style Cantonese restaurant. It's in a run-down section of town, in an unpretentious building that doesn't

look nearly as big as it is—650 seats. But the edges are a little rough, the waiters haven't got time to discuss the menu and probably would rather not anyway, and prices are low. Bring the kids. Pink Pearl has a comfortable, family feel, and no one can possibly be bothered by a crying baby in the midst of the bustle. Live seafood tanks near the door hold crab, shrimp, geoduck, oysters, abalone, rock cod, lobsters and scallops—all offered in a dozen or more ways.

Try clams in black bean sauce as a first course and crab sautéed with five spices as a main course. The crispy-skinned chicken will please everyone from the most adventurous palate to the most discerning critic of Chinese food. Arrive early for *dim sum* if you don't want to wait in line. On a weekend night, you may run into several wedding parties here—it won't be quiet. Lunch and dinner daily.

Kirin Mandarin Restaurant $$$
1166 Alberni near Bute
682-8833

The Kirin was one of the first restaurants to serve Chinese food in style. It was all a bit disconcerting at first: white linen tablecloths and a trendy postmodern decor, waiters who were fluent in English and trained to do more than slap dishes on the table with the aplomb of the old-style Chinese waiter. Stay out of the shark's fin and abalone sections of the menu in order to keep the price down. Peking duck does not have to be ordered in advance here; the menu is a mix of Szechuan, Shanghai and pan-regional party food, with a few Cantonese favourites, such as scallops in black bean sauce—the scallops from the live tank, served in their shells. Lunch and dinner daily.

Szechuan Chongqing $
2802 Commercial at 12th
254-7434

1668 W Broadway
734-1668

This unpretentious white-tablecloth restaurant in a revamped fried-chicken outlet serves the best Szechuan food in the city. Two dishes to try: fried green beans Szechuan style, steamed and tossed with spiced ground pork, and Chongqing chicken, boneless chicken on a bed of fried spinach that has the crispness of dried seaweed and a taste that is salty, rich and nutty all at once. Food here is hearty northern-style, with plenty of garlic and red peppers. Order steamed buns—plain or deep-fried so that the outside sixteenth of an inch is golden brown and sweet—instead of rice and use them to mop up the sauces. Lunch and dinner daily.

Won More Szechuan Cuisine $
1944 W 4th at Maple
737-2889
1184 Denman near Davie
688-8856

The one on Denman is the old Won More, the 4th Ave Won More is newer, fancier and just a tiny bit more expensive. Both follow the same pattern. The cooks work up front in a glassed-in kitchen, so you can watch them while you wait for a table; the functional dining room is in the back.

The Won More offers good, gutsy food, heavy on meat and even heavier on garlic—there's a vampire-free zone for several hundred metres around the restaurant.

You can get *mu shu* shrimp, beef and chicken here, but the classic shredded pork stirfry, wrapped in thin mandarin pancakes and flavoured with *hoisin* sauce, is still best. The fried dumplings are good, and so is the green onion pancake—a flat, 15 cm (6-inch) round of flaky pastry with flecks of green onion. Don't miss the eggplant with minced pork in hot garlic sauce—the best in

Serving steaming dim sum *in Chinatown. (Rosamond Norbury)*

Vancouver, and the leftovers make exotic filling for omelets the next day. On 4th Ave, lunch and dinner daily; on Denman, dinner only.

Hon's Wun Tun House $
108–268 Keefer at Gore
688-0871
Hon's Wonton House on Main had been there forever, with great cauldrons of chicken stock steaming up the windows; cooks at work on noodles in soup, fried noodles, fried rice and steamed and fried dumplings; arborite tables; and minimal service. But Hon's has moved into a new and plusher building around the corner on Keefer. It's the old menu, though prices are a little higher.

The speciality here is noodles—you'll want to try shrimp and meat dumpling with noodle (noodles and dumplings in a clear broth), potstickers (meat- or shrimp-filled dumplings fried to a golden crisp on their sweet little bottoms) and *gai lan,* a kind of Chinese broccoli, stirfried and

topped with oyster sauce. Lunch and dinner daily.

Dim Sum

Grand King Seafood Restaurant $$
705 W Broadway at Heather
876-7855
The fact that this restaurant is located in a Holiday Inn yet is lauded as the city's finest for Chinese cuisine is due to chef Lam Kam Shing. Shing gathered a following while he was at the Dynasty Restaurant (now closed) and they've followed him across the city to this new restaurant, which was named "best Chinese" in a recent *Vancouver Magazine* annual restaurant review.

There's a multi-paged menu with mouth-watering selections (in the shark's fin section alone there are six choices). The formal *dim sum* is an ideal introduction to Grand King's. These steaming hot offerings—deep-fried taro root dumplings and barbecued pork filo pastry, to name a

Dim Sum

Dim sum originated in Canton, so most dishes are subtle and lightly cooked, usually steamed. (Northern restaurants serve their own version of *dim sum*.)

Carts piled with bamboo steamers of hot food are wheeled around the tables. A steamer usually contains a plate with two or three dumplings of some sort. Savoury dishes are on the top of the carts, and sweet ones below; the Chinese intermingle the sweet and the savoury during the meal. After eating your fill, signal a waiter, and he will tally your bill by counting the number of dishes on the table. Average cost is $8 per person.

Dim sum is a family affair; the more friends, children and grandparents the better. It is served from about 10 AM to 2 PM every day.

The laws of *dim sum* are:

1. Go to a busy restaurant where the selection is varied and freshly steamed.
2. Don't sit in a corner or you'll be watching most of the carts pass you by.
3. Keep in mind that after 1 PM the selection shrinks.

---

couple—are an up-scale *dim sum* at its best.

The room is large and bright and always seems to be full. This is not a casual spot; it seems to attract the business crowd. Lunch and dinner daily.

New Diamond Restaurant $
555 Gore near Keefer
685-0727

The New Diamond isn't new at all— it's been serving *dim sum* for over 25 years in its Chinatown upstairs location. And it looks as if the decor and the price list haven't changed much over the years. Plastic coverings on the tables, plush red seats, an end wall decorated with the typical golden dragon on brocaded red—this is the real Chinatown experience. Also, there are few non-Chinese faces in the *dim sum* crowd.

As women wheel carts laden with bamboo steamers and call, "*Har kow . . . siu mai . . . cha siu bao . . . ,*" you raise your hand to indicate your choices.

If you are really curious about what you are eating (many of the *dim sum* servers don't speak English), or if you need some help with choosing, call Simon Ng, one of your friendly hosts. "Highly recommended," says Simon of the shrimp dumplings and shredded pork with bamboo shoot wrapped in rice noodle. The barbecued pork in a sweet sesame seed bun is delicious, and the sticky rice comes the traditional way, wrapped in a lotus leaf and steaming hot. For dessert try the water chestnut cake.

Dim Sum is served 7:30 AM–3. The busiest times—and the times when there will be the most *dim sum* carts being manoeuvred through the large room—is what Simon calls the "golden time," between 11:30 and 2. Most dishes here cost $2.30, and two or three, with lots of tea, will satisfy most appetites. For groups over six, make reservations. Closed Wed.

Also
Pink Pearl, see Chinese

Contemporary

Bishop's $$$
2183 W 4th near Yew
738-2025

For many years now, this modest little restaurant on 4th Ave has had a major reputation for what owner John Bishop likes to call contemporary home cooking. That means a mixture of Northern Italian, nouvelle cuisine and East-West crossover with a fine eye for dramatic presentation. The daily specials are always worth ordering. There are offerings like pan-seared scallops scented with lemon grass and chervil topped with a crisp potato pancake, or roasted rack of lamb, sautéed spinach and summer squash with red Vermouth and basil.

Everything about the restaurant— all white except for vibrant expressionist paintings, all of them by B.C. artists, including some by Jack Shadbolt—is simple, stripped down and in very good taste, the better to focus your attention on the food. Team service is friendly and professional; a "dessert technician" will visit your table after dinner and rhyme off an astonishing list of choices.

Bishop's has one flaw: you can arrive with dinner reservations and still not get seated for an hour. Best insurance: reserve for no later than 7:30. Dinner daily.

RainCity Grill $$
1193 Denman at Morton
685-7337

On a busy West End corner, this restaurant is a winner. The menu changes weekly but is always intriguing—prawn basil dumpling or barbecued lamb pizza have tempted the lunchtime set, and shark in green tea marinade with barley risotto and arugula aioli have pleased the curious for dinner. What doesn't change is the grilled Caesar salad—yep, the romaine is grilled—and the dressing is rich and creamy. There's a super selection of wines and ales, and a beverage is suggested for each dish. (Bowen Island Pale Ale with the lamb pizza, for example.) Freshness is guaranteed by daily trips to Granville Island.

It's always reassuring when a restaurant has an open kitchen; the decor is understated, with wood and greenery, soft greys and white linen. It's fancy enough for a special occasion, but you won't feel out of place if you've just walked the seawall. The small outdoor patio offers people-watching as well as the panorama of English Bay.

The RainCity gets an incredible amount of drop-in traffic, so reservations are recommended. Brunch is served Sat and Sun, 10:30–4:30; lunch and dinner daily.

Raku Kushiyaki $$
4422 W 10th near Trimble
222-8188

Some find it austere or think the portions are too small, but Raku has been a big hit in this town since it opened a couple of years ago. The food is East-meets-West fusion, borrowing heavily from Asia but also from the Middle East, Europe, the Caribbean and California. The decor is stylishly spartan.

Grilled skewered morsels make up the core of the menu, but it branches out to such dishes as orange-spiced lamb shanks, eggplant with garlic and goat cheese, or grilled shiitake mushrooms. Everything is served in small portions, three or four of which would make a meal. *Sake* or large bottles of Japanese beer are the perfect accompaniment. Lunch Tues to Sat; dinner daily.

Continental

William Tell $$$
765 Beatty at Robson

Georgian Court Hotel
688-3504
The ultimate in luxury and coddling, this Vancouver restaurant is now heading into its second quarter-century under the amiable hand of owner and maitre d' Erwin Doebeli.

At dinner the tables gleam with plate liners and flower vases of silver. Chef Christian Lindner cares enough about the quality of ingredients to keep a Fraser Valley farmer growing organic vegetables for the restaurant. Start with the Swiss specialty *bündnerfleisch,* paper-thin slices of air-dried beef; then try the roast Fraser Valley duck with dried apricots and a light orange-maple butter. A glorious place for a self-indulgent lunch or a big-occasion dinner. Lunch Mon to Fri; dinner Mon to Sat.

East Indian

Noor Mahal $
4354 Fraser near 27th
873-9263
A *dhosa* is a light, lacy pancake made of bean flour, rice flour and semolina, mixed into a batter and fermented overnight. Cooked and rolled around fillings—onions, green chilles and spices; cauliflower and potatoes; shrimp—it's the most popular street snack in southern India.

Paul and Susan Singh, the entire staff of Noor Mahal, make a dozen or so *dhosas,* all hearty and substantial; most of them are priced around $7. Prices are equally modest on the rest of the menu, which includes a good broad range of breads and curries. East Indian videos, elaborate beaded chandeliers, framed arrangements of tropical butterflies, red vinyl table-cloths—it's truck stop simple decor with cross-cultural touches. Superb value for the money. Dinner daily.

Rubina Tandoori $$
1962 Kingsway near Victoria

874-3621
Rubina Tandoori is an utterly reliable restaurant, the first place we would choose to indulge ourselves with a feast of East Indian food. Yes, it's worth the drive. The Jamal family owned a restaurant in London before coming to Vancouver; son Shaffeen is the maitre d' and has a phenomenal memory for faces.

Walk in past the display cases of desserts and *chevda,* a nuts-and-bolts salty snack you can buy by the pound, and watch them make *naan* (the wonderful flat bread) in the tandoori oven.

The menu covers the range of subcontinental cuisines, from south Indian seafood to meat dishes from the north. Lunch Mon to Fri; dinner Mon to Sat.

Vij's Restaurant $
1453 W Broadway near Granville
736-6664
This is a tiny hole in the wall, but don't let that put you off. Vikram Vij, formerly of Bishop's and RainCity Grill, is your host. When you walk through the door, see his smiling face, smell the curry and sip your welcoming *chai,* you'll know you're in the right place. When he opened his own restaurant, his goal was "homey cooking, clean and fresh" and he went to his family for their favourites. There's his mother-in-law's pork curry, his mother's chicken curry, and homemade samosas, but there are also dishes like Australian lamb and a savoury crepe filled with vegetable pickle.

Anyone who has been to India knows they do wonderful things with potato. Try the mashed potatoes with tumeric—it's memorable. Reasonably priced menu items are printed on a chalkboard and change weekly. There's only room for 14 diners and no reservations are taken, so arrive early. Vij's quickly joined the ranks of favourite Asian restaurants in the city so it might be a good idea to check the phone book in case popularity forces a move. Lunch Mon to Fri; dinner Mon to Sat.

Ethiopian

Nyala Ethiopian Restaurant $
2930 W 4th near Macdonald
731-7899
Whether you find Ethiopian food to your taste generally comes down to a question of bread. Made from a grain called *tef*, the staple food of Ethiopia, *injera* is a flat, spongy bread served cold. You get it in two ways: as a plate, on which all of the main dishes are served, and on the side, folded up like a napkin.

Ethiopian food is meant to be eaten with your fingers: tear off a little piece of *injera* and use it to pick up a bit of whatever you're eating. There are lots of choices here for vegetarians. If you want to try the national dish of Ethiopia, order *yedoro-watt*, chicken in a spicy red sauce. Dinner daily.

French

Chez Thierry $$
1674 Robson near Cardero
688-0919
The West End's best neighbourhood restaurant is a 35-seat storefront on Robson serving French country food. Thierry Damilano, windsurfing enthusiast and *sabreur*—he slices the corks off champagne bottles with a sabre—is the host. Damilano brushes cheeks with repeat clients (*zeez* Frenchmen!) and keeps a wine list with at least one choice from every major French growing region.

You can always get a simple piece of grilled fish, and if you don't like the way the day's catch is offered, you can have it prepared your way. Choc-

olate desserts, of the dark, bittersweet variety, are not to be missed. Dinner daily.

Le Crocodile $$$
909 Burrard at Smithe
669-4298
The Vancouver French restaurant that leads the pack in critical acclaim is a pleasant, informal bistro that serves traditional French bistro food, superbly. Be sure to try the sweet onion tart appetizer—a reminder of chef-owner Michel Jacob's Alsatian origins.

If you've made a point of visiting Le Crocodile whenever you're in town, you'll be pleasantly surprised by the new larger location—the closest thing this city has to a corner of Paris. Always make reservations: Le Crocodile has a loyal following. A few outdoor tables in good weather. Lunch Mon to Fri; dinner Mon to Sat. Closed Sun.

Le Gavroche $$$
1616 Alberni at Cardero
685-3924
There's no better place for a romantic dinner: a turn-of-the-century house, a bit of a view over Coal Harbour, ever-so-slightly-superior Gallic service and rich, inventive, passionate food along the lines of smoked pheasant breast on a purée of celeriac, shallots and wine with a light truffle sauce. Should you feel nostalgic, you can always get owner Manuel Ferreira to mix a Caesar salad by your table—and perhaps remember why everyone made such a big fuss over Caesars before the advent of salad bars. Le Gavroche handles seafood particularly well, so pay attention to the daily specials. If it's a special occasion with a big budget, ask for the reserve wine list. Lunch Mon to Fri; dinner daily.

Greek

Le Grec $

1447 Commercial at Grant
253-1253

Mezethes are the Greek answer to *tapas*—small servings of freshly prepared delicacies—and no one does them better than Le Grec. Everything on the menu is under $8.75, but there's more to lure guests back than a reasonably priced meal. Start with the 11-grain pita bread dipped in olive oil and balsamic vinegar (or hummus, of course) and savour the *melitzanes ragout* (eggplant with mushrooms and tomatoes), which is one of several authentic Greek dishes that don't grace other local Greek menus. Then work on the prawns done in ouzo and artichokes. Or share all of these with a friend and nibble on his or her prawn *souvlakia* marinated in wine, dijon and herbs. The vegetarian moussaka has a devoted following.

All this is served in contemporary Greek surroundings of cool tile floors, mustard-toned walls and a bright blue ceiling.

It's quiet during lunch but busy all evenings. Originally the restaurant didn't take reservations and evening line-ups were long but now you can reserve. Lunch and dinner Mon to Sat.

Simpatico Ristorante $

2222 W 4th at Vine
733-6824

Simpatico has been a fixture on 4th Ave since 1969, an enduring source of nourishing meals at low prices. Order one of the whole-wheat-crust pizzas—every table has a black metal pizza stand—or venture off into the Greek menu. Cornish game hen with rice, potatoes and Greek salad is a hearty, robust meal. Decor is generically Greek, with pathos plants, white walls, wooden floors and tables, blue-and-white checked tablecloths. Students eat here, and young families, and the rest of that vast army of us with more appetite than cash. Lunch and dinner daily.

Vassilis Taverna $$

2884 W Broadway near Macdonald
733-3231

Greek food is simple. What distinguishes Vassilis is fresh food, generous portions, reasonable prices and an amazing consistency. Years go by, and apart from the passing of Dino, the restaurant canary, nothing changes.

Vassilis's *kotopulo*—a chicken pounded flat, rubbed with herbs and grilled—is the standard other Vancouver Greek restaurants can be measured by. *Skordalia,* a velvety, sinful potato and garlic purée, is served cold as an appetizer. Don't miss the homemade *navarino,* a creamy custard square topped with whipped cream and ground nuts. Lunch Tues to Fri; dinner Tues to Sun.

Italian

Il Giardino di Umberto $$$

1382 Hornby at Pacific
669-2422

Umberto Menghi's first of many successful restaurants, Il Giardino wraps you in the ambience of a Tuscan villa with cool tiled floors, soft lighting and beamed ceilings. In summer, the sun-dappled patio is one of *the* places to dine. The city's stockbrokers, lawyers and social set all come here both for the cuisine and to be seen. Il Giardino is known for piping hot, hearty pastas and game dishes—although this is "raised" game as opposed to "wild," recipes are often traditional ones. Another favourite with the locals is the veal chop grilled with herbs and lemon.

The service is always good. Despite

the soft-toned surroundings, Il Giardino is more lively than quietly romantic. Always make a reservation since even Monday at lunch you'll find a full house. Lunch Mon to Fri; dinner Mon to Sat.

Piccolo Mondo $$

850 Thurlow near Robson
688-1633

Don't let the modern brute ugliness of the outside of Piccolo Mondo put you off. Inside it's an elegant brown-and-beige room, walls covered with framed menus, candles winking, silver gleaming. Expect to spend a while with the menu; there are serious decisions to be made here. Should you start with grilled prawns served in a light basil cream sauce with artichokes poached in an aromatic broth? Is a salad of roasted rabbit wrapped in pancetta with mixed greens and eggplant caviar more tempting? Which will go better with the broiled creamy salt cod with pine nuts and raisins? Or perhaps the risotto with duck, red pepper and gorgonzola would be more appealing. Serious decisions.

The choice of wines is among the city's best—Piccolo Mondo received two gold medals for its extensive selection at the 1995 Vancouver International Wine Festival.

Lunch Mon to Fri; dinner daily except Sun.

Villa del Lupo $$$

869 Hamilton near Smithe
688-7436

Go to Villa del Lupo for a special occasion, go because you have a free evening or go when your taste buds cry for a treat, but do go. Tucked between a firehall and a modern apartment block, the "house of wolves" is a narrow, Victorian house with dark green trim. Inside it is cozy and tastefully finished—rosy pink walls, stained glass, an oak- trimmed fireplace and

comfy, high-backed chairs.

The service and food won't let you down either. You'll be inclined to wolf down your made-on-the-premises, slightly crispy focaccia, but save room. There's salad that's a work of art adorned with a few edible flowers and served with tangy orange vinaigrette. And the choices of entrées leaves little to be desired—Fraser Valley duck breast broiled with red wine, cherries, blackberries and pears marinated in grappa and served with carrots, butternut squash and caramelized shallot purée gives you some idea of the choices here. Pasta lovers will revel in the seafood cannelloni or the linguini with grilled scallops, fresh eggplant, basil, capers and tomato marinara. The lemon tart is highly recommended as the final course. Villa del Lupo is perfect for a celebration or a romantic dinner. Open daily for dinner.

Arriva $$

1537 Commercial near Grant
251-1177

Commercial Dr was once the centre of Vancouver's Italian community. Now Little Italy is making room for Little Vietnam, Little Nicaragua, Little Greece—you name it. But the Italian delis are still on the Drive, and so are a number of good Italian restaurants. Our favourite is Arriva, for its uncluttered design and its commitment to authentic Italian food. If you must have spaghetti and meatballs, you can, but there's also fusili with wild game, spicy prawns and linguine in white wine sauce or a large selection of vegetarian pastas.

The antipasto plate is heaped with octopus, shrimp, roasted red peppers, cheese, sausage, and fat lima beans in a herby marinade. And the soups made here are thick, fresh and filling.

In many ways Arriva is the best of neighbourhood restaurants; it bustles in the early evening (reserve after 8 PM for a quiet dinner) and the waiters greet you like an old friend. And they're more apt to greet you in Italian than English—always reassuring in an Italian restaurant. When owner Paolo Frau has a moment, he loves to chat about two of his favourite subjects—pasta and golf.

Lunch Mon to Fri; dinner daily.

Japanese

Tojo's $$

777 W Broadway at Willow
872-8050
The best Japanese food Vancouver money can buy is made by Hidekazu Tojo, a meticulous, demanding, inventive artist among sushi makers. If you'd like your knowledge of Japanese food enlarged, pick a slow night, sit at the sushi bar, and ask Tojo to feed you something different. He always can. Tatami rooms are blond wood with kimonos hung on the walls for decoration. Seats by the north-facing windows have a splendid view of False Creek and the North Shore mountains.

Prices reflect the quality of the food; they're higher than in other Japanese restaurants but still far from expensive, gauged against prices you find at comparable French or Italian restaurants. Dinner Mon to Sat.

Shijo Japanese Restaurant $$

1926 W 4th at Cypress
732-4676

Sushi

We can't imagine finding better sushi anywhere in Canada. If you're new to sushi, imagine fish—the freshest you've ever had—with a delicate rather than a fishy taste.

There are three kinds of sushi. One kind is a small patty of rice that is covered with a thin slice of raw tuna, salmon, mackerel or other fish, and is called *nigiri*. Another is *maki,* a roll of rice covered with a paper-thin sheet of crisp seaweed and filled with tuna, salmon, salmon roe or cucumber. The third is crisp seaweed or salmon skin rolled into a cone and filled with rice and fish.

If you are trying sushi for the first time, order just enough for an appetizer—an assorted sushi plate will do for two to four people. If you're more adventurous or experienced, wait for a seat at the sushi bar, where you can be part of the banter and watch the sushi master at work. At the bar you can order particular types of sushi, one or two pieces at a time.

After sitting down you will be presented with a hot towel for your hands, because sushi is eaten with the fingers or chopsticks. Sake, green tea and beer are all appropriate and should be ordered from the waitress, though you order your sushi directly from the sushi chef.

You can also order soup (to be drunk from a bowl) from your waitress, but traditionally nothing but sushi is eaten at the bar.

Pick up a piece of sushi, dip it fish-side down into the little dish of soy sauce, and then pop it into your mouth (still fish-side down). The taste is clean, pure and delicious. The hotness comes from a thin layer of green horseradish called *wasabi* between the rice and the fish. Refresh your palate in between courses of sushi with a piece of shaved pickled ginger.

Shijo is the chic sushi bar, a convivial place one flight up from Kitsilano's main artery, filled with light and thoroughly modern, with a team of sushi and robata chefs cracking jokes behind the bar. Jazz plays discreetly in the background. Handsome lamps with patinated bronze finishes, lots of black wood: this is the aesthetic of modern Japan—oddly enough evoked by Vancouver designer Tony Robins, who has gone on to design a string of restaurants for Japanese clients. Ask for Japanese eggplant cooked on the robata and, if they're available, shiitake mushrooms cooked in foil. Lunch Mon to Fri; dinner daily.

Chiyoda $$
1050 Alberni at Burrard
688-5050
A robata bar serves food grilled to order in front of the customers—the essential sushi bar experience for people who won't eat raw fish. Chiyoda was designed in Japan, right down to the shapely little beer glasses. The bar is a set of concentric circles: a wood counter, a band of ice with the day's offerings displayed in wicker baskets, an inner circle of grills and then the chefs, who hand over your food on long paddles that look like pizza peels. Snapper, prawns, oysters, eggplant, mushrooms, onions, potatoes: there are about 30 choices to be grilled, seasoned with soy, lemon and *ponzu* sauce and served looking pretty, of course. Chiyoda's bar can be hilariously convivial. Lunch Mon to Fri; dinner Mon to Sat.

Jewish

Kaplan's Deli, Restaurant and Bakery $$
5775 Oak at 41st
263-2625
Tucked into a mini-mall on the road that leads to Seattle and to the Victo-ria and Gulf Islands ferries, Kaplan's is the traveller's last chance for authentic Jewish deli food. Eat in at one of the booths, or take your chopped liver, herring, lox and homemade corned beef with you. The cinnamon buns are justly famous. Open for breakfast, lunch and dinner daily, except on Jewish holidays.

Mexican

Topanga Café $
2904 W 4th near Macdonald
733-3713
A Kitsilano institution, the Topanga has been serving heaping plates of Cal-Mex food at low prices for over 15 years. Kids can colour blank menu covers while waiting for food; adults can scan the hundreds of framed copies of patrons' coloured menus (done by young and old) on the walls for inspiration. No reservations. There are only 40 seats, so arrive before 6:30 or after 8 if you don't want to wait in line. Lunch and dinner daily except Sun and holidays.

Spanish

La Bodega $$
1277 Howe near Davie
684-8815
The dark, cozy *tapas* bar under the Chateau Madrid fills every night. Endless plates of *patatas bravas*—potatoes fried and doused in a spicy, garlicky tomato dressing—mussels in vinaigrette and *chorizo* sausage are washed down with gallons of beer, tubs of wine and pitchers full of sangria.

Eat as little as you like, or as much, come in a big noisy party, or with your one best friend, have lunch, or stay till midnight—La Bodega is a kind of rolling Spanish theatre that lets you do precisely what you please. The staff here stays forever; consequently, there is always a familiar face to greet you. Flamenco music plays, sangria flows and conversations are animated and often on the loud side. Lunch Mon to Fri, dinner Mon to Sat.

Thai

Malinee's Thai Food $$
2153 W 4th near Yew
737-0097
If you'd like an introduction to Thai food, Malinee's is the best place in Vancouver. Chef Maneewan Hill is from Bangkok, and owner Stephen Bianchin lived in Thailand for two years. Malinee's only produces authentic and very good Thai food.

Specials are worth ordering; once it was a steamed whole red snapper, marinated in oyster sauce, ginger, cilantro, red pepper and lime juice—superb. Steamed fish with ginger, pickled plums and red chili sauce is on the regular menu. Dinner daily.

Sawasdee Thai Restaurant $
4250 Main near 27th
876-4030
Line-ups formed outside the door when this pleasant, skylit restaurant—the oldest Thai restaurant in Vancouver—first opened. Now Thai restaurants are popping up everywhere from New Westminster to Kitsilano, and the competition is fierce. Sawasdee on Main still offers some of the best Chinese-influenced Thai food in town. You won't find the subtleties of Malinee's here. There are more stirfries and food that tastes like what you'd find at a plain, home-cookin' restaurant in Thailand.

The tiny chilies the Thais call rat turds wait like land mines for the unwary—be careful when you eat the excellent stirfried spinach. Seafood comes in a red spicy curry sauce, and for the adventuresome, the Crying Tiger Beef is sliced marinated grilled beef, served with extra hot spicy sauce. Homemade coconut ice cream is sometimes available. Service here is so gentle and friendly that you start to believe in the Land of Smiles as something more than just a travel agent's cliché.

Lunch Tues to Fri, dinner daily.

British Columbia Wines

In recent years B.C. wines have been scooping medals at high-profile competitions out from under the noses of their international counterparts.

Travel the backroads of the Okanagan, Similkameen, Fraser and Cowichan Valleys and you'll find premium wineries that are making the most of B.C.'s northerly latitudes. Like other northern growing areas, this one leans towards whites, both table and dessert wines. Some of B.C.'s grape varieties are familiar: Riesling, Gewürztraminer, Pinot Blanc and Chardonnay. Newcomers, like Auxerrois (oh-zair-WAII), Ehrenfelser (AIR-en-fel-zer), Bacchus and Ortega, tend to be subtly fragrant and fruity. Reds include Pinot Noir, Merlot and lesser-known varieties such as Chancellor, Marachal Foch and Chelois. The makers of premium wines promote their product through the Vintners' Quality Alliance, whose "VQA" symbol on the neck of a bottle indicates that the wine meets strict standards.

For more information, contact the British Columbia Wine Institute at 986-0440 in Vancouver or 1-800-661-2794 from elsewhere in the province.

—*Elizabeth Wilson*

Vietnamese/Cambodian

Pho Hoang $
3610 Main at 20th
874-0810

Pho—a steaming bowl of beef soup—is the Vietnamese equivalent of a hamburger. Pho restaurants, serving up to 30 varieties of beef soup, have been popping up lately on Vancouver streets. Pho Hoang is the oldest and one of the most welcoming to those new to the routine: soup comes with fresh herbs, chilies and lime wedges on the side, for you to add to taste. Drink Vietnamese coffee, filter-brewed at your table. No alcohol, no credit cards. Lunch and dinner daily.

Phnom-Penh $
244 East Georgia near Gore
682-5777
955 W Broadway near Oak
734-8898

On a quiet back street on the fringe of Chinatown, the Phnom-Penh serves the best garlic and pepper whole prawns—head, shell and all—in the city. The dish is called Special Prawns and there is an equally good Special Crab dish. To avoid disappointment, order these when you make your reservation and the seafood will be set aside for you. Compared with the rest of the items on the menu, these are pricey dishes, but they'll make a memorable meal.

In this robust food, the Chinese part of Vietnam's culinary heritage is especially evident. Try the warm beef salad; the slices of beef are crusted with ground salt and pepper. The Phnom-Penh is a family restaurant with modest furnishings and a genuine feeling of hospitality. Lunch and dinner daily, except Tues.

West Coast

Raintree Restaurant & Bar at the Landing $$
375 Water near Cordova
688-5570

Go to the Raintree if you want to put your finger on the pulse of regional food in Vancouver. Owner Janice Lotzkar first introduced northwest coast cuisine to the city's restaurant scene years ago, and today chef Andrew Skorzewski maintains the same dedication to serving West Coast entrées that have made this restaurant a success. Skorzewski's extraordinary culinary work results in homey dishes seething with freshness. And the freshness at Raintree always comes from just next door: Pender Harbour spot prawns, Queen Charlotte Islands Dungeness crab and organic ranch beef from central B.C.

Now in Gastown, the still-elegant restaurant has the quintessential Vancouver view of mountains and ocean and has added a bar and bistro. And, get this, the prices at Raintree have actually gone down since their move—almost unheard of in the world of restaurants.

For lunch, consider a scallop spinach salad with pickled ginger sesame vinaigrette or a hearty burger which will be organic whenever organic beef is available. For dinner, you may choose the organic pesto roasted cod with garlic mashed potatoes, but keep in mind that the desserts—which vary with the seasons—are delightful. Plaudits are piled on the Okanagan apple pie served with Armstrong cheese. You can sample the Raintree's resolutely Pacific Northwest wine list in half-glass taster sizes.

Lunch Mon to Fri; dinner Mon to Sun.

Liliget Feast House $$
1724 Davie near Denman
681-7044

Formerly Quilicum West Coast Native Indian Restaurant, the Liliget still serves the original northwest coast cuisine in a basement "longhouse" that's more reminiscent of a clearing in a forest: a narrow path between raised concrete platforms, a dozen or so log columns, low tables and walls and columns hung with northwest coast art (most of it for sale).

Heavenly bannock bread, baked sweet potato with hazelnuts, alder-grilled salmon and, for the adventuresome, soap-berries for dessert—Liliget specializes in seafood and wild game and is much more than just a novelty restaurant. Dinner daily.

Some of this chapter has been been written by Eve Johnson, food editor at the *Vancouver Sun*.

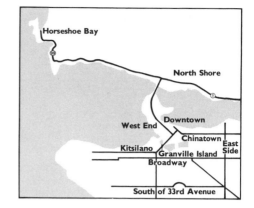

By Location

Broadway (between Main and Granville)

Ecco Il Pane, see Bakery Cafés
Grand King Seafood Restaurant, see Chinese, *Dim Sum*
Phnom-Penh, see Vietnamese/Cambodian
Szechuan Chongqing, see Chinese
Tojo's, see Japanese
Vij's, see East Indian

Chinatown

Hon's Wonton House, see Chinese
New Diamond, see Chinese, *Dim Sum*
Phnom-Penh, see Vietnamese/Cambodian

Downtown

Bacchus, see Lunch
La Bodega, see Spanish
Café Fleuri, see Breakfast/Brunch
Chartwell, see Lunch
Chiyoda, see Japanese
Le Crocodile, see French
Gallery Café, see Lunch
Il Giardino, see Italian
Kirin, see Chinese
Piccolo Mondo, see Italian
Raintree Restaurant at the Landing, see West Coast
Settebello, see Outdoors
Starbucks, see Espresso Bars
Water St Café, see Lunch
William Tell, see Continental

East Side

Arriva, see Italian
Cannery, see With a View
Japanese Deli House, see Lunch
Marineview Coffeeshop, see Seafood
Noor Mahal, see East Indian
Pink Pearl, see Chinese
Phnom-Penh, see Vietnamese/Cambodian
Pho Hoang, see Vietnamese/Cambodian
Rubina Tandoori, see East Indian
Sawasdee, see Thai
Szechuan Chongqing, see Chinese
Tony's Neighbourhood Deli, see Lunch

Granville Island

Bridges Restaurant, see Outdoors
Isadora's Co-operative Restaurant, see
  Breakfast/Brunch

Kitsilano/West Side

Benny's Bagels, see Late Night
Bishop's, see Contemporary
Flying Wedge, see Pizza
Gladys, see Breakfast/Brunch
Malinee's, see Thai
Naam, see Vegetarian
Nyala, see Ethiopian
Raku, see Contemporary
Shijo, see Japanese
Terra Breads, see Bakery Cafés
Topanga Café, see Mexican
Vassilis Taverna, see Greek
Won More, see Chinese

North Shore

Capers, see Breakfast/Brunch
Dundarave Concession, see Outdoors
Salmon House on the Hill, see With a
  View
Savary Island Pie Company, see Bak-
  ery Cafés
Tomahawk, see Breakfast/Brunch

South of 33rd Avenue

Kaplan's, see Jewish
Seasons in the Park, see With a View

West End

Chez Thierry, see French
Delany's on Denman Coffee House,
  see Espresso Bars
Liliget Feast House, see West Coast
RainCity Grill, see Contemporary
Starbucks, see Espresso Bars
Teahouse at Ferguson Point, see Out-
  doors
Won More, see Chinese

Getting Around

Public Transit 67
City Buses, SeaBus, SkyTrain

Coach Lines 71

Cars 71
Rentals, Parking

Taxis 72

Limousine Service 72

Trains 72

Ferries 74
Schedules, Fares, Travel Tips, Short Ferry Trips

Vancouver International Airport 77
Getting There, The New Look of Vancouver International, Airport Parking

Flights to Victoria 80
Downtown Victoria, Victoria Airport

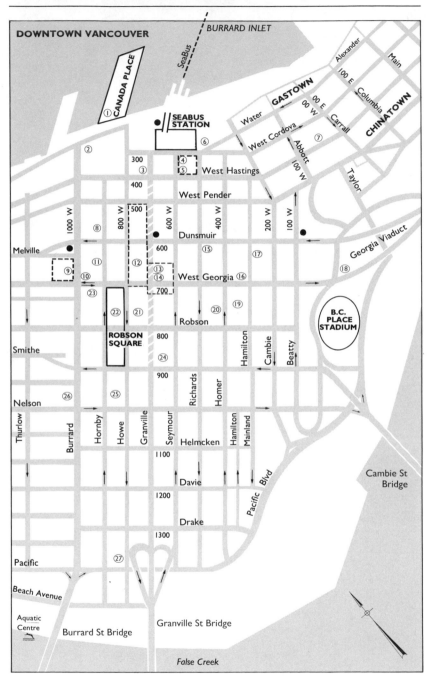

DOWNTOWN VANCOUVER

BURRARD INLET

CANADA PLACE

SeaBus

GASTOWN

Alexander

Main

100 E

Columbia

CHINATOWN

Water

Carrall

Taylor

West Cordova

Abbott

00 E

00 W

100 W

SEABUS STATION

West Hastings

West Pender

Dunsmuir

1000 W

800 W

500

600 W

400 W

200 W

100 W

Melville

600

Georgia Viaduct

West Georgia

700

ROBSON SQUARE

Robson

B.C. PLACE STADIUM

Smithe

800

Hamilton

Cambie

Beatty

900

Richards

Homer

Nelson

Thurlow

Burrard

Hornby

Howe

Granville

Seymour

Helmcken

Hamilton

Mainland

Cambie St Bridge

1100

Davie

Pacific Blvd

1200

Drake

1300

Pacific

Beach Avenue

Aquatic Centre

Burrard St Bridge

Granville St Bridge

False Creek

Public Transit

City Buses

B.C. Transit buses accept exact coin fares, tickets and passes. Coin fare is $1.50 adult and 75¢ concession.

Concession fares apply to senior citizens, children aged 5 to 13, and high school students aged 14 to 19 with GoCards. Transfers, issued only when the fare is paid, are valid for 90 minutes for *two-way* travel and are good on buses, the SeaBus and the Sky-Train. Thus, you can make a stopover and return on the same transfer.

Tickets and passes are sold at retail outlets (look for a blue and red "Fare-dealer" sign in the window), not by transit operators.

Tickets are sold in booklets of 10 for $13.75 for adults. Monthly passes are $54 for adults. These are one-zone fares but are valid for travel across several zones as long as it's not rush hour. To get to and from the suburbs during rush hour, you pay more. Day passes ($4.50 for adults) are good for unlimited travel after 9:30 AM weekdays, and all day Sat, Sun or holidays. These are sold by machines at SeaBus and SkyTrain stations (but not before 9:30 AM weekdays), and at retail outlets.

Transit information is available at 521-0400 seven days a week, 6:30 AM–11:30 PM. Persevere and you will eventually get through to this busy number.

Service on most routes ends about 1 AM. Then "Night Owl Service" (a bare-bones service on major streets) comes into effect until about 3 AM.

A *Transit Guide*, published by B.C. Transit, shows all the bus routes. The guide is reasonably priced and is available at newsstands. Bus shelters at major intersections often have route maps posted on them. The main branch of the Vancouver Public Library has a rack of current route schedules. Travel Infocentres and major hotels have a free guidebook, called *Discover Vancouver on Transit,* that describes transit routes to all Lower Mainland attractions as well as to Victoria.

On the North Shore

To travel to West Van—roughly anywhere west of the Lions Gate Bridge on the North Shore—call West Van

---

1 Vancouver Trade and Convention Centre
2 TouristInfo Centre
3 Sinclair Centre
4 Harbour Centre
5 SFU Downtown Campus
6 The Landing
7 Army & Navy Dept Store
8 YWCA
9 Royal Centre Mall
10 Christ Church Cathedral (Anglican)
11 Canadian Craft Museum/Sri Lankan Gem Museum
12 Pacific Centre Mall
13 The Bay Dept Store
14 Vancouver Centre Mall
15 Holy Rosary Cathedral (Catholic)
16 Main Post Office
17 Queen Elizabeth Theatre/ Playhouse
18 GM Place
19 Library Square
20 Ford Theatre
21 Eaton's Dept Store
22 Vancouver Art Gallery
23 Hotel Vancouver
24 Orpheum Theatre
25 Law Courts
26 YMCA
27 Executive Inn
▨ Buses/Taxis only
● SkyTrain station
⌐⌐⌐Underground shopping
→ Traffic direction

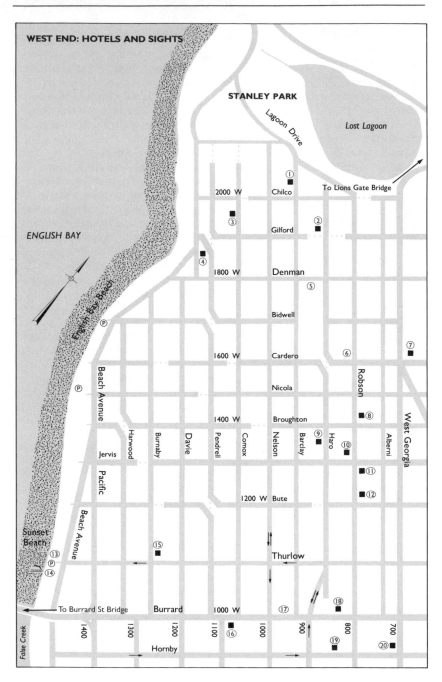

WEST END: HOTELS AND SIGHTS

STANLEY PARK

Lagoon Drive

Lost Lagoon

To Lions Gate Bridge

ENGLISH BAY

2000 W   Chilco

Gilford

English Bay Beach

1800 W   Denman

Bidwell

1600 W   Cardero

Beach Avenue

Nicola

Robson

1400 W   Broughton

Harwood

Burnaby

Davie

Pendrell

Comox

Nelson

Barclay

Haro

Alberni

West Georgia

Jervis

Pacific

1200 W   Bute

Beach Avenue

Sunset Beach

Thurlow

To Burrard St Bridge   Burrard   1000 W

False Creek

1400   1300   1200   1100   1000   900   800   700

Hornby

1 Rosellen Suites
2 Buchan
3 English Bay Inn
4 Sylvia
5 West End Community Centre
6 Robson Street Market
7 Westin Bayshore
8 Riviera
9 West End Guest House
10 O'Doul's
11 Pacific Pallisades
12 Blue Horizon
13 Aquatic Centre
14 Granville Island Ferries dock
15 Sunset Inn
16 Wall Centre Hotel
17 YMCA
18 Sutton Place Hotel
19 Wedgewood Hotel
20 Hotel Vancouver

Lagoon, or at stops on Denman or Stanley Park Dr. Frequency ranges from every 20 minutes to every hour, depending on the weather.

- **#250 Horseshoe Bay** bus to West Van and along Marine to Horseshoe Bay. Catch this blue West Van bus downtown on Georgia going west. This is about a 50-minute trip each way.
- **#1 Gastown/Beach** bus through Gastown, downtown and the West End and along Beach Dr from English Bay. This short loop should take only about 45 minutes to get you back where you started. Catch this bus downtown going either direction on Burrard.
- **SeaBus** to North Vancouver (described below).
- **SkyTrain** to the New Westminster Public Market (described below).

transit information at 985-7777. Although the blue West Van buses are part of a separate system, transfers from B.C. Transit are valid; transfers from the West Van buses are also valid on B.C. Transit.

In North Van—that is, east of Lions Gate Bridge—buses are part of the B.C. Transit system.

Airport Bus

See Coach Lines (Vancouver Airporter) and Vancouver International Airport, later in this chapter, for details.

Scenic Routes

A few Vancouver bus routes are particularly scenic and offer an easy, cheap way to see the city. As always, it's best to avoid rush hour. Some suggestions are:

- **#52 Around the Park** bus in Stanley Park. From Apr 1 to Oct 29, the #52 Around the Park bus takes in Stanley Park on Sat, Sun, and holidays, 10–6. Catch it at the loop at the foot of Alberni by Lost

SeaBus

Crossing Burrard Inlet every 15 minutes during the day since 1977, the SeaBus connects downtown to North Vancouver, reducing the rush-hour snarl on the bridges. Two 100-passenger catamaran ferries, the *Burrard Otter* and the *Burrard Beaver*, make the 13-minute trip. Unfortunately, there is no open-air deck, but the views from inside are spectacular.

The SeaBus is part of the B.C. Transit system; the same fares and rules regarding transfers apply. It leaves from the SeaBus Terminal located in the lovely old CPR Station on Cordova near Granville and goes to Lonsdale Quay, where there's a lively public market. The market has everything from clothing boutiques and toy stores to vegetable stalls (food downstairs and shops up).

A sunny plaza off the market has a tremendous view of Burrard Inlet and downtown. The restaurants, fast food outlets and pub will come in handy once you've finished exploring.

The SeaBus departs every 15 minutes Mon to Sat during the day and every 30 minutes on Sun and during the evening until just after midnight. In the summer, late June to early Sept, there are also 15-minute departures on Sun.

Avoid the northbound trip during afternoon rush hour.

Connections with SkyTrain can be made at the downtown SeaBus terminal.

Bicycles are allowed on the SeaBus at no extra cost, although during rush hours you may be asked to wait.

SkyTrain

The SkyTrain is Vancouver's rapid transit system. It runs 29 km (18 miles) from Surrey, through Burnaby and New Westminster, to the Canada Place Pier (Waterfront Station) downtown. (For SkyTrain information call 521-0400.)

At the centre of the city the Sky-Train goes underground, but most of the line is elevated, somewhat like the Seattle monorail. So far it is a single line with 20 stations.

Four-car trains depart every three to five minutes and reach 80 km/h (50 mph). A trip from one end of the line to the other takes 39 minutes. The driverless trains are run by computers monitored at SkyTrain headquarters. Security and information officers ride the trains and are at stations.

Tickets are sold by machines at each station; exact change is not necessary. The machines accept $2, $5 and $10 bills, as well as coins.

If you're curious about SkyTrain, the New Westminster Quay Public Market is a fine destination. Take the train to the New Westminster Station; the market is about half a block away on Front, right at the edge of the Fraser River. There's a large indoor market with fresh vegetables, fish and pasta, a wine store, an excel-

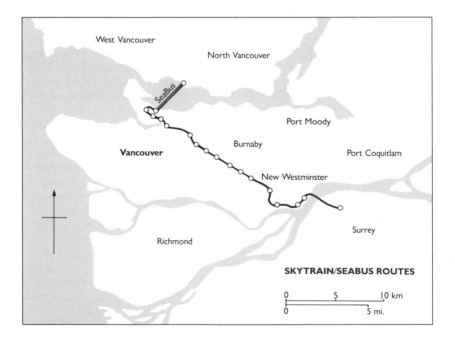

West Vancouver

North Vancouver

SeaBus

Port Moody

Vancouver

Burnaby

Port Coquitlam

New Westminster

Surrey

Richmond

SKYTRAIN/SEABUS ROUTES

0   5   10 km

0   5 mi.

About 29 km (18 miles) of elevated and underground track lead the SkyTrain from downtown to New Westminster and Surrey.

lent bakery and many small kiosks selling arts and crafts. You can walk along the Fraser and watch the tugs and leisure craft, or you can board one of the river touring boats, which depart from here. See Sightseeing (By Water).

The Paddle Wheeler Neighbourhood Pub is ideal for lunch. For dinner, Restaurant Des Gitanes (524-6122) is a short walk from the SkyTrain station (Columbia at 4th St). The Swiss-French cuisine is excellent.

Coach Lines

The bus depot is located in the Pacfic Central Station. Formerly a train terminal, it now services motorcoach and train travel. Although it is not in the city centre, it is close to the Main Street/Science World SkyTrain station.

Vancouver Airporter
244-9888
Leaves Level 2 of the airport every 15 minutes, 6 AM to midnight. There are pick-up points from major downtown hotels and the bus depot every 30 minutes. At Hotel Vancouver and Hotel Georgia, departures are every 15 minutes. The fare is $9.

Greyhound
662-3222
Service across Canada and to Seattle.

Maverick Coach Lines
255-1171
Buses go north up the Sunshine Coast to Powell River, and up the mainland coast to Squamish, Whistler, Blackcomb and Pemberton. Buses also go to Nanaimo on Vancouver Island.

Pacific Coach Lines
662-8074
Buses go to Victoria. See also Ferries (Bus Passengers).

Cheam Tours
1-604-792-9357 (Chilliwack)
Pick-up at the Vancouver International Airport, Level 1. Buses travel to destinations in the Fraser Valley as far as Hope.

Quick Shuttle
244-3744
Quick bus service to Bellingham Airport, downtown Seattle and SeaTac Airport. The 3½-hour trip from downtown to downtown costs $28.

Cars

Rentals

Avis
757 Hornby near Georgia
606-2847

Budget
450 W. Georgia at Richards
668-7000

Hertz
1128 Seymour near Davie
688-2411

Tilden
1140 Alberni near Thurlow
685-6111

Rent-a-Wreck
180 W Georgia at Cambie
688-0001
Cheap car rentals.

For something grander—a Porsche, Corvette convertible, Mercedes or Ferrari—call:

Exotic Car Rentals
1820 Burrard at W 2nd
644-9128

Parking

Finding parking may be a challenge. The main parkades are at Pacific Centre (entrance on Howe at Dunsmuir), the Bay (entrance on Richards near Dunsmuir) and Robson Square (entrances on Smithe and Howe). You may get lucky at the lot at Granville Square at the end of Granville or the multi-level lot on Seymour just after you pass Pender. Many downtown parking lots, both attended and metered, will take credit cards as well as cash.

Parking meter time limits are strictly enforced, and cars are towed (even if you have out-of-province plates) from rush-hour "no parking" areas. Check the parking meter and street signs for times. Parking in commercial alleys is illegal. See also Essential Information (Motor Vehicles).

Taxis

Vancouver has never been an easy city in which to hail a taxi other than in city centre. There are moves to improve this—in the spring of 1995, TAXIHOST, a four-year program to im-

prove the service in the city, was launched by Vancouver Tourism and the city's taxi companies. To find a cab quickly, the best bet is to head for a downtown hotel (there are cab stands at the Hotel Vancouver and the Hyatt) or call:

Black Top
731-1111, 681-2181
Request a Checker car with "collar-and-tie service," which is a black late-model car, guaranteed spotless, along with a neatly dressed, knowledgeable and friendly driver. All at no extra cost.

MacLure's
731-9211, 683-6666

Vancouver Taxi
255-5111, 669-5555
Has oversized cabs for wheelchairs or other large items.

Yellow Cab
681-3311, 681-1111
Yellow will take you for a personal tour of the city on its suggested routes. Prices are the regular meter rate. See Sightseeing (Other Tours).

Limousine Service

There are about 50 limousine companies in the city. For information, call the Talking Yellow Pages at 299-9000 and dial 9717.

The recorded message gives comprehensive information on hiring for specific requirements.

Trains

VIA Rail
1-800-561-8630 toll free (Canada)
The two major railways in Canada amalgamated their cross-country service into VIA Rail. The transcontinental train arrives and departs from the Pacific Central Station at Main and

Station St three days a week. Call the above number for reservations and information.

Call 669-3050 for arrivals and departures.

Amtrak
585-4848

In May 1995 Amtrak service between Seattle and Vancouver was reinstated after a 14-year absence. The Mount Baker International departs daily from Seattle at 7:15 AM and returns from Vancouver at 6:30 PM from Pacific Central Station. The trip takes about four hours and stops in Bellingham, Mount Vernon and Everett. Cost of the round trip is $64. Reserve at least a day in advance.

B.C. Rail
631-3500

Operates out of the train station at 1311 W 1st St in North Vancouver. If you have an inclination to see more of British Columbia—the Coast Mountains, forests and some small interior towns—take the B.C. Rail passenger train 253 km (157 miles) northeast to Lillooet. You can get there and back in a day, with a two-hour stopover for lunch and exploration. The train leaves every day in summer at 7 AM and travels via Horseshoe Bay, Squamish and Whistler, arriving in Lillooet at 12:30 PM. (You could go on to 100 Mile House, Quesnel or Prince George, but that would be at least a two-day trip.) The train arrives back in North Vancouver at 8:45 PM. The return fare is $116, with discounts for seniors and children, and includes breakfast and dinner. All passenger trains are non-smoking.

See also Sightseeing (Royal Hudson/MV *Britannia*).

Rocky Mountaineer Railtours travels from Vancouver to the Rockies in daylight hours. (Rocky Mountaineer)

Rocky Mountaineer Railtours
1-800-665-7245 toll free (Canada and U.S.)

To enjoy the rugged beauty of the Rockies by daylight, The Rocky Mountaineer has a two-day trip from Vancouver to Jasper, Banff or Calgary.

This route, which includes a one-night hotel stay in Kamloops, has been called "the most spectacular train trip in the world." Only the well-travelled Paul Theroux would know if that's an exaggeration, but this trip is a major event for tourists and train nuts. Rocky Mountaineer recently added a dome car, which means an even better view of the scenery. Even if you've travelled the highway a dozen times, you'll find that this route, which follows the tracks of Canada's first transcontinental railways, gives the best perspective of the wild, undeveloped backcountry.

People from all over the world take this trip, so book early.

Ferries

B.C. Ferries Corp has one of the largest and most modern ferry fleets in the world (certainly the largest in North America), transporting over 22 million people and 8 million vehicles annually.

The ferries include some extraordinary vessels—like the *Queen of Cowichan, Coquitlam, Surrey* and *Oak Bay*, which have bridges, loading facilities, propellers and rudders at both ends, so they can sail in either direction. The newest and largest additions to the fleet of 40 ferries are the *Spirit of British Columbia* and the *Spirit of Vancouver Island*. Designed and built in B.C., each carries 2100 passengers and 470 vehicles.

B.C. Ferries Corp undertook some innovative remodelling to accommodate the increasing traffic between the mainland and Vancouver Island.

The key principle was to stretch and lift. The first renovation in 1968 was to suspend an additional car deck, like a mezzanine, from the ceiling of the existing car deck, increasing the capacity from 110 to 150 cars. Then, a year later, the company started cutting some of the boats in half vertically, inserting a 25 m (82-foot)

midsection and welding the three sections together to increase capacity to 200 cars. A few years later it even cut four of the stretched boats in half horizontally! Another car deck was inserted, making these ferries both stretched and lifted. The *Queen of Esquimalt, Saanich, Vancouver* and *Victoria* have been converted so that they each carry over 300 vehicles.

The larger boats each have a restaurant, snack bar (some have cappuccino machines), newsstand/giftshop, video arcade, children's play area, and ship-to-shore telephone. Smoking is allowed only on the outside decks. Pets must remain on the car deck.

Schedules

For sailing times call 277-0277 (24 hours) for a recorded announcement or pick up a schedule at the Vancouver TouristInfo Centre at 200 Burrard St or at major hotels.

Vancouver is near two ferry terminals. Tsawwassen is an hour's drive south of downtown. Sailings from this terminal go to Swartz Bay (a 30-minute drive from Victoria), Nanaimo and the Gulf Islands.

Horseshoe Bay, the other ferry terminal, is a 30-minute drive north from downtown. Sailings from here go to Nanaimo, to Bowen Island and up the Sunshine coast.

The busiest routes are from the mainland to Vancouver Island. These crossings take 90 minutes to 2 hours. From June to Labour Day, there are hourly sailings from both Tsawwassen terminal and Swartz Bay 7 AM–10 PM. Sailings from Horseshoe Bay and Nanaimo are less frequent. The rest of the year, except for holidays, sailings are generally every two hours. There are exceptions to this— always double-check the schedule.

Fares

There are 24 routes with different fares; see the latest B.C. Ferries schedule. B.C. seniors, but not their vehicles, travel free Mon to Thurs, except holidays. Seniors must show their B.C. Gold Care Card to confirm their age and full-time residency in B.C.

Bus fare from downtown Vancouver to downtown Victoria, including the ferry, is $22.50 one-way.

Travel Tips

Car Passengers

Reservations for vehicles are accepted only on the routes from Tsawwassen to the Gulf Islands, from Port Hardy to Prince Rupert, and from Prince Rupert to the Queen Charlotte Islands. Call 669-1211 for reservations.

All other routes are first come, first served. Reservations must be accompanied by payment. Reserve by phone and use Visa or MasterCard. Summer and holiday reservations

should be made as far in advance as possible.

At any time during the summer it is wise to arrive early if you are taking your car. Once you are on the ferry, don't lose your car—it's the quickest way to be spotted as a tourist. Some boats have three car decks—all are numbered—so remember which one your car is on.

Constant upgrading and adding of vessels gives B.C. Ferries the capacity to carry some 26,000 passengers and 6000 vehicles between the mainland and Vancouver Island every day during the summer; however, it's still advisable to avoid peak times like weekends and holidays.

The worst times are Fri afternoon and evening, Sun afternoon and evening, and holiday weekends. Also, try to travel before sunset; you'll miss the scenery if you sail in the dark.

Leave your car behind if possible, especially at busy times. But on holiday weekends don't count on leaving it at the Tsawwassen parking lot. Although there is parking for 1100 cars, the lot is frequently full. Parking is not allowed along the lengthy causeway to the terminal, but there is a privately operated Park and Ride service at the foot of the causeway. Consider travelling as a foot or bus passenger.

Foot Passengers

Foot passengers can avoid car line-ups and walk right on board. It's a costly trip by taxi from Vancouver to either ferry terminal—about $55 to Tsawwassen and $35 to Horseshoe Bay. Taking public transportation to Tsawwassen from Vancouver is a long trip and not practical if you have luggage. Take #601 South Delta from Pacific Central Station and change at the Ladner Exchange to bus #640 Tsawwassen Ferry. Call B.C. Transit (521-0400) to check schedules.

To reach the Horseshoe Bay termi-

Orcinus orca, the Killer Whale

More killer whales are found off the coast of British Columbia than anywhere else in the world. Of the local population of 350 whales, 80 reside in southern waters—the Strait of Georgia, Juan de Fuca Strait and Puget Sound. On a B.C. Ferries trip you will occasionally see a group of dorsal fins 60 to 120 cm (2 to 4 feet) long as the whales cruise the waters near Tsawwassen. Killer whales live and travel in pods of 5 to 50.

Orcinus orca is 6 to 8 m (20 to 26 feet) long and can swim at 20 km/h (12 mph), leaping out of the water when it travels at top speed. Because it is a toothed whale and a successful predator, it has ended up with the unfortunate name of killer whale. It generally feeds on salmon but also preys on porpoises, seals, sea lions, birds and even other kinds of whales.

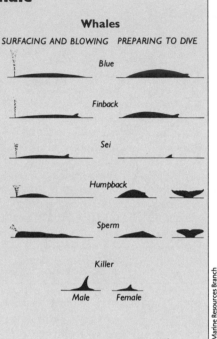

Whales

SURFACING AND BLOWING   PREPARING TO DIVE

Blue

Finback

Sei

Humpback

Sperm

Killer

Male   Female

Marine Resources Branch

---

nal, take the blue #250 West Van bus to Horseshoe Bay from downtown (it picks up passengers at bus stops on the north side of Georgia). The bus takes you to within walking distance of the Horseshoe Bay terminal. Call 985-7777.

Foot passengers must purchase tickets at least 10 minutes before sailing time (at Tsawwassen, it can take that long to walk from the ticket booth to the ferry). If you require bus transportation upon your arrival, listen for announcements giving bus information during the trip. Tickets are purchased on the ferry, and you board the bus before the ferry docks. Buses take you to downtown Victoria, Nanaimo or Powell River or to designated stops in these areas. (Note that some ferries do not have bus service during the winter schedule.) Foot passengers can

check luggage at the ferry terminal where tickets are sold. Don't forget to mark the destination on your bag. You can carry your bags onto the ferry, but there are no lockers and space is often at a premium.

Bus Passengers

Buses are the first vehicles on and off the ferries. To get to Victoria, take a Pacific Coach Lines bus. It leaves from the bus depot in downtown Vancouver 75 minutes before almost every sailing. No reservations are necessary, and the fare ($22.50) includes the cost of the ferry. You can board the bus at the bus depot or at designated stops on the way. To arrange for the bus to stop and pick you up, you must phone Pacific Coach Lines (662-8074) at least an hour before the bus leaves.

If your destination is Nanaimo or

the Sunshine Coast, catch a Maverick Coach Lines bus (255-1171). Buses to Nanaimo are generally every two hours, and two times daily for the Sunshine Coast. Maverick is the line to take for all departures from Horseshoe Bay.

Ferry Food

B.C. Ferries is the largest fast food outlet in the province after McDonald's, and it has never been known for its wonderful fare. An effort is being made to improve on-board dining, however—vegetarian dishes have been added, and some vessels, like the new *Spirit of British Columbia* and *Spirit of Vancouver Island*, have buffets where freshness is emphasized. And let's face it, you can't beat the view from a ferry's dining room. Another solution, particularly for famiies, is to pack a picnic. Or, if you are departing from Tsawwassen, you can get into the ferry line-up early and grab a snack at Galley West, a large new food fair at the terminal, before you board.

Short Ferry Trips

Personally, we're sold on the ferries. Nothing can beat the scenery and salt air as you lounge on the deck on a sunny day. If the weather is good, take a jacket and binoculars out on deck to watch the marine traffic: fish boats, freighters, sailboats, yachts, tugs and other ferries. You may even catch sight of seals, otters or whales.

Some of the following short ferry trips are perfect if you want a little fresh air as well as a chance to see the coastal waterways. Save these trips for a sunny day; it makes a big difference.

Horseshoe Bay to Bowen Island

This is the shortest of the B.C. Ferries runs, about 20 minutes to go 5 km (3 miles) one way. It is possible to do this trip from Vancouver in an afternoon, even with a stopover on Bowen.

Take the bus to Horseshoe Bay and travel as a foot passenger or take a car. Phone B.C. Ferries Corp for times and prices.

See also Accommodation (Bed and Breakfast).

Sunshine Coast

Another pleasant day trip. The mainland coast north of Vancouver is accessible by a road-and-ferry system for only about 160 km (100 miles) because of the rugged fiord-cut terrain. Phone Maverick Coach Lines (255-1171) for times and fares to Gibsons. The ferry ride from Horseshoe Bay to Langdale takes 40 minutes, and then there is a short bus ride along the craggy coast into Gibsons. Call B.C. Ferries Corp for sailing times and fares if you are taking your car.

Gulf Islands

Sail to the peaceful Gulf Islands from Tsawwassen, perhaps to Galiano or Mayne, the two closest islands. Both are popular bicycling destinations; Mayne is more compact and not as hilly. If you are taking a car, make sure you have a ferry reservation, especially on summer or holiday weekends.

See also Excursions from Vancouver (Gulf Islands).

Granville Island Ferries

See Sightseeing (Granville Island).

Vancouver International Airport

The airport is on an island at the mouth of the Fraser River, 13 km (8 miles) from downtown. It is Canada's second-busiest airport, with 325,000 takeoffs and landings handling 11 million passengers a year. The major

The Spirit of Haida Gwaii, The Jade Canoe *is the work of Haida artist Bill Reid.*

airlines at the main terminal are: Air Canada, Canadian Airlines, Air B.C., United, Delta, American, Horizon, KLM, Malaysia Airlines, Northwest Airlines, Alaska Airlines, Air New Zealand, Cathay Pacific, Air China and Japan, and Singapore, Mandarin and Korean Airlines. The smaller South Terminal services regional airlines.

Transportation between the two terminals is not regular. Call the connecting airline to arrange transportation, or take a taxi.

Getting There

Getting to the airport by cab costs about $23 from downtown. It's cheaper to take the Vancouver Airporter (244-9888) for $9. It leaves every 30 minutes from the major downtown hotels. You can also flag it down at Broadway and Granville or at 41st and Granville.

Airlimo provides a flat-rate, 24-hour limousine service between the airport and various locations ($29 to downtown). Phone 273-1331 to book.

Public transit buses to and from the airport unfortunately involve a transfer and so are not recommended if you have luggage. But if you want to go by bus from downtown, take a #20 Granville south to 70th and Granville and then transfer to the #100 Airport, which goes to the airport terminal. Going into town, take the #100 New Westminster Station and transfer at 70th to the #20 Victoria.

The New Look of Vancouver International

Vancouver International's new terminal will open in June 1996, making life easier for some 4.8 million international travellers who pass through this airport. The original 30-year-old terminal has been overcrowded and inconvenient ever since the tourism world discovered Vancouver in 1986.

The International Terminal will be the new wing of the original airport and will handle international and U.S. traffic; the original terminal will handle domestic flights. Departing passengers must pay the Airport Improvement Fee, which varies according to your destination. The fee can be paid at machines that take cash or credit cards or at staffed booths located near the security gates. You must pay the fee before you go through security.

Departures are on Level 3 of the new terminal. International check-in is in the southwest wing (Concourse D), and U.S. check-in is to the southeast (Concourse E). The focal point of the airport is between these two areas in an amphitheatre that holds *Spirit of Haida Gwaii, The Jade Canoe*, a large bronze work by world-renowned Haida artist, Bill Reid. The carving, which is approximately 4 m (13 feet) high and 6 m by 3 m (20 feet by 10 feet) in area, is backed by floor-to-ceiling glass art depicting waves. Throughout the terminal, large, open spaces, glass walls, soaring skylights and Squamish rock pillars create a feeling of spaciousness even at the most crowded times. There is an information centre on each level. Level 3 facilities include a food fair (with mezzanine seating) as well as a lounge and restaurant, newsstands, retail outlets, duty-free shops and children's play areas, and there are several currency exchanges and bank machines (near check-in counters in both wings, beside security in the east wing and in the international departure lounge). Throughout the terminal, five moving sidewalks ease movement. Airline lounges for first-class and business passengers are located past security on Levels 3 and 4 in the International Terminal.

Passengers arriving by air are greeted with superb views of the West Coast mountains through floor-to-ceiling windows. The short walk and escalator ride to Canada Customs and the arrivals hall on Level 2 is enhanced by Musqueam art. The *Spindle Whorl*, a 4 m high (13-foot-high) cedar carving, which depicts eagles, man, salmon, the moon and the earth, dominates a wall; weavings hang from the ceiling; and water cascades beneath an escalator. At the bottom of the escalator, arriving passengers meet the *Welcome Figures*. Carved from one red cedar log, the 5.2 m high (17-foot-high) carved figures of a Native man and woman display a traditional Coast Salish welcome.

Goods and Services Tax rebate forms for non-Canadians are available 24 hours from Canada Customs. The arrivals hall has tour and cruise operators (there are baggage belts here where cruise passengers can deposit their luggage), car rentals (after February 1997 these will be moved to Level 1 of the parkade), a currency exchange, a tourist information area and a chapel. Arriving passengers can enjoy the *Spirit of Haida Gwaii* from this level as well as it sits above the meet-and-greet lobby in an open area. Through the exit doors, the first curb is for buses, taxis and limousines, and the next curb is for general pick-up traffic.

Domestic departures leave from Level 3 in the domestic terminal (Concourses A, B and C), and arrivals are on Level 2. There is a children's nursery and large play area on Level 3 in the passageway that connects the Domestic and International Terminals.

Airport Parking

Covered walkways connect the Domestic and International Terminals to what will eventually be a four-storey parkade with 2400 parking spaces. (The second phase of the parkade will open in February 1997; at that time rental car outlets will move to Level 1 of the parkade.) Baggage carts are available in the parkade as well as inside beside the baggage carousels and curbside outdoors.

Flights to Victoria

Downtown Victoria

Air B.C.
688-5515
Harbour-to-harbour seaplane service. Depart from Vancouver Harbour near the Bayshore Inn and land 35 minutes later in front of the Empress

Hotel on Victoria's Inner Harbour. The fare is $195 return, but weekend and greatly reduced excursion rates are available.

Helijet Airways
273-1414
A 12-passenger Sikorsky helicopter will transport you from the Vancouver Harbour heliport to the Victoria heliport, a few minutes' drive from the harbour and city centre. A free shuttle service is provided to downtown. The fare is $250 return, with weekend and greatly reduced excursion rates.

Victoria Airport

It is generally cheaper to fly from airport to airport, but it can be less convenient since it involves a 30-minute drive to and from the city at both ends. Call Air B.C. (688-5515) or Canadian Airlines (279-6611).

Sightseeing

The Sights 82

Granville Island 82
What to See, Special Events, Places to Eat, For a Cool Drink,
Getting to the Island

Royal Hudson/MV Britannia Excursion 87

Chinatown 89

Touring Vancouver 93
By Air, By Land, By Water, Other Tours

Special Interest Tours 99

Calendar of Events 99

The Sights

Thanks to the mountains, ocean and climate—and the history of the place—there are things in Vancouver that you can't do or see anywhere else. Many sights are described in this section and elsewhere in the book, but don't miss the top 10, listed below in no particular order:

1. **Granville Island**; see this chapter
2. **The Royal Hudson**; see this chapter
3. **Robson Street**; see Shopping (Shopping Areas)
4. **Museum of Anthropology**; see Museums/Art Galleries
5. **A walk in the forest**; see Parks/Beaches/Gardens
6. **A ferry ride**; see Getting Around (Ferries)
7. **Chinatown**; see this chapter
8. **Stanley Park seawall**; see Parks/Beaches/Gardens
9. **Dr Sun Yat-sen Classical Chinese Garden**; see Parks/Beaches/Gardens
10. **Jericho Beach to Spanish Banks**; see Parks/Beaches/Gardens

The Public Market is the place to fill shopping bags with everything from fresh produce to baked delicacies. (Judi Lees)

Granville Island

Granville Island, dredged out of the mud flats of False Creek in 1915, was first known as Industrial Island, since it was a busy centre of sawmilling, ironworks and other heavy industry. Always joined to the rest of Vancouver by a causeway, the island boomed in the twenties and thirties, but after the war many of the large plants left the island. It remained unnoticed until 1973, when the federal government decided to rescue it. Most of the remaining industries were persuaded to leave, but buildings were kept and given a face-lift. The public market opened in 1979 and became a raging success. Now Granville Island is a hub of enjoyment, and the federal government regulates the businesses, gearing most to food, marine activities, and arts and crafts.

The island is a hodge-podge of unusual buildings—the exteriors of the

A fruit grower's day stall at Granville Island Public Market. (Rosamond Norbury)

industrial structures have been jazzed up with bright blues, greens and yellows. They were never architectural wonders—in fact, some were not much more than sheds—but the idea was to blend the old and the new, and it works.

Granville Island is a people place. It is not too trendy or touristy, and there is far more to do than just shop. Even though the public market is the star attraction, one can spend hours wandering the craft and art galleries, enjoying the waterfront scenes and simply being part of the easygoing atmosphere.

What to See

Granville Island Information Centre
1592 Johnston St near the Public Market
666-5784
You'll find maps, brochures and helpful information officers here, as well as a continuous 12-minute slide presentation on the history of Granville Island. There is a currency exchange and bank machine in the same building.

Granville Island Public Market
Nothing can beat the market for one-stop food shopping. Where else can you get boneless chicken breasts, a litre of fish stock, fresh basil, salmon roe, Callebaut chocolate, cheese-and-onion buns and serrano chilies, all under one roof? If you're making a picnic (perhaps to take to Kits Beach, a few blocks away), here is a cornucopia.

On a dull day, the market building is dry, warm and full of fragrances, bright colours, lively people and wonderful things to taste. In hot weather, huge glass doors lift so that you are right out on the shore of False Creek, where you can sit, sample your purchases, enjoy buskers and watch tugs and sailboats go by.

The market is open 9 AM to 6 PM every day in the summer (May to Sept) and is closed Mon in the winter. See also Shopping.

Art and Crafts Galleries
Many of the galleries on the island are in the Net Loft building, which is across from the Public Market. Circle Craft displays jury-selected B.C. crafts, Kingsmill Pottery Studio contains murals that are worth checking out, Wickaninnish Gallery features

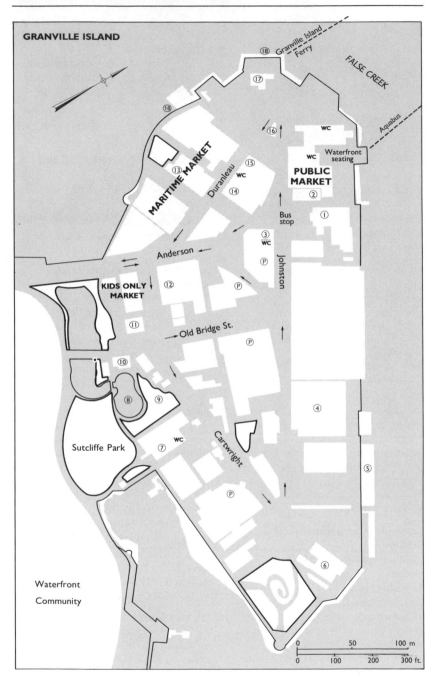

GRANVILLE ISLAND

FALSE CREEK

Granville Island Ferry

Aquabus

MARITIME MARKET

PUBLIC MARKET

Duranleau

Anderson

Johnston

KIDS ONLY MARKET

Old Bridge St.

Cartwright

Sutcliffe Park

WC

Bus stop

Waterfront seating

Waterfront Community

traditional and contemporary Native art, and Paperworks Gallery and Malaspina Printmakers (1555 Duranleau) exhibit limited edition prints.

As you wander the island, you will discover a wonderful mix of local crafts, and many craftspeople will welcome you into their studios to observe their techniques. Some are the tapestry makers at Fibre Art Studio and silk painters at Maiwa Handprints (both in the Net Loft building on Johnston), weaver Diana Sanderson (15–1551 Johnston, tucked behind a narrow walkway near Mulvaney's Restaurant), the glassblowers at Newsmall and Sterling (1440 Old Bridge), the quilters at Textile Context (1420 Old Bridge) the gold- and silversmiths at Forge and

Form (1334 Cartwright) and Joel Berman, maker of contemporary glass (1244 Cartwright).

The Gallery of B.C. Ceramics and Crafthouse, both on Cartwright, are excellent places to enjoy and purchase local crafts.

See also Museums/Art Galleries (Craft Galleries).

Emily Carr Institute of Art and Design

The Charles H. Scott Gallery has changing exhibits of visiting artists; weekdays, 12–5; weekends, 10–5; free admission.

The Concourse Gallery displays students' work; hours vary.

Sea Village

The only residents of the island live here in one of Vancouver's few houseboat communities.

Boat Rentals

You can rent kayaks from Ecomarine Ocean Kayak Centre, power boats from the Granville Island Boat Rentals or Pacific Boat Rentals and canoes or kayaks from Adventure Fitness. Experienced sailors can rent from a number of outlets in the Maritime Market. See Sports/Recreation for more details.

Water Park

One of the most imaginative playgrounds in the city, located beside Isadora's Restaurant. The wading pool has stationary fire hoses for dousing "intruders."

Tennis

The courts beside the False Creek Community Centre are free and open to the public.

Theatres

Three theatres are on the island: the Arts Club, the Arts Club Revue and the Waterfront. See Entertainment/ Culture (Theatre).

---

1 Arts Club Theatre
2 Arts Club Revue Theatre
3 Granville Island Info Centre
4 Emily Carr College of Art
5 Sea Village floating homes
6 Granville Island Hotel
7 False Creek Community Centre
8 Water Park
9 Adventure Playground
10 Isadora's Restaurant
11 Waterfront Theatre
12 Granville Island Brewery
13 The Lobster Man
14 Net Loft
15 Blackberry Books
16 La Baguette et L'Échalote
17 Bridges Restaurant
18 Boat rentals
WC Washroom
☐ Park

Brewery Tour
Island Lager, made on the island by Granville Island Brewery, is the best beer in British Columbia. For more details, see Special Interest Tours later in this chapter.

Net Loft
This small warehouse is jammed with unusual stores selling handmade hats, beads for jewellery making, Native silver work, kitchenware, crafts, books, handmade papers, fabric-dyeing supplies and specialty postcards.

Kids Only Market
See With the Kids (Day Trips).

Special Events

Granville Island is a popular location for festivals celebrating such things as bluegrass, comedy, jazz, wooden boats, writers and crafts. Free events often take place at the front and the back of the market building. Check at the Information Centre to see what's going on.

Places to Eat

There are many take-out stands in the market, and you can get gourmet take-out food from La Baguette et L'Échalote. Create a picnic and sit outside by the water behind the market, or eat at one of the island's restaurants.

Isadora's Co-operative Restaurant
A casual place with outdoor seating and some super vegetarian dishes. Perfect for families. See Restaurants (Breakfast/Brunch).

The Keg
A steakhouse.

Bridges Restaurant
Pub food in the pub, light meals in the bistro and elegance upstairs. The wonderful outdoor deck makes you feel as though you're in Marseilles.

See Restaurants (Outdoors)

For a Cool Drink

Arts Club Back Stage Lounge
A small lounge with outdoor seating and a great view.

Bridges Neighbourhood Pub
A lively pub atmosphere.

Getting to the Island

By Boat
For those with their own boat, there is free two-hour moorage directly behind Granville Island Public Market.

Two companies run small ferries from downtown to the island.

Granville Island Ferries (684-7781) run continuously from the south foot of Thurlow behind the Vancouver Aquatic Centre to Granville Island for $1.50 for adults, with discounts for children and seniors. The trip takes about five minutes. Daily service 7 AM–10 PM in the summer; 7 AM–8 PM in the winter. The ferry also goes to Vanier Park daily 10–8 in the summer, weekends only in the winter. During summer the ferry also goes to Stamps Landing at False Creek 8–6.

Aquabus Ferries (689-5858) run from the foot of Hornby St, leaving every two or three minutes, for Granville Island and False Creek. During summer the hours are 7 AM–10:30 PM; during winter, 7 AM–8 PM. Price is $1.50 for adults, with discounts for seniors and children. Bikes travel for 50¢; there is one specially designed ferry that transports 12 cyclists and bikes at once.

By Bus
Catch a #51 Granville Island bus at Broadway and Granville; it runs until 6:20 PM. The #50 False Creek South from downtown stops a five-minute walk away from the island.

*It's a five-minute ride on a small ferry from the West End to Granville Island.
(Judi Lees)*

By Car

If you're not a patient driver, go by boat or bus. Line-ups and parking on the island can be horrendous. During the day free parking is limited to three hours; after that you are quickly towed away. Covered pay parking is available; credit cards are accepted by the machines. There is less traffic on weekdays (the earlier in the day, the better). On weekends, you can try parking on W 2nd or W 3rd Ave east of Burrard; it's a 10-minute walk to the market.

Royal Hudson/MV Britannia Excursion

This is the best day trip from Vancouver, combining a train ride and a boat ride up and down the spectacular B.C. coast.

The Royal Hudson is a regal steam locomotive that runs up the coast to the logging town of Squamish, 64 km (40 miles) north of Vancouver. The train steams out of the B.C. Rail train station in North Vancouver at 10 AM and chugs through picturesque West Vancouver (beach cottages and lavish waterfront mansions perched on cliffs and surrounded by mammoth Douglas firs). But suddenly you are in the wilds of the Coast Mountains and the train tracks are hanging onto a cliff with the ocean 30 m (100 feet) below. Waterfalls plummet beside you and hawks circle above.

Find a seat at the back of the train so that you can see the engine as you round curves, and be sure to sit on the left side for the journey north or you'll be looking at the cliff.

Recently the Royal Hudson introduced its Parlour Class, which offers fine dining (lunch en route to Squamish and tea and desserts on the return) in the grandeur of a historic railway car.

The trip to Squamish takes about two hours, and you have 1½ hours to explore or have lunch before the return trip. Unless you're from a small B.C. town and have seen it all before, use the time to wander

One of the last operational steam locomotives in Canada, the Royal Hudson, on a trip up the coast to Squamish. (Province of British Columbia)

around and have the barbecued salmon buffet later on the boat. There are several optional side trips from Squamish: a 20-minute flight over the glaciers of the Coast Mountains, a guided walking tour of Shannon Falls Provincial Park or, a favourite with train buffs, the West Coast Railway Heritage Park.

The MV *Britannia* is a step or two above B.C. Ferries' boats. There are two seating levels with huge windows and a sun deck on top. The boat follows the same route as the train, but the view from the water is entirely different. (Bring binoculars—the West Van houses look even more sumptuous from the water.) You cruise through Howe Sound, Burrard Inlet, English Bay and Vancouver Harbour, sailing past Stanley Park and downtown, and then dock at Coal Harbour by the Bayshore Inn at 4:30 PM. A free shuttle bus will take you to the train station in North Van to retrieve your car, or you can walk downtown in 10 minutes.

The pacing of the train and boat excursion is perfect—you are never bored, left waiting or rushed. You return relaxed even after a full day.

We recommend taking the train up and the boat back because the boat can be cool in the morning, but you could reverse this. The train and boat trip is $60, with discounts for children and seniors.

It is also possible to take the Royal Hudson both to and from Squamish ($35 adult, return fare), but the boat is definitely worth the extra money.

The boat/train day trip is operated by 1st Tours (688-7246). Tickets must be purchased 48 hours before departure; this can be done over the phone with Visa, MasterCard or American Express. You can also purchase tickets from the 1st Tours Royal Hudson dock at Coal Harbour beside the Bayshore Inn, at the B.C. Rail Station in North Vancouver (1311 W 1st St) or from the Vancouver TouristInfo Centre at 200 Burrard (663-6000). The train runs Wed to Sun from June

Shoppers in Chinatown. (Rosamond Norbury)

to mid-Sept. Reserve well in advance for weekends.

Try to avoid driving to the B.C. Rail station, even though parking is free. You will be returned there at the height of rush hour and will have to inch back across Lions Gate Bridge. Instead, take the #740 Royal Hudson special bus that goes from downtown to the station and back. It stops at some hotels. Get more bus information when you buy your tickets.

Chinatown

Walking into Chinatown is like stepping onto a movie set or entering another time and place, with all the sights, smells, sounds and tastes of another culture. Street life is one of the reasons Chinatown is so distinctive; the sidewalks are bustling, often jammed with curious foodstuffs spilling out from stores. And it's noisy as enthusiastic vendors call out their specials. Lichee nuts, anyone? The best time to visit is on a sunny afternoon when it is at its liveliest.

The heart of the Chinese commu-

nity is Pender from Carrall to Gore, and Keefer from Main to Gore. Parking has always been difficult, but the situation improved with the opening of the Chinatown Plaza Parkade, which added 1000 additional parking spots. Most lots in Chinatown have meters, so take lots of change. Better yet, come by bus or walk. Chinatown is only a 20-minute walk from Georgia and Granville.

The Chinese are Vancouver's oldest ethnic group. They first came in 1858 to join the Fraser Valley gold rush and were later contracted in large numbers to construct the Canadian Pacific Railway. Today Vancouver has the second-largest Chinese community in North America after San Francisco. There are about 150,000 people of Chinese origin; few live in Chinatown, but many shop there. In the adjacent residential community east of Gore you will notice bilingual street signs because the residents are mostly Chinese.

The best examples of the distinctive architecture found only in Vancouver's Chinatown—recessed balconies,

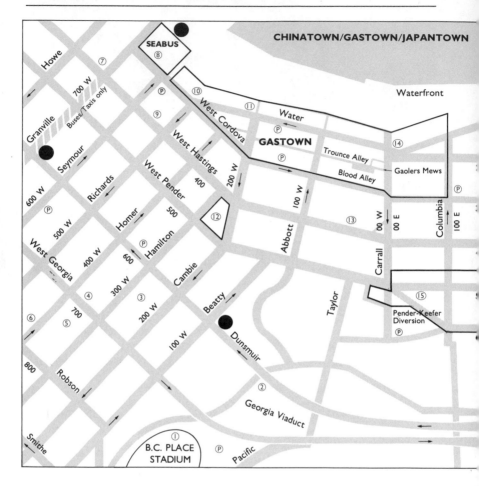

Map: CHINATOWN/GASTOWN/JAPANTOWN

ornamental roof lines and curved roof tiles—are the two blocks of Pender west of Main. These buildings were constructed at the turn of the century by Chinese clan associations or benevolent societies, which provided for the welfare of new immigrants and needy families, since the Chinese were not allowed citizenship and had no rights until 1949.

Today the Chinese community is active and respected in all aspects of city life.

Like the rest of the city, Chinatown has seen changes during the nineties,

but care has been taken to blend the new with the old; modern buildings are finished in soft-toned red brick, for example. As well as adding parking, the **Chinatown Plaza Parkade & Shopping Centre** at 180 Keefer adds retail space and Canada's largest Chinese restaurant—the Floata Restaurant seats 1000. Apartments and a care facility were added to meet community needs, and the **Bank of Hong Kong** showed confidence in the economic growth of Chinatown by moving into a new tower at Main and Keefer.

At 50 E Pender is the **Chinese Cul-**

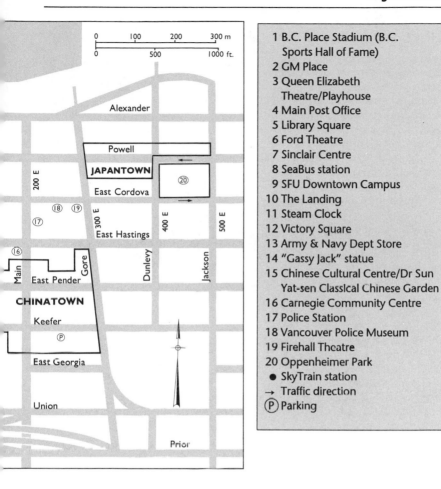

1	B.C. Place Stadium (B.C. Sports Hall of Fame)
2	GM Place
3	Queen Elizabeth Theatre/Playhouse
4	Main Post Office
5	Library Square
6	Ford Theatre
7	Sinclair Centre
8	SeaBus station
9	SFU Downtown Campus
10	The Landing
11	Steam Clock
12	Victory Square
13	Army & Navy Dept Store
14	"Gassy Jack" statue
15	Chinese Cultural Centre/Dr Sun Yat-sen Classical Chinese Garden
16	Carnegie Community Centre
17	Police Station
18	Vancouver Police Museum
19	Firehall Theatre
20	Oppenheimer Park
●	SkyTrain station
→	Traffic direction
Ⓟ	Parking

tural Centre, which holds classes in English and Chinese, Chinese arts and crafts, and *tai chi*. The building is the entrance to **Dr Sun Yat-sen Classical Chinese Garden**. This garden was designed in the People's Republic and built with the help of $6 million worth of labour and materials donated by the people of China. The Ming Dynasty–style garden is the only classical Chinese garden outside of China. The garden is walled to preserve the sanctuarylike feeling of this type of garden. Adjacent to the garden is a public Chinese park, not as authentic as the Sun Yat-sen but

quite lovely. See also Parks/Beaches/Gardens.

Along Pender between Carrall and Main are stores selling rattan, porcelain, silk and inexpensive gifts. Stop in at **Ming Wo** at 23 E Pender, one of the best cookware stores in town, crammed with every imaginable kitchen utensil. Just a couple of doors away is **China West** at 41 E Pender, a treasure chest of cheap toys, novelties, calligraphy equipment, and Chinese jackets and slippers.There are many of this type of stores here, and they are excellent places to purchase small gifts for children.

Library Square

No one is ambivalent about the city's new library. Some see the Colosseum-style structure as a bold and original piece of architecture, whereas others view it as pretentious and inefficient. Love it or hate it, you must see for yourself.

Designed by Moshe Safdie, a Canadian architect now working in Boston who collaborated with the Vancouver firm of Downs/Archambault, the 9-storey, 35 000 m^2 (323,000-square-foot) library takes up a full city block. The Georgia St entrance leads into a 6-storey light-filled atrium, which serves as a promenade connecting the circular library with an adjoining 22-storey office tower.

There is an outdoor feel to the promenade as you look up to view the soaring glass and soft-brown stone façade (it's a pre-cast concrete made from granite quarried locally) above. There are retail shops, espresso bars, kiosks and a bookstore on the office tower side. Library tours are available (call 331-4049), and there's a designated meeting place in the promenade.

The Children's Library on the lower level is delightful. It includes child-size furnishings, bright colours and a reading/play area that borders an outside glassed wall where a waterfall cascades. There is also a pint-size house where a child can sit and read.

Truly a library of the nineties, it has vertical and horizontal electronically controlled conveyors that move books and materials throughout the building, automated checkouts, a computerized lab where patrons use a variety of software (call 331-3685 to book), the Online Public Access Catalogue (OPAC), Internet, Freenet access and specialized databases. A language library allows self-tutoring in 90 languages. The seventh floor has a glass-enclosed section for rare, historic books, and three meeting rooms are available for public use (call 331-4045 for information), as well as a pre-function area.

Visitors may obtain a temporary library card (call 331-3600). The library is open Mon to Wed, 10–9, and Thurs to Sat, 10–6 from May until Sept. From Sept through April it's also open Sun, 1–5.

The book'-märk is run by the Friends of the Library. This shop is on the ground level and has gift items as well as children's souvenirs. Hours are Mon to Sat, 10–6, and, during winter, Sun, 1–5.

Just before Main is **New Town Bakery** at 158 E Pender, our favourite of the Chinatown bakeries. You can take out or sit at the back and have baked goods and tea. Try a barbecued pork bun (slightly sweet dough with barbecued pork inside), a coconut or custard tart, or a coconut-filled bun.

Once you cross Main you are in the thick of the food markets. Prices in Chinatown are cheaper (and quality often higher) than anywhere else, especially for produce, fish, poultry and meat. Stop at one of the bigger markets (try **Yuen Fong** at 242 E Pender) and you'll find dozens of cans, bottles and packages of foods you've never seen before. Yuen Fong also has a large selection of Chinese cooking and eating utensils.

On this block you can watch butchers skillfully wield their cleavers to chop up barbecued pork or duck in the windows of the meat markets. Half a barbecued duck costs only $5 and makes a great picnic with some coconut tarts and fruit.

Turn right at Gore, walk past more markets and then turn right at Keefer. At the corner of Keefer and Main

is the **Ten Ren Tea and Ginseng Co**, which sells an enormous variety of Chinese teas that promise simple refreshment or a cure of all ailments —and cost up to $68/kg ($150/lb.). Ginseng is a specialty here, and the store serves samples. The store also sells a range of attractively packaged teas that make great gifts or souvenirs. Another perfect gift is the Chinese tea sets found here and in other small shops.

The best Chinese restaurants unfortunately are no longer in Chinatown, but there are some good lunch spots, including **Hon's Wun Tun House** for noodles or **New Diamond** for *dim sum*. The best Vietnamese/Cambodian restaurant in town, the **Phnom-Penh**, has a location in Chinatown and is open for lunch and dinner. If possible, order ahead for the Special Prawns dish—you won't taste prawns better than this. See Restaurants (Chinese, Vietnamese).

The Symphony of Fire

Each summer the four nights of fireworks, called the Symphony of Fire, are bigger, splashier and more expensive, attracting 400,000 spectators. They are set off in the middle of English Bay and can be seen from Kitsilano, the West End and West Vancouver. Traffic used to be horrendous in the West End that evening; now the area is closed to cars on fireworks nights. Take transit, park downtown and walk, or watch from Kitsilano or West Vancouver.

Touring Vancouver

In Vancouver you can see the sights by bus, trolley, boat, steam locomotive, helicopter, Rolls-Royce, float plane or paddle wheeler.

By Air

Harbour Air
688-1277
A variety of trips are available, ranging from a 20-minute tour of the city ($69 a person) to a 2½-hour outing to a secluded mountain lake with a picnic lunch ($204 a person, but the price is reduced when more people attend).

In the spring and summer there are daily commuter flights to the Gulf Islands from Vancouver Harbour and to Saltspring only from Vancouver Airport's south terminal.

Sea Lions at Steveston

Since 1980 Steller sea lions from as far north as Alaska, and California sea lions from as far south as Baja, have been congregating on the Steveston jetty at the mouth of the Fraser River. Each spring more and more sea lions arrive, possibly lured by the warm currents of El Niño. Most recently more than 700 were counted sunning themselves on the jetty. Seeing that 1992 had the largest run of eulachon (a smeltlike fish of the northern Pacific) in the Fraser River in 30 years, they'll probably be back for more.

All the visiting sea lions are males, here to fatten up before returning home to breed. Breeding takes place on land, and the males are forced to fast for about six weeks while protecting their harem. Some mature Stellers reach 1120 kg (2500 pounds).

Unlike the territorial hostility between the males at the breeding grounds, or rookeries, confrontations at Steveston are usually lim-

ited to a dominant male shoving a smaller one off a choice sunning rock. It can get to be a lively and social scene, with the Californias barking and the Stellers growling like bears, but mostly the sea lions are intent on lazing in the sun. They feed at night, and during the day at the height of the season every boulder on the end of the 8 km (5-mile) jetty has a sea lion draped over it. (Imagine the beach at Fort Lauderdale during spring break and you've got the idea.)

Sea lions are protected in American and Canadian waters but are hated by fishermen because of their voracious appetites and the damage they do to nets—California sea lions off Vancouver Island alone consume 600 tonnes of salmon a year, and that's just 10 per cent of their diet. In recent years the numbers of Californias have been increasing; the Steller population is stable.

Harbour Air's terminal at Vancouver Airport is worth a visit. The Flying Beaver, a restaurant/pub, adjoins it, and in summer you can eat on a sunny deck that juts over the river and watch the float planes land. In colder weather, there's a fireplace, comfy seating and the same terrific views. There's finger food, pastas, fresh seafood and beer on tap.

Vancouver Helicopters
270-1484
Tours leave from either the Vancouver Harbour heliport or from Grouse Mountain. City and mountain tours from Grouse Mountain start at $40 a person for a six-minute tour; a two-hour coastal mountain tour with a stop on a glacier costs $295 a person.

By Land

Vancouver Trolley Company
451-5581
The turn-of-the-century trolleyless trolley cars you occasionally see on Vancouver streets let you take a tour of the major attractions at your own speed. The trolleys have a two-hour circuit including 15 stops. You can get out at each stop and reboard a subsequent trolley—they come every 30 minutes. Each trolley has a guide on board to narrate the trip. Fares, $17 for adults with discounts for children, can be paid to the driver and are good for one circuit (cash only).

Bus tour companies seem to fall into two categories: the big companies

The Pacific National Exhibition

The PNE, classified as an agricultural fair, has been held every summer since 1910. It opens mid-Aug and ends on Labour Day. A parade from downtown to the PNE grounds starts the fun.

This fair is one of the largest in North America. You'll see horse shows, prize livestock, horticultural displays and craft shows. There are logger sports, a petting zoo, an international food pavilion and entertainment stages. You can wander through educational and cultural exhibits or eat Tom Thumb doughnuts and corn dogs on the midway after a 95 km/h (60 mph) roller coaster ride.

Babysitting is provided by St John's Ambulance staff at a nominal rate. Phone B.C. Transit regarding special PNE buses. For the daily schedule of events, check the newspaper or phone 253-2311.

Gates are open daily 10:30–10:30; grounds are open until midnight and the casino until 2 AM. Admission is charged, but there are free days for seniors and children. After 1996, the location of the PNE will be changed.

See also With the Kids (Playland).

---

that use big buses, where you'll find yourself with about 50 people, or smaller companies with small buses that hold about 20 people.

The trips themselves don't vary that much between the big and the small companies. There's a trip to the North Shore, including Grouse Mountain, the Capilano Suspension Bridge, a salmon hatchery and sometimes Lonsdale Quay market. The city tours usually include downtown, Gastown, Chinatown, Robson Street, Canada Place, Stanley Park, Shaughnessy, Queen Elizabeth Park and Granville Island.

The small bus companies are:

West Coast City and Nature Sightseeing
451-1600

LandSea Tours
255-7272

Skyland Tours
669-2521

The two largest tour companies are:

Pacific Coach Lines
662-7575
1-800-661-1725 (Canada and U.S.)

Gray Line of Vancouver
879-3363
1-800-667-0882 (Canada and U.S.)

See also Getting Around (Public Transit, Taxis).

By Water

Starline Tours
272-9187, 522-3506 (seasonal)
If you're in Vancouver in the spring, the sea lion boat trips from Steveston are a must. Since 1980 sea lions from both Alaska and California have converged on the Steveston jetty to fatten up on Fraser River fish. You may see as many as 700. The trips are 1¾ hours long and cost $17 for adults, with discounts for seniors and children. Phone to check times. The sea lions generally arrive in March and leave in May.

Starline Tours also has other trips. There is a three-hour cruise on the busy Fraser, where you'll see tugs, log booms, freighters—a fascinating look

A horse-drawn carriage tour is one of the many ways to enjoy Stanley Park. (Judi Lees)

at a working river. The cost is $22 for adults, and it departs from New Westminster across from the SkyTrain station. A relaxing and scenic six-hour cruise on Pitt Lake costs $50. The Starline crew is knowledgeable about the rivers, local history, and flora and fauna.

Harbour Ferries
687-9558

Tour the harbour in a paddle wheeler! In a 90-minute tour of Burrard Inlet you'll see Lions Gate Bridge, Stanley Park, the city skyline and the workings of a busy port. Cost is $16 for adults, with discounts for seniors and children. The company also has a sunset dinner cruise.

Bluewater Adventures
3–252 E 1st St, North Van
980-3800

Weeklong natural history trips to wilderness spots such as the Queen Charlottes or northern Vancouver Island for bird-watching, whale watching or exploring abandoned Native villages and old-growth forests. All trips are on a 21 m (68-foot) yacht and are accompanied by a naturalist.

Lotus Land Tours
684-4922

For a quick entry into wilderness, take a day trip kayaking in Indian Arm. Lotus Land picks up from hotels or residences and transports you to Deep Cove for a six-hour trip that includes paddling a wooded marine park. Harbour seals, cormorants, herons, eagles, starfish, jellyfish—there are many bonuses on this soft adventure. There's a barbecued salmon lunch on Twin Island and lots of time to explore the beach and forest—all less than an hour's drive from city centre. No kayak experience is necessary. Cost is $120. (Lotus Land also does hiking and cycling excursions.)

For private charters, see Sports/ Recreation (Cruising). For short, scenic ferry trips, see Getting Around (Ferries).

Other Tours

Historical Walking Tours of Gastown
683-5650

Gastown's namesake, raison d'être and first non-Native inhabitant was a saloon owner named Gassy Jack Deighton back in 1867. After the big fire that destroyed Vancouver in 1886, the area was rebuilt with ware-

10 Best Buildings

This list favours big landmark buildings on Vancouver's downtown peninsula. Only Simon Fraser University's Burnaby campus is beyond walking distance of the core.

1. **Marine Building**, 1930
    355 Burrard at Hastings
Vancouver's only art deco skyscraper, carefully detailed with period-transportation bas reliefs and a sumptuous lobby.

2. **St James Anglican Church**, 1937
    Cordova at Gore
Go inside. Sir Adrian Gilbert Scott's essay in concrete is a masterpiece outside, a spiritual redoubt within.

3. **Daon Bulding**, 1981
    888 W Hastings at Burrard
Carefully massed to maximize the view to the north and honour the Marine Building opposite, this modestly proportioned temple of commerce exhibits good manners and design finesse.

4. **MacMillan Bloedel Building**, 1969
    1075 W Georgia at Thurlow
A return to load-bearing walls, Arthur Erickson's most ionic building was the most elegant corporate headquarters of its time.

5. **Robson Square**, 1979
    800 block Robson
By knitting together law courts, government offices and the Vancouver

Art Gallery over three blocks, Erickson gave the city its heart.

6. **Toronto-Dominion Bank** (now SFU Downtown), 1920
    580 W Hastings at Seymour
A romantic Mediterranean temple by the best architect of Vancouver's pre–World War I boom, New York–trained Marbury Somervell.

7. **B.C. Hydro and Dal Grauer Substation**, 1957, 1954
    570 Burrard at Nelson
In top form, Vancouver's greatest firm of architects (Thompson Berwick Pratt) brings modern architecture uptown.

8. **Sylvia Motel addition**, 1987
    1861 Beach at Gilford
Richard Hanriquez sets a new standard with this sympathetic but utterly contemporary extension to a formerly ordinary character building on a landmark site.

9. **Sinclair Centre**, 1986
    757 W Hastings at Granville
Henriquez fuses four significant heritage buildings of different styles and structures into more than the sum of their parts.

10. **Simon Fraser University**, 1965
    Burnaby Mountain
Erickson's most seditious work, cradle of student rebellion, risks livability in search of timelessness.

—Sean Rossiter

houses and hotels. Once the depression hit, it became a skid row and remained derelict until the late 1960s, when it was declared a historic site. Gastown underwent a beautification program: trees were planted, antique lamp standards and cobblestone

streets were installed, and overhead wires were buried.

Today Gastown is attractive and the architecture significant. The buildings are the city's oldest, and most predate 1900. It is a pleasant place to stroll and shop on a sunny after-

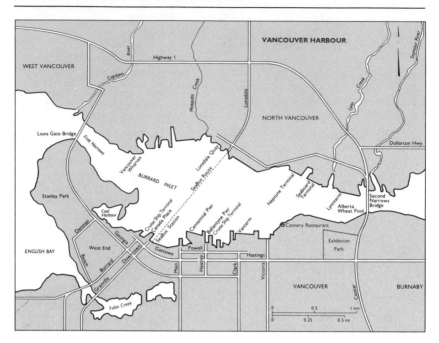

noon. Water St from Richards to Columbia is where you want to be.

At the corner of Water and Cambie is an odd contraption, the world's first steam clock. It is powered by an underground steam system used to heat the neighbouring buildings. Every quarter-hour the whistle blows, and on the hour steam spews from its works. A statue of the loquacious Gassy Jack stands in Maple Tree Square at the other end of Water.

A popular walking tour of Gastown is conducted daily during the summer. The free, 90-minute tour leaves from the Gassy Jack statue in Maple Tree Square (Water and Carrall) at 2 PM.

Horse and Carriage Triple A Tours
681-5115
A one-hour narrated tour of Stanley Park takes you through the forest, past the rose gardens and along the waterfront in a 20-passenger carriage. It leaves every half-hour from the information booth in the first parking lot from the Georgia St entrance. $10 adult. Private tours in a two- to six-person carriage can also be booked during summer.

Fridge's Early Motion Tours
687-5088
See the city in a 1930 Model A Ford Phaeton touring convertible. A one-hour tour of downtown, Stanley Park, Chinatown and Gastown costs $80. Follow the suggested route or devise your own. The car holds four passengers.

Yellow Cab
681-3311, 681-1111
Yellow will take you for a personal tour of the city on their suggested routes or your own. One route is to Stanley Park, downtown, Chinatown, Gastown and English Bay. The cost is about $60. Another is to the mountains and parks of the North Shore for $75. The third is to the beaches of Kitsilano and Point Grey, UBC, Queen Elizabeth Park and the mansions of SW

Marine Dr and Shaughnessy for about $70. Taxis take up to five passengers.

Special Interest Tours

Port of Vancouver
666-6129 or 666-0815
At the Vanterm container facility at the north end of Clark is a public viewing area, open year-round Mon to Fri, 9–noon and 1–4.

Granville Island Brewery
1441 Cartwright, Granville Island
688-9927 or 687-2739
Tour this small high-tech brewery run by a German brewmaster. Tasting room and retail sales. Half-hour tours are offered seven days a week at 2 PM Mon to Fri and at 1 and 3 on Sat and Sun.

Seymour Demonstration Forest
987-1273
This 5600 ha (14,000-acre) wilderness is for outdoor enthusiasts. For a family outing, take the 90-minute walk with a professional forester, who will identify local vegetation and discuss forest management techniques. Tours are conducted during the summer, usually on weekend afternoons; call for times. This Ecology Loop Trail is an easy one, but others, like the 22 km (14-mile) hike to Seymour Dam, are more challenging. Opened to the public in 1987, this area has 50 km (30 miles) of paved and gravel trails and draws mountain bikers and in-line skaters as well as walkers and hikers. Take the Lillooet Rd exit from the Upper Levels Hwy. A guide-yourself brochure is also available at the park.

University of British Columbia
Free walking tours Mon to Fri, May–Aug; call 822-5355.
　　The science-minded can discover the many uses of subatomic particles at TRIUMF, which has the world's largest cyclotron. Free 90-minute tours

are given Mon to Fri, twice daily in summer, twice weekly in winter. No reservations necessary except for large groups. Located on Wesbrook Mall 1 km (0.6 mile) south of 16th Ave; call 222-7354 or 222-7355.

Rogers Sugar Refinery
123 Rogers
253-1131
See the sugar museum and an 18-minute film on the history of Rogers Sugar, which started in 1890 and is almost as old as the city. Mon to Fri, 9:30–3:30. Call ahead to book.

Alberta Wheat Pool
South end of Second Narrows Bridge
684-5161
A one-hour tour of the wheat-loading facility at the Port of Vancouver, Tues at 10 and Thurs at 1. Must be 16 years or older. Phone for reservation.

Simon Fraser University
Free tours of the campus are conducted by students year-round, Mon to Fri. Call for reservations; there is no set schedule. Call 291-3397.

Calendar of Events

January 1 Polar Bear Swim Club dips into English Bay, 732-2304.

Late January Women in View Festival: Celebration of works of women in various areas of the arts. Venues are usually in the city's East Side. 685-6684.

Late January to mid-February (date varies) Chinese New Year is celebrated with the traditional Dragon Parade in Chinatown on a Sunday afternoon. Chinese Cultural Centre, 687-0729.

March Vancouver Storytelling Festival is held for three days at a variety of West End venues. There's a wonderful mix of ethnic stories; translators assist in five different languages. 876-2272.

Mid-March to mid-May Sea lions at Steveston jetty, 272-9187.

March or April Vancouver Wine Festival, 873-3311.

Easter Antique Car Easter Parade to Queens Park in New Westminster, 522-6894.

May Vancouver International Marathon, 872-2928. Vancouver International Children's Festival, 687-7697. Port Day, open house featuring free harbour cruises sponsored by the Port of Vancouver, 666-3226.

Late May New Westminster Hyack Festival celebrates Queen Victoria's birthday, 522-6894.

June Canadian International Dragon Boat Festival on False Creek, 688-2382.

June through September Bard on the Beach (Shakespeare in Vanier Park), 737-0625.

Late June to early July Du Maurier International Jazz Festival, 682-0706 (Jazz Hotline).

July 1 Canada Day Celebrations, Canada Place. Gastown Grand Prix bicycle race, 737-3034. Steveston Salmon Festival, 277-6812.

Mid-July Vancouver Folk Music Festival, 602-9798. The Seafest, 684-3378. Nanaimo-to-Vancouver Bathtub Race, 1-604-758-2040.

Late July to early August Early Music Festival, UBC School of Music,

732-1610. Vancouver Chamber Music Festival, St George's School, 602-0363. Symphony of Fire, international fireworks competition, 688-1992. Vancouver International Comedy Festival, Granville Island, 683-0883.

Early August Abbotsford International Airshow, 1-604-852-8511.

Late August Pacific National Exhibition, 253-2311. Wooden Boat Festival, Granville Island. 688-9622.

Early September Indy Vancouver car race, 684-4639.

September Vancouver International Fringe Festival (alternative theatre and performance art), 873-3646.

Late September or October Vancouver International Film Festival, 685-0260.

Late October Vancouver Writers Festival, 681-6330.

Early November Snow Goose Festival at George C. Reifel Migratory Bird Sanctuary, 946-6980.

Mid-November Hycroft Christmas Fair, 731-4661. Christmas Craft Market, Granville Island, Circle Craft Co-op, 737-9050.

Early December Carol ships in English Bay and Burrard Inlet, 682-2007. Sinterklaas arrives by steamboat in New Westminster, 522-6894.

December Festival of Lights, VanDusen Garden, 878-9274.

Parks/Beaches/Gardens

IN THE CITY

Dr Sun Yat-sen Classical Chinese Garden 102

Jericho Beach to Spanish Banks 103

Queen Elizabeth Park/Bloedel Conservatory 104

Stanley Park 104
On Foot in Stanley Park, Getting around the Park,
Vancouver Aquarium

VanDusen Botanical Garden 111

AT THE UNIVERSITY OF BRITISH COLUMBIA

Nitobe Memorial Garden 112

UBC Botanical Garden 113

Pacific Spirit Regional Park
(University Endowment Lands) 114

ON THE NORTH SHORE

Capilano River Regional Park 115

Grouse Mountain 116

Lynn Canyon Park 117

Lighthouse Park 117

Mount Seymour Provincial Park 118

Seymour Demonstration Forest 119

OTHER

George C. Reifel Migratory Bird Sanctuary 119

Dr Sun Yat-sen Classical Chinese Garden

The Dr Sun Yat-sen Garden is the only classical Chinese garden outside of China.

Ever since the city's 1886 resolution to purchase 405 forested hectares (1000 acres) and make it a park, Vancouver has had a high regard for green spaces. Today Stanley Park is among the continent's largest city parks, and the equivalent of 20,000 blocks is devoted to space where, rain or shine, Vancouverites walk, jog, cycle, picnic, play and just generally have a good time in their parks. Some are prettily manicured; others are wilderness. Some stretch along the waterfront; others offer magnificent views—there is a bounty for visitors to choose from.

IN THE CITY

Dr Sun Yat-sen Classical Chinese Garden

This beautiful walled garden at 578 Carrall near Pender in Chinatown is the result of a co-operative effort by the people and governments of China and Canada, and it is a significant local treasure. The Ming Dynasty–style garden is the first classical Chinese garden to be built outside of China. In 1985, 52 artisans from China spent 13 months creating the garden, using only traditional methods and materials. Most of the materials came directly from China (donated by the Chinese government, as was the labour), and no nails or screws were used in the construction.

You leave the hustle and bustle of Chinatown behind when you enter this enclosed garden sanctuary. The emphasis here is very different from that of Western gardens—don't expect flashy displays of brightly coloured flowers. The garden is tiny, only 1300 m² (⅓ of an acre), yet as you stroll through pavilions and over bridges and pebble-mosaic pavement, you'll feel a spaciousness created by the careful arrangement of rocks, plants, water and architecture.

The garden is characterized by both harmony and contrast: craggy evergreens and contorted limestone rocks suggest a miniature landscape, contained within architecture boasting whitewashed walls, curving tiled roofs and shiny lacquered beams.

To understand the symbolism of particular plants or architectural elements, join one of the excellent guided tours that are offered from 10:30 to 4 in summer and from 10:30 to 2:30 in winter.

Hours are from 10 to late afternoon, depending on the season. (Call 662-3207 to check hours.) Admission is $4.50 for adults, with discounts for children, seniors and families.

Adjacent to the classical garden is Dr. Sun Yat-sen Park, which is a free public park. Although somewhat less elegant than its neighbour, the park is also a walled enclosure that is a very pleasant place to stroll or rest. It features a Chinese pavilion (the Pavilion of Gratitude), set in a large pond, and walkways through local and Asian shrubbery. The park also has an entrance on Columbia at Keefer. Hours are the same as at the classical garden.

Jericho Beach to Spanish Banks

Heritage West, David McIntyre

The chain of beaches from Jericho to Spanish Banks is active with windsurfers, swimmers, sailors, picnickers and sun-bathers but is over 3 km (2 miles) long and so is never congested.

Start your walk at the foot of Alma at Point Grey, where there is a small wooden structure, the Hastings Mill Museum. Built in 1865, it is the oldest existing structure in Vancouver, one of a handful of buildings to survive the great fire that destroyed the city in 1886. (See Museums.) Cross the small park and go past the Royal Vancouver Yacht Club, the Jericho Tennis Club and Brock House (a restaurant and senior citizens' centre). Jericho Beach Park is straight ahead. There are paths through the park and around a duck pond, or you can walk along the beach. The Department of National Defence once owned this land and built the huge concrete wharves, where you can see the foundations of airplane hangars that stood here until the mid-1970s. The Vancouver Hostel, the large white building set back from the beach, is a former RCAF barracks.

Jericho Sailing Centre is next, and then Locarno Beach and Spanish Banks. Directly across Burrard Inlet are the Point Atkinson Lighthouse and Bowen Island. Keep going around the farthest point, Point

Grey, if you want to sun-bathe nude at Wreck Beach.

There are concession stands and washrooms en route.

From downtown take the #4 Fourth Ave or UBC bus or the #7 Dunbar. Get off at 4th and Alma, and walk four blocks north to the Hastings Mill Museum.

Queen Elizabeth Park/ Bloedel Conservatory

Queen Elizabeth Park is a spacious, beautifully landscaped park with ornamental flowerbeds, shrubs, trees and lots of grass. The park is on Little Mountain, the highest spot in the city. At the top are two abandoned quarries that have been transformed into huge sunken rock gardens full of blossoms and shrubbery, with ponds and waterfalls at every level. It's a fabulous display of landscaping and a favourite location for wedding and graduation pictures.

The park facilities include a restaurant with a smashing view, 20 tennis courts, a pitch and putt golf course, lawn bowling, Frisbee golf and picnic spots. The big attraction at Queen Elizabeth Park is the Bloedel Conservatory at the top of the mountain. The building is a Plexiglas dome, 43 m (140 feet) in diameter, covering a small rain forest and desert. It is a multisensory experience: you feel the heat and humidity, see and smell the lush tropical growth, watch a hundred brightly coloured tropical birds flying freely, and hear parrots squawking and a stream rippling beside you. A path takes you on a short circular walk and ends up in a desert. Guaranteed to cheer you up on a rainy day.

Queen Elizabeth Park is off Cambie, between 29th and 37th Ave. The conservatory is open every day but Christmas; in summer Mon to Fri, 9–8, and Sat and Sun, 10–9; and in winter 10–5 daily. Admission is $3.10 for adults, with discounts for seniors, children and families. Phone 257-8570 for more information.

From downtown, take the #15 Cambie bus.

Stanley Park

City parks usually bring to mind lawns, picnic tables, civic monuments and a few stately old trees. You'll find these at Stanley Park, but it's the enormous area, the wildness and the ocean that make this park one of a kind. Stanley Park is *huge,* and though the edges tend to be manicured, the dense forest in the centre is a natural area with only paths and a road cutting through. The ocean almost encircles the park, and along the shore are sandy beaches and a seawalk that offers spectacular views.

The aquarium is the biggest attraction, but there are dozens of other activities for exercise, fun or a lazy time in the sun. Stanley Park is one of the largest inner-city parks on the continent, and it is a mere 15-minute walk from downtown. Originally its 400 ha (1000 acres) were swamp and rain forest. The forest was a dense growth of Douglas fir, cedar and hemlock; the swamp that filled the low-lying area is now Lost Lagoon. Several culturally important Coast Salish villages were once on the land, and former Native trails have become park paths.

The area was logged in the 1860s and later became a military reserve. With great foresight (considering that the population of the city then numbered about 1000), one of the first city council resolutions in 1886 was to petition the federal government to turn the military reserve into parkland.

The park was opened in 1888, and an official ceremony with Governor General Lord Stanley took place a year later.

Getting there: catch the #19 Stanley Park downtown on Pender, and it will take you to the park entrance at the foot of Alberni. If you're on foot, Alberni or Beach Ave are the best entrances. Stanley Park is a very popular spot. It is not advisable to take your car into the park at all on summer weekends unless the weather is bad. If you do drive around the park, remember that vehicle traffic runs one way, counterclockwise, so you must use the Georgia St entrance. There is a charge for parking in the park—on the roadside as well as in the lots. The cost is $1 for two hours and $2 for all day. There are many parking meter machines scattered throughout the park; they take loonies and quarters. Park attractions are well marked.

Siwash Rock on the Stanley Park Seawall is a popular stop for cyclists, anglers, walkers and joggers. (Judi Lees)

The Stanley Park Forest

The forest is made up of western red cedar, spruce, hemlock and giant Douglas fir, the largest tree native to Canada. The biggest Douglas firs in the park were logged in the 1860s, and the trees that look so huge today were actually culls. The enormous stumps in the pitch and putt course give an indication of the size of the original trees, which were about 60 m (200 feet) high—equal to a 16-storey building! The remaining trees are thought to be about 800 years old. On Cathedral Trail, which goes north from the west side of Lost Lagoon, are the Seven Sisters, huge first-growth cedars that are perfect examples of the trees used by the Northwest Coast Native people for totem poles.

Pacific Trees

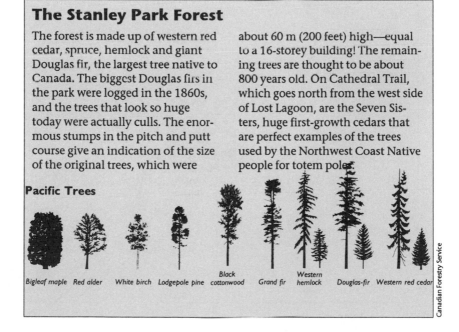

Bigleaf maple   Red alder   White birch   Lodgepole pine   Black cottonwood   Grand fir   Western hemlock   Douglas-fir   Western red cedar

Canadian Forestry Service

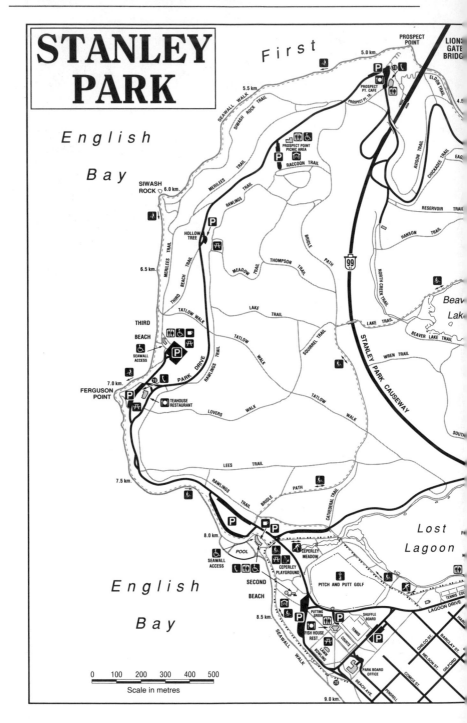

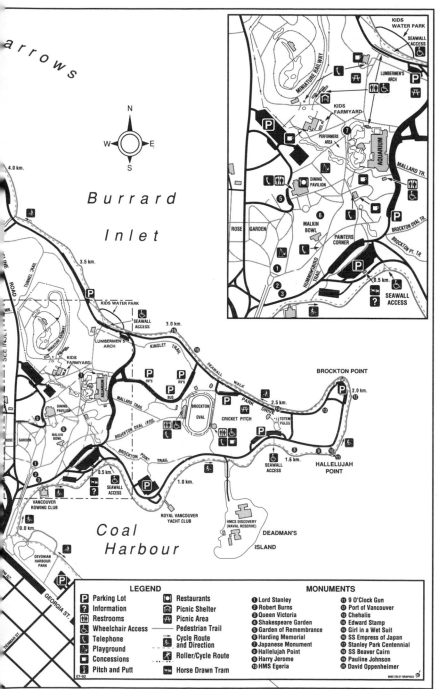

LEGEND

P	Parking Lot		Restaurants
?	Information		Picnic Shelter
	Restrooms		Picnic Area
	Wheelchair Access		Pedestrian Trail
	Telephone		Cycle Route and Direction
	Playground		Roller/Cycle Route
	Concessions		Horse Drawn Tram
	Pitch and Putt		

MONUMENTS

1. Lord Stanley
2. Robert Burns
3. Queen Victoria
4. Shakespeare Garden
5. Garden of Remembrance
6. Harding Memorial
7. Japanese Monument
8. Hallelujah Point
9. Harry Jerome
10. HMS Egeria
11. 9 O'Clock Gun
12. Port of Vancouver
13. Chehalis
14. Edward Stamp
15. Girl in a Wet Suit
16. SS Empress of Japan
17. Stanley Park Centennial
18. SS Beaver Cairn
19. Pauline Johnson
20. David Oppenheimer

Map courtesy of Vancouver Board of Parks and Recreation

107

On Foot in Stanley Park

The park is a peninsula rimmed by a seawall and walkway along the water. The walk introduces you to the ocean, the harbour and the forest, and provides fabulous views of the mountains and the city—all this within the two hours that it takes to walk the 10.5 km (6½ miles).

If you do only one thing in Vancouver, walk around the seawall. It gives you the best idea of what living in this city is like. Go on Sunday if you want to be part of the parade of joggers, cyclists, dogs (which must be leashed), anglers and hundreds of people out strolling. Go on a weekday morning if you prefer quiet. The seawall path is clearly divided—one side for pedestrians and the other side for cyclists—but look out anyway.

Start at either English Bay or the park entrance at the foot of Georgia. Walking east from the Georgia St entrance, you pass by the Vancouver Rowing Club and the Royal Vancouver Yacht Club. A causeway leads to the naval reserve training base, called the HMCS *Discovery* (the last remnant of the original military base), on Deadman's Island, a former Salish burial ground. Hallelujah Point is next, where Salvation Army revival meetings were once held.

On the water side of the path is a large metal box enclosing a cannon, the Nine O'Clock Gun. Beginning in 1890, the gun was sounded to signal the curfew that ended weekend fishing. Now it is a time signal electronically fired at 9 PM.

At Brockton Point, once a pioneer cemetery and now occupied by a small lighthouse, you can see Lions Gate Bridge ahead. The totem poles on your left were carved on the north coast of B.C. by the Kwakiutl and Haida in the late 19th century. They were the initial stage of a reconstruction of a Native village that was never completed. Two Native canoes, each carved from a single cedar log, are under cover near the totems. Some dugout canoes have measured as long as 18 m (60 feet).

Directly west of the totems is a grassy area used for cricket, field hockey and rugby. Next is Brockton Oval, a cinder jogging track. Rugby and soccer games are held in the centre of the oval, and there is a pavilion with washrooms, hot showers and a refreshment stand.

The seawall path passes the *Girl in a Wetsuit*, a statue sitting on a rock off the shore. You'll notice a similarity between it and the famous mermaid statue in Copenhagen Harbour. The sculptor who made this piece was inspired by the Danish work but transformed it to show a more modern, adventurous and down-to-earth figure.

Pauline Johnson (1862–1913)

This legendary Indian "princess" was born in Ontario, the daughter of a Mohawk chief and an Englishwoman. She gained acclaim for her poems about Native life and spent much time touring North America and England giving recitations. She settled in Vancouver and learned local Native legends from Chief Capilano; she retold these in a collection entitled *Legends of Vancouver*.

Pauline Johnson often went canoeing at Lost Lagoon in Stanley Park, and her ashes are buried near Ferguson Point, where there is a memorial to her. She is best known for her poem "The Song My Paddle Sings" and a poetry collection entitled *Flint and Feather*.

Next is a replica of the figurehead of the *Empress of Japan,* a luxurious liner that sailed at the turn of the century to and from Asia. At Mile 2, a children's water playground is on your right. On your left is Lumbermen's Arch, made of rough Douglas fir and erected in 1952 to honour workers in the logging industry. This was the site of one of the original Native villages.

Lions Gate Bridge marks the halfway point of the walk around the park. Slightly beyond is Prospect Point, named for the stunning viewpoint 60 m (200 feet) above. The SS *Beaver,* a Hudson's Bay Company vessel and the first steamship on this coast, was wrecked in 1888 on the rocks here. Just past the point are cormorants nesting on the rock cliff above.

The seawall turns to the southwest, and along this section you will see the impressive Siwash Rock. The story of Siwash Rock is Vancouver's best-known Native legend. Long ago, a young Native man was about to become a father. He decided to swim the waters of English Bay until he was utterly spotless so that his newborn child could start life free from the father's sins. The gods were so impressed that they immortalized him in the form of Siwash Rock. Two smaller rocks, representing his wife and son, are up in the woods overlooking Siwash Rock.

You may run into anglers fishing for bottom fish, and occasionally you even see them get lucky. The first beach you encounter is Third Beach. If you're hungry and prefer eggs Benedict to fish and chips, walk up to the lovely Teahouse Restaurant at Ferguson Point for lunch. Back on the seawall, the view is soon of English Bay, Kitsilano and the conical roof of the planetarium at Vanier Park.

About 800 m (½ mile) past Ferguson Point is the swimming pool at Second Beach. If you've had enough walking and want to return to your starting point, cross the road behind the pool and head back to Lost Lagoon. Water birds on the lagoon include Canada geese, trumpeter swans, mallards, wood ducks and coots. Pictures on a signboard on the west side of the lagoon help identify them. Lost Lagoon, originally a tidal inlet, was so named that by Mohawk poet Pauline Johnson because the water often disappeared at low tide. Today the main road through the park acts as a dike to keep the lagoon at a constant level.

If you want to continue along the water, the seawall extends for several kilometres past Stanley Park. Or you can take advantage of the sports facilities between Second Beach and the lagoon. There is an inviting pitch and putt course and putting greens where you can rent equipment. (This is one of the best spots to see the remains of the ancient fir trees that were logged in the 1870s; you can clearly see springboard holes in the stumps.) The Lawn Bowling Club is open to visitors, and there are also tennis and shuffleboard courts. The Fish House Restaurant by the tennis courts has both casual and more elegant dining rooms as well as outdoor decks for lunch and dinner.

In this same area, between the road and seawall, is an old fire engine for children to scramble over, and nearby there is an adventure playground. The tarmac in this area is used for ethnic dancing and square-dancing on summer evenings, and everyone is welcome to join in. On weekday afternoons in July and Aug (weather permitting), the Vancouver police run the Kids' Traffic School here for children 5 to 8 years old. Children drive pedal cars through "streets" and learn about intersec-

Children love the old fire engine at Ceperley Playground in Stanley Park. (Rosamond Norbury)

tions, crosswalks, traffic lights and so on. It starts at 12:30; show up early because it's first come, first served.

The Children's Farm Yard is heaven for small children. Most of the animals are in a large open area and are free to move around together and with the children. All the usual barnyard animals are there, eager to be patted. There are pony rides for children under 12. Beside the Children's Farm Yard is a miniature steam locomotive that takes children and adults on a ride through the forest. Because it's the hit of the park, there are often line-ups. It's best to come early in the day. The train runs daily in the summer and on weekends in the winter, weather permitting.

Directly south of the Children's Farm Yard is the cafeteria-style Dining Pavilion with a view of 275 varieties of roses and an outdoor theatre, Malkin Bowl, which stages Broadway productions in the summer. See Entertainment/Culture (Theatre).

Getting around the Park

During the summer you can take advantage of the #52 Round the Park bus that runs around Park Dr on Sat, Sun and holidays. Ask for a transfer (good for 90 minutes) when you board the bus so that you can get on and off as often as you like for one fare.

Nothing beats walking in the park, but one of the best views, from Prospect Point, is hard to get to on foot. The lookout there is perched on top of a cliff, and the view of the North Shore is unforgettable. The mountain directly in line with Lions Gate Bridge is Grouse Mountain, recognizable by the ski runs. The two craggy peaks just west of Grouse are the Lions. (From an easterly perspective they actually do look like reclining lions.) These peaks were so named by Pauline Johnson because they reminded her of the lions in Trafalgar Square. Lions Gate gets its name from these "lions" looming over the narrow entrance to the harbour. The grassy area at the foot of the far side of the bridge is the Capilano Indian Reserve. (The Capilano Indians also own the land on which Park Royal Shopping Centre, to the left of the bridge, is built.)

Vancouver Aquarium

The Vancouver Aquarium, Canada's largest, has more than 8000 animals.

Near the entrance is a marine life exhibit called the B.C. Hall of Fishes. Tanks depict specific coastal regions, such as Vancouver shores, the west coast of Vancouver Island and the rocky bottom of the Strait of Georgia. The Rufe Gibbs Hall displays fish and plant life from the lakes and rivers of inland B.C. There is also a fascinating display about salmon, showing their life stages and spawning habits.

The MacMillan Tropical Gallery presents marine life from the tropical Pacific: sharks, sea turtles and magnificently coloured tropical fish from Indonesia, Micronesia and the Philippines. From here you enter the Amazon rain forest exhibit. Tropical birds fly freely, tropical plants grow around fish-filled pools, and tropical bugs, such as giant cockroaches and tarantulas, crawl around behind glass. You'll see boa constrictors, poisonous frogs and tanks of piranhas. Once an hour thunder, lightning and the deluge of a tropical rainstorm shatter the calm. It's a short but gripping walk.

The aquarium has outdoor pools for the belugas and killer whales, with underwater viewing windows. Smaller exhibits hold playful seals and sea otters. The marine mammal staff interact with these animals frequently during the day, and you can watch feeding, play and research sessions.

Other galleries focus on particular ecological areas such as the Truk La-goon of Micronesia and Lancaster Sound off Baffin Island.

Recently opened, the Ducks Unlimited Wetlands Discovery Centre focusses on the rich and complex ecosystems of wetlands. Visitors have the opportunity to come face to face with turtles, sticklebacks and a variety of wetland amphibians and aquatic plants. There are some entertaining exhibits here. Games like the migration obstacle course are both fun and educational, and you can get bird-feeding tips at the Bird Break Café.

Admission is $11 for adults in summer and $9.50 for adults in winter, with discounts for seniors, children and families. (The beluga and harbour seal pools are also visible from the park outside the aquarium.) Open daily year-round. Summer hours are 9:30–7; winter hours are 10–5:30. Phone 268-9900 for more information.

Note that the ClamShell Gift Shop in the aquarium is the best spot in town for souvenirs.

VanDusen Botanical Garden

Originally a 22 ha (54-acre) golf course, VanDusen (at Oak and 37th) is now the largest botanical garden in the city and has been named one of the 10 best botanical gardens in the world by *Horticulture* magazine. Tranquillity envelops you as you wander around the ponds, lawns and thousands of varieties of trees, shrubs and flowers. Some of the walks are wonderful as well as educational. The rhododendron walk, with one of the best collections in Canada, is spectacular in its prime in May and illustrates botanical relationships.

All of the plants are well labelled and are arranged by species and place

Nitobe Memorial Garden exudes tranquillity. (June West)

of origin for those interested in horticulture; for the rest of us, it's an enjoyable stroll.

Month by month, the floral highlights are: January, witch hazel, silk tassel bush, Himalayan box; February, early rhododendrons, helleborus, winter aconite and crocus; March, early flowering bulbs, spring heathers; April, magnolias, spring flowering bulbs; May, rhododendrons, trilliums, camellias, laburnum; June, primulas, hydrangeas, the meadow garden; July, lilies, waterlilies, Southern Hemisphere bulbs; August, hibiscus, silk tree, hanging baskets, annuals; September, fall heathers and perennial flowers, ornamental grasses; October, eastern North American forest (109 different kinds of maples), ginkgo trees; November, fall berries, broadleaf evergreen shrubs; December, the extensive holly collection of 118 varieties. The Festival of Lights, in December, features a section of the garden lit with 19,000 Christmas lights.

A favourite with children is the Elizabethan maze planted with a thousand pyramid cedars—don't worry; it's only 1.5 m (5 feet) high, and parents can watch from a grassy knoll. Families also enjoy trying to find turtles that bask around the lakes or experiencing the gentle motion of the floating bridge in Cypress Pond.

The garden opens daily at 10 AM; closing time varies according to daylight hours. The Festival of Lights in December is open 5–9:30 PM.

Guided tours (and cart tours for those with limited walking ability) are offered every afternoon from Easter to Thanksgiving, weather permitting. Seasonal self-guided tour sheets are available at the entrance. Admission is $5 for adults, with discounts for seniors, children and families. Phone 878-9274. There is a restaurant with an open-air deck at the entrance.

From downtown, take the #17 Oak bus to the park.

AT THE UNIVERSITY OF BRITISH COLUMBIA

Nitobe Memorial Garden

The Nitobe garden at the University

of British Columbia is a gem. It is an authentic Japanese tea and stroll garden complete with teahouse. Japanese landscaping objectives of harmony, balance and tranquillity are clearly met by the blend of indigenous fir and cedar with classical arrangements of shrubbery, waterfalls and small bridges over gurgling streams. The garden was started 25 years ago and has an established, serene feeling. There are no lawns, and you must stay on the paths, but there are benches on which to pass a quiet moment.

The garden is off NW Marine, a short walk west from the Museum of Anthropology, so go to both; they are fine examples of Pacific Rim cultures. From mid-Oct until mid-Mar, Nitobe is open weekdays 10–2:30; during the summer, daily 10–6. Admission is $2.50 for adults, with discounts for seniors, students and children. Combination tickets to Nitobe and the UBC Botanical Garden are available for $5.50.

For access by public transit, see UBC Botanical Garden.

J. K. Henry Lake is in the UBC Botanical Garden. (June West)

UBC Botanical Garden

The parking lot and entrance to the botanical garden is off SW Marine, 3 km (1 mile) past Nitobe Memorial Garden. The beauty of this garden is more subtle than that of display gardens like VanDusen. The purpose is to inspire gardeners by showing new and creative ways to use plants. The garden also displays and sells new and rare varieties and is especially known for its fine examples of espaliered fruit trees and for its giant 4 m (13-foot) Himalayan lilies. In all, 10,000 types of trees, shrubs and flowering plants are displayed here.

There are several parts to this 28 ha (70-acre) garden. The Asian Garden is on the west side of Marine; Moongate tunnel, a pathway under the road, leads you to the Food, Physick, Contemporary, Arbour, Winter, Alpine, Perennial Border and B.C. Native gardens.

The Asian Garden is a unique combination of native cedar forest underplanted with Asian plants: 400 varieties of rhododendrons, the giant lilies, climbing hydrangeas, magnolias and more. The Food Garden has a spectacular display of espaliered fruit trees—imagine an apple tree hedge thick with fruit but no higher than your chest. The Physick Garden is a formal 16th-century herb garden with plants from the Chelsea Physick Garden in London. In the B.C. Native Garden you can walk from a coastal rain forest into the semiarid environment of the interior of the province, all within 3 ha (7½ acres).

The shop at the garden has the best selection of gardening books in town, gardening gizmos and tools, gifts and an assortment of unusual plants for sale. Tours of the garden are strongly recommended because they allow you to catch the seasonal highlights that you might otherwise miss. During the summer tours are offered, and on summer Sundays there are detailed tours of particular parts of the garden or types of plant. Phone 822-4208 to check times. Admission to the garden is $4.25 for adults, with discounts for seniors, students and children.

In the summer the #42 Spanish Banks/Chancellor bus takes you right to Nitobe and the botanical garden from 10th and Alma. From downtown take the #10 UBC bus to this transfer point.

Pacific Spirit Regional Park (University Endowment Lands)

The University Endowment Lands (UEL) were originally a 1200 ha (3000-acre) parcel of land given to the University of British Columbia in 1923 to be sold off for housing as the university needed revenue. Because there was little demand during the depression and the war, most of the land remained intact except for the logging that had been done in the 1890s. The existing forest is now about 100 years old, and a few remnant trees from the original 500-year-old forest can be seen on the western fringes of Point Grey and on the southern cliffs over the Fraser River.

The Endowment Lands now consist of 1000 ha (2500 acres), of which almost 800 ha (2000 acres) is Pacific

Spirit Regional Park. This park is considerably larger than Stanley Park, but it's used by relatively few people. Even though the 53 km (33 miles) of trails are perfect for hiking, jogging, mountain biking and horseback riding, you can sometimes meander through the forest and not encounter a soul. No need to worry about getting lost; the park is cut by three major roads that provide landmarks, and every trail junction is signed. There are also park volunteers, who wear yellow armbands.

The wildlife is varied but elusive. Squirrels, chipmunks, voles, moles, bats, weasels, mink, raccoons, otters, owls, skunks and coyotes all live in the park, but you will see them only if you are a keen observer. Bald eagles are easy to spot soaring overhead or perched on treetops near the shoreline.

There is a park information centre at 4915 W 16th Ave. There are interpretive programs led by naturalists; inquire at the park centre or phone 432-6359 for times. The centre is the best place to pick up maps; there is also parking.

If you are heading out without a guide, you will find Pacific Spirit to be a welcoming place with fairly easy trails. Trail #24, Swordfern (in the southwest corner of the park), is recommended as a typical B.C. coastal forest with cedar and fir trees. The trail starts from SW Marine opposite the viewpoint and historical monument (marking Simon Fraser's 1808 trip down the Fraser River). On the same side of the street as the monument, another trail descends sharply to the Fraser and the largest log-boom grounds in Canada. Here you will pass a remnant of old-growth forest.

Another section of the park recommended for hiking is above Spanish Banks. The East and West Canyon

Trails, #7 and #27, form a convenient loop through an alder and broadleaf maple forest. They slope gently down to the water, making the return walk a little strenuous. Start from Chancellor.

Pacific Spirit Regional Park is simply a refreshing walk in the forest, a chance to get away from the city, just 20 minutes by car from downtown traffic.

By public transit from downtown, take the #10 or #4 UBC bus to campus or the #25 Brentwood from Brentwood Mall in Burnaby to enter the park via 16th Ave.

ON THE NORTH SHORE

Capilano River Regional Park

This North Shore park is on a strip of land along the Capilano River running from Grouse Mountain to Burrard Inlet. The park is wide at the top and very narrow from the middle down. The river is tempestuous (it is used for whitewater kayaking) and has gouged a deep canyon along its course. Although park trails are well kept, the surroundings are dramatically wild: rapids, plunging cliffs and huge timber, all in a misty rain forest setting.

At the very top of the park is the Cleveland Dam, which separates Capilano Lake from the river and regulates the city's water supply.

Park your car at the dam. You can walk across the top of the dam for a view in either direction. Maps of the trails are available at a signboard near the parking lot.

A salmon hatchery is a 10-minute hike down the path on the east side. It hatches about 3 million salmon eggs a year and releases the fingerlings into the Capilano River and other local waters. The outdoor displays and fish tanks are open 8–8 in summer; they close earlier in winter months. (Call 666-1790 to check hours.) There is a brochure available for self-guided walks. In late summer and fall, if the river is high enough, you may witness coho jumping up the fish ladders at the hatchery.

Because it's a popular spot on the bus tour route, the hatchery can be jammed with people—avoid midmorning and midafternoon if possible.

From the dam you can hike the trails on either side of the river above Dog's Leg Pool. On the west side you can hike all the way down to the mouth of the river, about 7 km (4½ miles), but the park itself is sometimes not much wider than the trail, which occasionally goes through residential neighbourhoods. We recommend hiking halfway down on the west side until you reach a bicycle barrier, where the forest opens up and you can see the adjacent residential area, and then hiking back up to the dam on the same side. You might want to make a small detour to see the enormous fir on Giant Fir Trail. This is the biggest tree in the park— 2.4 m (8 feet) in diameter and 61 m (200 feet) tall—and is thought to be over 500 years old. The round trip will take you about 90 minutes.

The Capilano Suspension Bridge, a well-publicized attraction, is a swinging wood and cable bridge that hangs 70 m (230 feet) above the canyon. Unfortunately, it costs $8.25 to walk across. Although the bridge is spectacular and is an easy walk for people who don't want to negotiate the paths, the views from Capilano River Regional Park are free. If you must walk across a swinging bridge, there's no charge for the one at Lynn Canyon Park. See With the Kids (Day Trips).

Suspension bridges span canyons on the North Shore. (Rosamond Norbury)

There are two ways to get to the park by public transportation. From downtown, take the #246 Lonsdale Quay/Highland. At Edgemont and Ridgewood, transfer to the #232 Grouse Mountain. From mid-Apr to mid-Oct the #236 Pemberton Heights/Grouse Mountain bus leaves from Lonsdale Quay and goes right by the park. You can get to Lonsdale Quay easily from downtown via the SeaBus.

Grouse Mountain

Grouse Mountain is in the centre of the row of mountains that line the North Shore. You can easily distin-

guish it at night because of the brilliant arc lights along the ski runs. This 1200 m (4000-foot) mountain offers one of the best views of the city and is a fun family outing or a quick escape from the city—nothing too strenuous and lots to keep the kids amused. Go on a clear day if you want to take in the view.

Capilano Rd ends at the base of a tramway that takes you most of the way up Grouse Mountain. This 100-passenger tram, or Skyride, glides you up the steep mountainside, skirting treetops, with kilometres and kilometres of wilderness surrounding you. Over your shoulder, Vancouver and all of the Lower Mainland are laid out in miniature down below. In eight minutes you're 1100 m (3600 feet) above sea level and near the top of Grouse Mountain. The Skyride is $15 for adults, with discounts for seniors, children and families. The price is a bit steep but includes the Peak Chairlift, a multimedia show on Haida folklore and the history of Vancouver, and a logger sports show. (Around the Lower Mainland, the only other place to see logger sports is in Squamish, a healthy drive north of the city.) These competitions highlight traditional loggers' skills such as springboard chopping, ax throwing and races between hand-saws and power saws. The show is in a grass amphitheatre near the Peak Chairlift.

In winters when there is enough snow (artificial or otherwise), Grouse is a popular learn-to-ski spot, so don't be surprised to see ski runs when you get off the tram. Although the area immediately around the tram is developed, there is plenty of wilderness. If you're after the wilds, take the Peak Chairlift up another 120 m (400 feet). In winter, the price of the Skyride also includes a horse-drawn sleigh ride.

In summer, Grouse has picnic ta-

A horse-drawn sleigh ride is a favourite winter excursion on Grouse Mountain. (Grouse Mountain)

bles and lawns where you can find a quiet place to sun-bathe or read. If you're feeling more energetic, you can hike the well-marked interpretive trail around Blue Grouse Lake in less than an hour.

Helicopter tours of the mountains and lakes in back of Grouse Mountain leave from the lift at the top of the mountain. Costs range from $40 to $70 a person, depending on the length of the tour. Phone 270-1484.

Just behind the lodge is an adventure playground made of logs and ropes, with a kid-size suspension bridge and a hand rope tow.

The outdoor beer garden, beside the Peak Chairlift, is the most pleasant place to eat or sit in the sun with a cold drink. As you might expect, the main restaurant, Grouse Nest, has a knockout view. It's open for lunch and dinner and is expensive, but if you make advance reservations for dinner the Skyride up the mountain is free. Phone 984-0661 for more information. See also Sports (Skiing).

From downtown, take the SeaBus to North Vancouver. In the summer the #236 bus leaves from the SeaBus terminal on the North Shore for Grouse Mountain. Another way to get there from downtown is to catch the #246 Lonsdale Quay/Highland bus, which goes over Lions Gate Bridge. At Edgemont and Ridgewood, transfer to the #232 Grouse Mountain.

Lynn Canyon Park

See With the Kids (Day Trips).

Lighthouse Park

Point Atkinson Lighthouse, built in 1912, sits at the tip of a wilderness area not far from the city centre. Park trails take you past mammoth Douglas firs, rocky cliffs and smoothly sloping granite rocks that line the shore (a perfect sun-bathing and picnicking area). The water is not as warm as at the city beaches, but after you've lain in the sun on the hot granite for two hours, it feels just right.

A map in the parking area shows the two main trails to the lighthouse.

Point Atkinson Lighthouse in Lighthouse Park, a good hiking and swimming spot with one of the last stands of virgin timber in the Lower Mainland. (Rosamond Norbury)

Follow one path down and the other back for a round trip of about 5 km (3 miles) that takes less than an hour. At the point, you can see Point Grey and the University of British Columbia campus directly across Burrard Inlet; to the southwest across the Strait of Georgia are the mountain tops of Vancouver Island, visible on clear days.

Watch for bald eagles and their large, ragged nests in the forks of tall trees. The largest Douglas fir trees here, 61 m (200 feet) tall and 500 years old, are the best accessible example of virgin forest in the Lower Mainland. The arbutus, an unusual tree recognizable by its smooth, peeling, orange-red bark, is the only broadleaf evergreen native to Canada.

You can hike in Lighthouse Park all year, even on wet days, but it is popular and can be crowded on summer weekends. The Point Atkinson Lighthouse is a working lighthouse and is not open to the public.

To drive to the park, go west on Marine 10 km (6 miles) past Park Royal Shopping Centre. On your left at Bea-

con Lane is a small wooden sign directing you a short distance south to Lighthouse Park.

From downtown, take the blue West Van bus #250 Horseshoe Bay.

Mount Seymour Provincial Park

Mount Seymour is convenient for your first taste of hiking in the mountains because it's close to the city and a road goes part way up the mountain. Even if you don't feel like hiking, drive up the 13 km (8-mile) parkway for a picnic and the magnificent views. The best views are on the way down.

Most of the trails start at the top parking lot, which is at the end of the road. A signboard at this parking lot shows the paths and their distances. Trail maps are available at the signboard and the park office. The main trails are well maintained but can be wet, so wear sturdy shoes for walking and hiking boots for the more rigorous trails. Snow lingers until June at this altitude, so the best time to hike is from July to late Oct.

Remember that you are in very different climatic conditions than in the city. Clouds can move in quickly and reduce visibility dramatically. Pack a rain jacket, wear warmer clothes than you would down below, and keep to the trails.

The Goldie Lake Trail is the easiest. A 1½-hour walk will take you around the lake through a hemlock and cedar forest. The large Douglas firs in the park are 250 years old, and lower down on the slopes are a few 800-year-olds.

On your way back down the mountain parkway, stop at the Vancouver lookout. Use a city map to identify Lions Gate Bridge, Stanley Park, Simon Fraser University and the oil refineries of Ioco and Port Moody. On clear days distant points are visible. To the southeast, Washington State's Mount Baker rises majestic and alone out of the clouds. The range of mountains due south is the Olympics, also in Washington. Towards the west are the American San Juan Islands, the Gulf Islands and Vancouver Island.

Please remember that you are not allowed to remove anything from a provincial park and that pets must be leashed at all times.

In winter here you can ski downhill or cross-country, or you can take advantage of the snowshoe trails, cafeteria, day lodge, ski and snowshoe rentals, tobogganing and ski lessons. See also Sports (Skiing).

Access is by car only, via the Second Narrows Bridge and Mt Seymour Parkway.

Seymour Demonstration Forest

See Sightseeing (Special Interest Tours).

OTHER

George C. Reifel Migratory Bird Sanctuary

The bird sanctuary is located on Westham Island at the mouth of the south arm of the Fraser River, a 45-minute drive from downtown Vancouver. At the entrance you can buy a bag of seed and get a map of the 3.2 km (2 miles) of paths, and then you are on your own. Bring a bird book, binoculars and a warm jacket. Remember that this is a refuge, not a tourist attraction, so the amenities are for the birds. Take the path on the dike to see the marshy flatlands of the delta—it's dramatic country. A four-storey observation tower and several blinds (wooden shelters with viewing slats) give you views of the tidal marshes and of birds you won't spot anywhere else. The refuge is heavily populated in fall, winter and spring but is pretty quiet in the summer. One of the best times to visit is between mid-October and late November, when Westham Island is visited by some 25,000 snow geese. They can be viewed in the fields and flying to

The exotic-looking wood duck can be seen at the George C. Reifel Migratory Bird Sanctuary. (Judi Lees)

Ten Favourite Walks in the Forest

Although stumps from the original forest are visible in many parks, there is virtually no old growth in the Lower Mainland. You may see a solitary tree left because it was not choice material or because it grew on too steep a slope. Although second growth is not as dramatic as old growth, some trees are now 130 years old and are quite impressive.

Because 90 per cent of B.C. is covered in trees, you won't experience the real West Coast until you've gone for a walk in the forest. Here are suggestions for accessible trails that are easy family walks unless otherwise noted:

1. **Pacific Spirit Park, Swordfern Trail**. The trailhead is across SW Marine Dr from the viewpoint and historic monument. Less than an hour for the return trip. See Pacific Spirit Regional Park.

2. **UBC Botanical Garden, B.C. Native Garden**. This is a pretty tame walk, but it is pleasant. Green-thumbers will love it. Half an hour for the return trip. Admission charge for the garden. See UBC Botanical Garden.

3. **Stanley Park, Siwash Rock Trail**. The trail starts on the water side of Park Dr just past Prospect Point, parallels the shoreline on the cliff above the seawall and ends at a viewpoint of Siwash Rock and English Bay. (See map in Stanley Park section.) Less than an hour return.

4. **Mount Seymour Provincial Park, Mystery Lake Trail**. Many people are not happy unless they hike a mountain trail.

This trail head is at the end of the parking lot located at the end of the road. This is a pleasant area with picnic tables, washroom facilities and maps.

On Mystery Lake Trail you are instantly among stands of Douglas fir, cedar and hemlock. It's an uphill, occasionally rocky route with a few view spots. You reach the pretty little lake in less than an hour, a great spot for a picnic. You can return by the same route or go east around the lake and follow several well-marked trails that continue up the mountain or go back to the parking lot. Take a jacket, since weather changes quickly in the mountains, and wear good walking shoes or hiking boots. Be cautious if it is wet. See Mount Seymour Park.

5. **Lynn Headwaters Regional Park, Lynn Loop Trail**. Drive over Lions Gate Bridge to the Upper Levels Hwy, go north on Mountain Hwy and follow signs to the park. As in all Greater Vancouver Regional District parks, trails are very well maintained and marked, and maps are available at the park entrance. Walk the loop trail in a counterclockwise direction so that you are going downhill at the steep section. Don't miss the short detour to the viewpoint (it's marked) at the top of the loop. Some sections may be a bit steep for seniors and small children. Two hours return.

6. **Cypress Provincial Park, Yew Lake Trail**. Drive over Lions Gate Bridge, go west on the Upper Levels Hwy and take the turn-off to Cypress Park. The traversing road up the mountain

has magnificent views of the city and as far as Mount Baker and Vancouver Island.

The Yew Lake Trail leaves from the top parking lot across from the ski-lift ticket office. This is an easy 1.5 km (1-mile) interpretive trail (signs point out flora and fauna indigenous to the area) looping through forests of Douglas fir, mountain hemlock and yellow cypress, which the park is named for. At times the trail skirts the shore of the lake before returning you to the base of the black chair ski lift. This is a leisurely walk of about 45 minutes. Black bears have been spotted here, so keep alert. If you want a more demanding hike, dozens of trails are marked on the map. Some depart from this area; others are in the Hollyburn area (they are cross-country trails in winter), which is lower down the access road.

7. **Capilano River Regional Park**. Park your car at Cleveland Dam. The Capilano Pacific Trail takes you down the west side of the Capilano River. Although this area has been logged, there are some big trees to admire and several viewpoints that show off the canyon and North Shore mountains. Continue until the park narrows and residential neighbourhoods are visible; then hike back up to the dam. About 90 minutes for the return trip. This is a short version of a hike that can continue to Marine Dr. See Capilano Regional Park.

8. **Lighthouse Park**. The Valley Trail, parallel to but on the east side of the road, takes about an hour for the return trip to the

lighthouse side. See Lighthouse Park.

9. **Belcarra Regional Park**. Take the Barnet Hwy, turn off to Port Moody and turn west on Ioco Rd; follow signs to the park. It's a 45-minute drive from city centre, and this park offers excellent choices. Admiralty Point Trail hugs the shoreline above rocky outcrops and beneath an umbrella of evergreens. The one-hour walk to Admiralty Point has view spots overlooking the water, and the point is perfect for a picnic.

For more of a workout, take Jug Island Beach Trail, which leaves from the overflow parking lot. It's occasionally steep and takes about an hour and a half to reach a rocky beach that looks out on Jug Island. There's a lovely mix of greenery—evergreens, alders, maples, ferns and bush. On weekends it's fun to observe the boat traffic in Indian Arm. Avoid Belcarra on warm summer weekends; it's best midweek or during spring and fall weekends.

10. **Buntzen Lake**. Take Hastings St to the Barnet Hwy and go through Port Moody to Ioco. Watch for signs to Anmore and Buntzen Lake. It's an hour's drive from downtown, but this lake in the midst of the forest and mountains is beautiful. From the picnic area take the interpretive loop trail on a half-hour walk. The park is very busy on weekends; go midweek if possible. For a more ambitious but very rewarding walk, you can circumambulate the lake in about 3½ hours, not including stops.

and from the shoreline, where they feed. The Snow Goose Festival is held annually the first or second weekend in November. Choose another time to visit if you don't like crowds.

Open daily 9–4. Admission is $3.25 for adults, with discounts for children and seniors. For information call 946-6980. There is a two-hour guided walk every Sun at 10. All the paths are wheelchair accessible, and picnic tables are provided for your use.

Reifel is not accessible by public transit. To get there, drive south on Hwy 99, and after the George Massey Tunnel take the second exit (which is marked Hwy 17). At the lights, go right on Ladner Trunk Rd to the end and then left on River Rd to Westham Island, where the sanctuary is located.

Museums/Art Galleries

First Thursday 124

Major Museums 124
Vancouver's Favourite Museum, Vanier Park Museum Complex,
Other Major Museums

Other Museums 130

Public Art Galleries 132

Major Private Galleries 133

Artist-Run Galleries 133

Photo Galleries 134

Indian or Inuit (Eskimo) Galleries 134

Craft Galleries 134

First Thursday

On the first Thurs evening of every month many museums and galleries open their doors from 5 to 8 to welcome the public with free admission. A complete list of participating galleries can be found each week in the *Georgia Straight*; see Essential Information (Newspapers). The Vancouver Art Gallery has free admission every Thurs evening from 5 to 9.

Major Museums

Vancouver's Favourite Museum

Museum of Anthropology
6393 NW Marine, University of British Columbia
822-3825
If you visit only one museum in Vancouver, make it the Museum of Anthropology. It is stunning. The museum houses artifacts from all over the world but focusses on the arts of the First Nations peoples of the Pacific Northwest. Apart from what it contains, the award-winning building is an architectural stroke of brilliance, designed by Arthur Erickson and inspired by Native cedar houses.

As you walk through the carved front doors and into the Great Hall, you will be awe-struck by the monumental totem poles and carvings. You can almost feel the power of the carved spirits depicted on the poles in the form of ravens, bears, frogs and humans. At the back of the Great Hall is a 13.5 m (45-foot) glass wall that overlooks more totem poles, traditional Haida houses and the unspoiled cliffs of Point Grey, against a backdrop of inlet and mountains.

Other Northwest Coast Native works on display include exquisite gold and silver jewellery, intricate

The Raven and the First Men, *a carving by Bill Reid in the Museum of Anthropology, depicts the Haida legend of the beginning of man.*

sculptures of argillite (a jet-black slate found in British Columbia's Queen Charlotte Islands), bone carvings, baskets and a collection of amazing ceremonial masks.

Also featured is contemporary First Nations art such as the massive sculpture *The Raven and the First Men*, designed and carved by Bill Reid. Finished in 1980, it was created from a block of 106 laminated yellow cedar beams and took five people more than three years to complete. The carving is an enormous, menacing, smirking raven perched on a partially open clamshell. Teeming inside the shell are human figures strug-

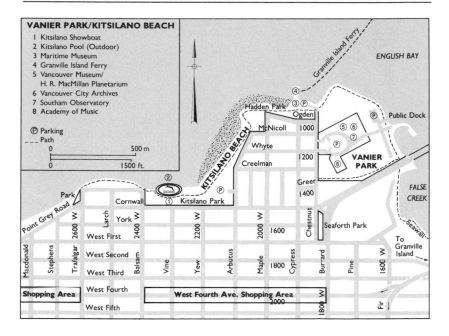

VANIER PARK/KITSILANO BEACH

1 Kitsilano Showboat
2 Kitsilano Pool (Outdoor)
3 Maritime Museum
4 Granville Island Ferry
5 Vancouver Museum/
  H. R. MacMillan Planetarium
6 Vancouver City Archives
7 Southam Observatory
8 Academy of Music

Ⓟ Parking
--- Path

gling either to emerge or retreat. These humans are unsure, terrified and awed; it is the Haida legend of the beginning of man.

The Museum of Anthropology's permanent collection is not locked away as in other museums but is completely accessible. Visitors are encouraged to pull out the glass-topped storage drawers.

Join a guided walk for an introduction to the collection (phone 822-5087 for times) or use the excellent booklet called "Guide to the UBC Museum of Anthropology." You should walk to the Great Hall and experience the totem poles for a few minutes before doing anything else.

A variety of special events takes place throughout the year, often on Sunday afternoons. There are also special changing exhibits, so the museum definitely warrants return visits.

The museum is on the University of British Columbia campus. To drive there, go west on 4th Ave until the road forks at NW Marine. Take the right fork and follow it until you are on the campus; then watch for the museum, which is on the north side of the road. Or take the #4 or #10 UBC bus, which will let you off in the middle of the university campus; the museum is a 10-minute walk northward (check the map at the bus stop when you get off). Admission is $6 for adults, with discounts for children, seniors and families. Free on Tues, 5–9 in summer and 11–9 in winter. Open Tues, 11–9; Wed to Mon, 11–5. Closed Mon in winter.

Vanier Park Museum Complex

Vanier Park is a wonderful stretch of waterfront on the Kitsilano end of the Burrard St Bridge and is the home of the Vancouver Museum; the H. R. MacMillan Planetarium and the Gordon Southam Observatory, which are both part of the Pacific Space Centre; the Maritime Museum; and the City

The deck of the St Roch, *the first ship to travel the Northwest Passage from west to east. A national historic site, the ship is housed in the Maritime Museum.*

of Vancouver Archives. The museum and planetarium are in the same building, a distinctive landmark because of its conical roof. The roof shape is patterned after the woven cedar-bark hats worn by the Northwest Coast Native people, a reminder that the land surrounding the museum was once the site of a Native village. Outside the building is a huge, stainless steel sculpture of a crab, which, according to Native legend, guards the entrance of the harbour.

Vancouver Maritime Museum
257-8300

The Maritime Museum, located close to the Vancouver Museum, is easy to spot because of the tall Kwakiutl totem pole that stands before it. Besides the spectacular Museum of Anthropology, the Maritime Museum is Vancouver's most fascinating mu-

seum. It is also just the right size—there is no museum burnout after visiting this one.

One of the highlights is the completely restored *St Roch,* a 1928 two-masted schooner that was the first ship to sail the treacherous Northwest Passage from west to east. (It took the captain and eight crew members more than two years to complete the voyage.) The *St Roch,* a Royal Canadian Mounted Police patrol boat, was also the first ship to circumnavigate North America. It is now an official National Historic Site, and you can take a self-guided tour. The ship is just as the crew might have left it—rum on the table, laundry by the bunks and huskies on deck.

Other exhibits reflect the maritime heritage of Vancouver and coastal B.C. The Children's Maritime Discovery Centre is an interactive display where the younger set learn about boats and the sea using computer games, an underwater robot and telescopes.

Many special events take place at the Maritime Museum, particularly in the summer. Restored heritage vessels are moored at the museum wharf, Heritage Harbour, in front of the museum.

Granville Island Ferries runs from the Aquatic Centre and Granville Island to the Maritime Museum wharf daily in summer and on weekends the rest of the year; call 684-7781.

Open daily in summer, 10–5; closed Mon in winter. Admission is $5 for adults, with discounts for children, seniors and families.

During summer discount coupons are available when you go to the Maritime Museum, the Vancouver Museum and the Planetarium in one visit.

The Vancouver Museum and Planetarium building, with its distinctive conical roof, in Vanier Park. (Rosamond Norbury)

Vancouver Museum
736-4431

A visit to the Vancouver Museum is an easy entry into Vancouver's past. Exhibits vividly depict the city's story from the time of exploration to the beginning of World War I. Among the memorabilia you will see a full-size trading post, the steerage section of an immigrant ship and a car from the first CPR passenger train to arrive in 1887.

This museum is a story in progress—as well as featuring the past, it looks at current issues and the future of Vancouver. The gift shop specializes in First Nations art and jewellery and is excellent.

The museum holds many special events evenings and on weekends: concerts, workshops, cultural demonstrations and lectures. Children's programs focus on natural history, science, storytelling, and arts and crafts.

Open seven days a week from May to Sept but closed Mon the rest of the year except holidays. Hours are 10–7 in the summer, 10–5 the rest of the year. Admission is $5 for adults, with discounts for children, seniors and families.

Parking is free, but the lot can fill up quickly when special events are held at Vanier Park.

H. R. MacMillan Planetarium at the Pacific Space Centre
738-7827

The planetarium explores the universe with shows each afternoon and evening. There is a mix of family shows, astronomy-oriented ones and the wild music/laser light show. Evening shows are not recommended for children younger than 8.

The rock music/laser light show is the second presentation every evening. (Be forewarned: this show is loud.) Arrive at least 20 minutes before showtime for any performance, since no latecomers are admitted.

The newest attractions here include

The courtyard outside the new Canadian Craft Museum downtown is a restful, secluded spot. (Producer's Workshop/ Images B.C.)

GroundStation Canada, an experiential theatre that explores Canada's achievements in space. There are also hands-on computer exhibits and the Cosmic Simulator, which gives you the sensation of a trip into space.

Closed Mon in winter. Admission to the astronomy show is $5.50 for adults, except on Tues, when it is $3.50. There are discounts for children, seniors and families; seniors are free on Tues. Admission to the rock music show is $7.75 with no discounts. In summer the museum is open daily; shows (not including the laser show) are held on the hour every hour, 11–4. Evening shows are 7:30 and 9; there is an extra show on weekend evenings. It is possible to see a second show by paying $1 when you are admitted, and shows are rotated so that you'll be seeing something different. Shows run about an hour.

Gordon Southam Observatory at the Pacific Space Centre
738-2855
The observatory is the small domed building beside the museum/planetarium complex and is open for public

stargazing. An astronomer explains how the 50 cm (19½-inch) reflector telescope works and how to use it. If you have a 35-mm SLR camera, phone for details on the observatory's "shoot the moon" program—you can take your own pictures of the full moon on clear evenings.

Open every evening during the summer (depending on the weather). During the winter, open Fri, Sat and Sun evenings when the sky is clear.

Call ahead to check. Admission is free.

City of Vancouver Archives
736-8561
The building behind the Southam Observatory that looks like a concrete bunker is the City of Vancouver Archives. Walking into it is like entering another world. The atmosphere is positively serene—it must be the most tranquil government office in the city. If you're fed up with traffic and crowds, it's the place to spend a few hours poring over local history.

In the main foyer is a changing exhibit, usually of wonderful old Vancouver photographs. The archives house public records from city hall, private papers of historical value, maps, newspaper clippings, books and, most interesting of all, historical photographs. Everything is indexed if you're looking for something specific, but the photographs are displayed in binders that you can leaf through for hours.

Open Mon to Fri, 9:30–5:30.

Other Major Museums

Canadian Craft Museum
639 Hornby near Georgia
687-8266
The museum started on Granville Island as the Cartwright Gallery, and its vision and mandate have expanded over the years to make it Canada's first national craft museum. Now the

Science World, along with the Omnimax Theatre, is housed in a geodesic dome on the shores of False Creek. (Science World)

museum is located on the ground level of Cathedral Place, a prestigious downtown office tower. The adjacent courtyard is one of the city centre's most pleasant resting spots; during summer there is often entertainment here, but it's still a peaceful retreat. The museum entrance is off this courtyard.

The museum is compact but showcases Canadian crafts with some international ones. It features contemporary as well as traditional works in everything from jewellery to baskets. The gift shop is worth a stop. The museum is open Mon-Sat, 10–5; and Sun and holidays, 12–5. Admission is $4 for adults, with discounts for children and seniors.

Science World
1455 Quebec near Terminal and Main
268-6363
This hands-on museum located in a geodesic dome blends entertainment with education. Many "please touch" exhibits help both kids and adults understand science while having a whole lot of fun. Demonstrations are

offered daily on such diverse topics as bubbles, illusions, water, air and fire.

In the Search Gallery, which is devoted to natural history, you can crawl through a beaver lodge, climb inside a hollow tree and watch a beehive in action. There's no end to the wonders—you can play a tune on a giant walk-on synthesizer in the Music Machine Gallery, light up a plasma ball in the Matter and Forces exhibition or search for gold in the Mine Games section.

The Omnimax Theatre, the world's largest domed screen, can take you on journeys into space or to explore Mayan culture; feature films change about every six months. The gift shop is sensational.

Admission to the museum is $9 for adults, with discounts for seniors and children; admission to the museum and Omnimax is $12 for adults, with discounts for children and seniors. Located across from the Main St/Science World SkyTrain station. Summer hours are daily, 10–6. Winter hours are weekdays, 10–5; and Sat and Sun, 10–6. Science World can be extremely busy—if you can't take crowds, go after 2 PM during the school year, on a sunny day in the summer or on Sat evening.

Vancouver Aquarium
See Parks/Beaches/Gardens (Stanley Park).

Other Museums

Burnaby Village Museum
6501 Deer Lake, Burnaby
293-6500
You walk a pathway lined with fragrant flowers and then cross a rustic bridge surrounded by woods to enter a peaceful 1920s village. This museum is a walk through history complete with costumed "townspeople" who chat about their everyday life. The dining room table is set for guests at the Elworth residence, a Charlie Chaplin flick is on at the Central Park Theatre, type is being set by hand in the print shop, the blacksmith heats iron bars at the forge . . . the scenes unfold in over 30 authentically restored buildings.

This is a wonderful place for children. Not only will they marvel at the things like the washboard and Brownie camera in the general store, but they can take part in activities, like playing games from the 1920s. And there is a beautifully restored 1912 carousel, which, in the 1950s, was at the Pacific National Exhibition. Young and old both enjoy this musical ride, which is truly a work of art.

In summer, vaudeville shows take place Sun afternoons. This can be an all-day outing—you can lunch in the ice cream parlour or bring a picnic.

Statutory holidays are special days—it may be a traditional craft weekend with doll making, quilting or a playroom full of turn-of-the-century toys, or an old-fashioned picnic with pie-

eating contests, sack races and the like. Christmas is one of the best times, with strolling carollers, musicians and traditional decorations and crafts.

From downtown, it is a 20-minute drive to the museum. Take the Trans-Canada Hwy #1 or #401 eastbound and exit at Kensington. Public transit is easy: take a #120 New Westminster Station bus from Burrard and Georgia directly to the museum, or take the SkyTrain to Metrotown Stn and then the #110 bus to city hall; the museum is a short walk when you turn left on Deer Lake Ave.

Open seven days a week from Apr to Sept, Thanksgiving weekend and most of Dec. Closed the rest of the year. Admission is $6 for adults, with discounts for children, seniors and families.

B.C. Sports Hall of Fame and Museum
B.C. Place Stadium, Gate A1
687-5520
It is apt that Canada's largest sports museum is located in British Columbia, where sports are, for many, a way of life. Although the history and development of sports are illustrated through photos, Olympic medals, trophies, personal mementos and equipment from all the big-name athletes, this museum is also about action.

In the Participation Gallery you can run, climb, throw, ride or row, and in the Discovery Gallery you learn what makes a champion. The museum also includes the Hall of Champions, galleries dedicated to Terry Fox and Rick Hansen; a salute to the province's coaches, referees, and others in the world of sports; a theatre where films focus on sports highlights; temporary exhibits; and, the latest to open, the History Gallery, which chronicles sports from the 1890s to the present. As you walk through each decade, you follow the progress of sports. Guided tours are available.

Open daily, 10–5; $2 a person; children under 5 free.

B.C. Golf Museum
2545 Blanca near University Blvd
222-4653
Appropriately, the entrance of this museum overlooks the 16th green and 17th tee of the University Golf Course. Housed in the original clubhouse of this picturesque course, the beamed 1920s building filled with antique furniture contains information on most courses in the province, golf paraphernalia—it's fun to compare today's equipment with that of the early-day clubs—a library of over 1200 volumes that cover history as well as everything you would like to know about this sport, and a video viewing area. There are also rotating exhibits. Admission is free, but donations are welcomed. Open Tues to Sun, 12–4.

Sri Lankan Gem Museum
925 W Georgia at Hornby
662-7768
The small, gem-packed museum located in Cathedral Place (same building as the Canadian Craft Museum) is the result of 20 years of travel and collecting by gemmologist Shelton di Silva.

The museum is like a small temple; the lighting is subdued, and it exudes an air of reverence—in this case, it's a reverence for the fine stones. Your gaze is first attracted to the floor, since it's inlaid with over 9000 Brazilian agates. Walls are lined with gold and hand-etched motifs, and the ceiling features 24 karat gold with enamelled drawings depicting Sri Lankan legends. The exhibits cover the world: there are moonstone and star rubies from India, crystals from Brazil, jade from China, an amazing topaz and star sapphire from Sri

Lanka and much more. Two eye-catchers are the map of Sri Lanka done in gemstones and the very large amethyst geode—the cavity, filled with crystals, is the size of a child's bathtub!

Hours are Mon to Sat, 10–5:30. The museum is always locked; you go to the jewellery store across the lobby and a guide takes you through. Admission is $3.50 for adults, with discounts for seniors and children.

Hastings Mill Museum
Point Grey at Alma
228-1213
This is like a country town museum with lots of artifacts—photos, Native baskets, early clothing and furniture, all jumbled together. Worth a stop if you're in nearby Jericho Park. Open seven days a week from June to mid-Sept, 11–4; winter hours are Sat and Sun afternoons only, 1–4. Admission by donation.

Vancouver Police Museum
240 E Cordova at Main
665-3346
The history of the Vancouver Police Department is told through displays on gambling, weapons, counterfeit money and notorious Vancouver crooks. Open seven days a week, 11:30–4:30; admission is free (donations appreciated).

Buddhist Temple
9160 Steveston Hwy, Richmond
274-2822
An impressive example of Chinese architecture that houses an active Buddhist temple. Leave your shoes outside to enjoy the traditional artwork in the heavily incensed interior. Open daily, 10–5; no admission charge.

Canadian Museum of Flight and Transportation
Hangar 3, Langley Airport
535-1115

Vancouver Art Gallery

A collection of vintage aircraft, including a Tiger Moth, a CF-100 Canuck and a Lockheed Starfighter, as well as a technical library and gift shop. The aircraft are on display from mid-May to late Oct, seven days a week, 10–4; the library and gift shop are open all year. Admission is $4 for adults, with discounts for children and families. Walkmans and a taped audio guide to the collection are available. An annual open house (free admission) is held the third weekend of June.

Public Art Galleries

Information about current shows at both public and private galleries can be found in *Vancouver Magazine*, the *West Ender*, and the What's On column of Thursday's *Vancouver Sun* and Friday's *Province*.

Vancouver Art Gallery
750 Hornby at Robson
682-5621
Vancouver's old courthouse, built in 1911, was transformed into the new Vancouver Art Gallery in 1983, completing the Robson Square complex. The architect of the courthouse, Francis Rattenbury, also designed the Empress Hotel and the Legislative Buildings in Victoria.

The elegance of the original courthouse remains: ornate plaster work and a glass-topped dome over a majestic rotunda that showers the centre of all four floors with natural light. The neoclassical style was popular for administrative buildings be-

cause of the weight and authority lent to them by Greek and Roman architectural features in the form of imposing columns, domes and entries guarded by lions. The main entrance has been moved to Robson St, but do look at the stately old entrance and square on the Georgia St side.

Off the main lobby is the gift shop, the Annex Gallery and access to the restaurant upstairs. Past the Annex Gallery is a stairway up to the gallery library (housed in the former law library). You can feel the tranquil atmosphere of the old law chambers here in the annex, with its quiet marble halls and heavy wooden doors. The former Supreme Court chamber, largely intact, is now the gallery boardroom.

The reference-only library is well stocked with art books, more than 100 different art magazines, files on contemporary Canadian artists and gallery catalogues from all over the world.

Be sure to see the permanent gallery on the third floor showing the work of Emily Carr, British Columbia's best-known artist. Her paintings from the early part of this century depict the power and mystery of nature as reflected in looming forests, foreboding skies, magnificent totem poles and abandoned Native villages.

When you reach the fourth and top floor of the gallery, take a look at the details on the walls and ceiling. In the original courthouse there was no fourth floor; it was introduced in a high-ceiling area to provide an intimate space for smaller art pieces. The effect is somewhat bizarre, since you can now see architectural details close up rather than from the intended vantage point of the floor below.

The gallery is closed Mon and Tues in winter, but the restaurant and gift shop are open every day. Gallery hours are Mon, Wed, Fri and Sat, 10–5; Thurs, 10–9; and Sun, noon to 5. Docent tours of exhibitions are available weekdays. Admission is $6 for adults, with discounts for students. Children and seniors are free. Pay what you can on Thurs after 5 PM. The Gallery Café has the best outdoor seating downtown.

Burnaby Art Gallery
6344 Deer Lake Ave, Burnaby
291-9441

Charles H. Scott Gallery
Emily Carr Institute of Art and Design
1399 Johnston, Granville Island
844-3811

Morris & Helen Belkin Art Gallery
1825 Main Mall, University of British Columbia
822-2759

Richmond Art Gallery
7700 Minoru Gate, Richmond
231-6440

Simon Fraser Art Gallery
Burnaby Mountain, Burnaby
291-4266

Surrey Art Gallery
13750–88th Ave, Surrey
596-7461

Major Private Galleries

Bau-Xi Gallery
3045 Granville at 14th
733-7011

Buschlen-Mowatt Fine Arts
1445 W Georgia near Nicola
682-1234

Crown Gallery
1017 Cambie at Nelson
684-5407

Diane Farris Gallery
1565 W 7th near Granville
737-2629

Equinox Gallery
2321 Granville at 7th
736-2405

Heffel Gallery
2247 Granville at 7th
732-6505

John Ramsay Contemporary Art
2423 Granville at 8th
737-8458

Artist-Run Galleries

Contemporary Art Gallery
555 Hamilton near Dunsmuir
681-2700

Federation of Canadian Artists Gallery
1241 Cartwright, Granville Island
681-8534

Or Gallery
112 W Hastings near Abbott
683-7395

Pitt International Galleries
317 W Hastings
681-6740

Students' Concourse Gallery
Emily Carr College of Art and Design
1399 Johnston, Granville Island
844-3811

Western Front
303 E 8th near Kingsway
876-9343

Photo Galleries

Exposure Gallery
851 Beatty near Robson
688-6853

Foto Base Gallery
231 Carrall near Cordova
687-7465

Presentation House
333 Chesterfield, North Van
986-1351

Indian or Inuit (Eskimo) Galleries

Gallery of Tribal Art
2329 Granville at 8th
732-4555

Images for a Canadian Heritage
164 Water near Cambie
685-7046

Inuit Gallery
345 Water near Richards
688-7323

Knot-La-Cha
270 Whonoak off Marine Dr, beside
the Capilano Indian Reserve, North Van
987-3339

Leona Lattimer Gallery
1590 W 2nd at Fir
732-4556

Marion Scott Gallery
481 Howe at Pender
685-1934

Wickaninnish Gallery
1666 Johnston St, Granville Island
681-1057

Craft Galleries

Circle Craft
1666 Johnston, Granville Island
669-8021

Crafthouse Gallery
1386 Cartwright, Granville Island
687-7270

Gallery of B.C. Ceramics
1359 Cartwright, Granville Island
669-5645

Oh Brothers
2356 W 41st near Vine
263-2122

See also Major Museums (Canadian Craft Museum).

Entertainment/Culture

Theatre 136

Classical Music 140

Dance 141

This festival tent allows rain-or-shine summer performances of Shakespeare on the shore of English Bay. (David Cooper)

The best places to check for entertainment listings are the daily newspapers (Thursday's *Vancouver Sun* and Friday's *Province* have detailed event listings) and the *Georgia Straight,* Vancouver's free entertainment weekly.

The Arts Hotline (684-ARTS) provides information about events in music, dance, theatre, visual arts and museums. Hotline hours are Mon to Sat, 9:30–5:30.

Tickets for most major events are sold through Ticketmaster outlets and can be purchased over the phone with MasterCard, Visa or American Express. Call 280-4444.

Theatre

Arts Club Theatre
1585 Johnston, Granville Island
2750 Granville near 12th
687-1644

The most active theatre in town, the Arts Club began over 32 years ago in a renovated former gospel house on Seymour. The location may have been peculiar, but the productions were consistently good, with a mix of classic plays, drama, comedy and musicals. Under the leadership of Bill Millerd, the Arts Club has burgeoned into the city's theatre success story. Come fall 1996, there will be three Arts Club locations in the city as the company opens its latest venue in the Stanley Theatre on Granville. Originally a vaudeville theatre in the thirties, then a movie house until the early nineties, the Stanley's exquisitely detailed art deco has been refurbished, and its 450-seat Lower Theatre features state-of-the art sound and lighting.

The Arts Club has two stages on Granville Island. The Arts Club Mainstage is a spacious, modern theatre beside the Public Market; it was converted from a chain forge and warehouse at the edge of False Creek. The Backstage Lounge overlooks the water and is a casual, fun hangout as well as a place to see the who's who of theatre in the city.

The Arts Club Revue Theatre is next door. It was a cabaret-style theatre for years, but in the fall of 1995 it changed to a multilevel, flexible-seating format to accommodate contemporary dramatic works. All three theatres have a year-round schedule of productions.

For reservations and tickets, call the

Show Boat *was the premier production in the new Ford Centre for the Performing Arts. (Catherine Ashmore)*

box office at 687-1644, Mon to Sat, 10–8.

Bard on the Beach
Vanier Park
737-0625
The setting of mountains, sea and the urban panorama of the West End high-rises adds magic to these Shakespearean performances. Productions run in repertory, rain or shine, in an airy, festival-sized tent behind the Vancouver Museum mid-June to mid-Sept. Ticket prices are reasonable and shows generally sell out, so you'll need to reserve by calling the box office at 739-0559. Bring a sweater.

Firehall Arts Centre
280 E Cordova at Gore
689-0926
Until 1975, 280 E Cordova was the original No. 1 Firehall. It's now a 150-seat theatre housing three companies: Touchstone Theatre, Axis Mime and the Firehall Theatre Co Dance events. Concerts are also staged here.

The Ford Centre for the Performing Arts
777 Homer at Robson
602-0616
The big event on the Vancouver theatre scene in the past few years was the opening of this magnificent, 1824-seat theatre. Designed by Moshe Safdie, who also created Library Square across the street, the three-level theatre offers patrons an exceptional view, since seating surrounds the stage on three sides. Despite the modernistic lobby with its eye-catching glass cone and mirrored staircase, the wood-panelled theatre has an intimate feel. To purchase CDs, and all sorts of paraphernalia related to musical shows (not just the ones that appear here), visit the Musical Theatre Store.

The Ford Centre's premier production, *Showboat*, created an excitement that is long-term for Vancouver audiences—the opening of this theatre heralds a new era in Vancouver theatre, since large-scale productions

Vancouver Opera performs Gilbert and Sullivan's The Pirates of Penzance. *(Vancouver Opera)*

can now be staged for long engagements.

For tickets call the Live Entertainment number: 280-2222.

Orpheum Theatre
Smithe at Seymour
665-3050

The Orpheum, home of the Vancouver Symphony Orchestra, is a mid-size theatre with excellent acoustics. (Glen Erickson)

The Orpheum Theatre is the home of the Vancouver Symphony Orchestra. Built in 1927 for the Orpheum vaudeville circuit based in Chicago, the theatre was converted into a movie house when vaudeville died out, and then deteriorated over the years. In the 1970s, its owner wanted to turn it into a movie theatre complex but was prevented by the "Save the Orpheum" campaign, which ended when the city purchased the building. The Orpheum became the home of the VSO after being restored to its 1920s style; many other musical events are held there as well.

The theatre is dramatically ornate, with huge, 1000-bulb crystal chandeliers, gilt ornamental plaster work, a painted domed ceiling and the original Wurlitzer organ. In 1983 a new entrance and foyer were added; unfortunately, they do not match the grandeur of the old theatre. And in 1995 renovations were made to improve the acoustics of the grand old theatre.

You may be able to persuade the man at the stage door (on Seymour)

Theatre Under the Stars in Stanley Park. (Jay Morrison)

to let you have a look around if you can't make it to a concert.

Presentation House
333 Chesterfield at 4th St, North Van
986-1351
A dynamic community arts centre combining a recital hall, a theatre, a museum, archives and a gallery specializing in photography.

Queen Elizabeth Theatre and Playhouse
630 Hamilton near Georgia
665-3050
The QE complex houses the huge, 2800-seat Queen Elizabeth Theatre and the smaller Vancouver Playhouse, a 650-seat theatre used by the resident Vancouver Playhouse Company. Usually six major Vancouver Playhouse productions run from fall to spring. Opera, dance and touring theatrical productions frequently hit the stage of the QE Theatre. Tickets are available at Ticketmaster (280-4444).

Theatre Under the Stars
687-0174
It does seem odd that one of Canada's rainiest cities has a tradition of outdoor theatre. Malkin Bowl, the theatre in Stanley Park, was built in 1934 as a bandshell and has been at the mercy of the elements ever since. The TUTS productions are often popular musicals such as *My Fair Lady* or *The King and I,* using professionals and amateurs. Shows are nightly, weather permitting, in July and Aug. Pick a dry night, pack a blanket and perhaps a thermos of sherry, and take in some outdoor theatre. You might even want to bring a picnic dinner. Curtain time is 8 PM.

Vancouver East Cultural Centre
1895 Venables and Victoria
254-9578
Perhaps it's a sign of the times that a turn-of-the-century East End church is now a bustling centre for the performing arts. It calls itself a neighbourhood theatre, and the Vancouver East Cultural Centre certainly has a neighbourly feel to it, but it would be unfair to leave the description at that. The VECC is one of the liveliest multipurpose performance spaces in the country, staging high-calibre theatre,

music and dance, as well as several Saturday afternoon children's series.

Phone seven days a week for reservations and information. All seats are general admission.

Vancouver TheatreSports League

Stanley Theatre, 2750 Granville near 12th
688-7013
Quirky and bizarre theatre is what TheatreSports is all about. The concept is comedy improvisational theatre in a sports context: generally two teams of three actors, a referee who makes calls ("Two minutes for obscenity!"), three judges and cheering fans. Themes are set, but there are no scripts. The skits are hilarious. (Audiences roared at "Greased," a spoof of the 1950s musical.) Theatresports has been around since 1980, and surely a sign of its success is its move to the art deco digs of the Stanley Theatre's 250-seat Upper Theatre in the fall of 1996. This troupe has become a cult in Vancouver, so reserve tickets. Shows take place Wed to Sun at 8 PM; Fri and Sat there are additional performances at 10.

Waterfront Theatre

Cartwright at Old Bridge, Granville Island
685-6217
Independent productions, family entertainment by Carousel Theatre and original works by B.C. playwrights (sponsored by the New Play Centre) are staged here.

In addition to these theatres, Vancouver has many small and innovative fringe theatre groups. For information about some 35 theatre companies, call Vancouver Professional Theatre Alliance, 879-2999.

Classical Music

New music, early music, choral music, symphony, opera, chamber groups, string quartets—the choice is yours. Information on current concerts is in the events listings in Thursday's *Vancouver Sun* and Friday's *Province* and at the two classical record stores in town, Sikora's and the Magic Flute; see Shopping (Recorded Music).

Festival Concert Society

736-3737
Sunday morning is an awkward time for visitors in any city. Unless you indulge in a three-hour brunch, there isn't much to do. The Festival Concert Society has an alternative—the Coffee Concert Series every Sunday morning from Sept through June at the Vancouver Playhouse, 630 Hamilton at Dunsmuir.

The concert may be jazz, folk, classical music, dance or theatre. Not only does it fill that Sunday-morning gap, but it costs only $5 and there's free babysitting and coffee. Buy tickets at the door the day of the concert; the box office opens at 10 AM and the show starts at 11 AM.

Vancouver Bach Choir

921-8012
The Vancouver Bach Choir performs three major concerts in its regular season, including a Handel's *Messiah* sing-along each Christmas. The 150-voice choir, considered to be the most impressive nonprofessional choir in the city, tours extensively and frequently wins international competitions. The Bach Choir performs at the Orpheum Theatre.

Vancouver Chamber Choir

738-6822
The Vancouver Chamber Choir is one of only two professional choirs in the country. It has an extensive interna-

tional touring schedule and records regularly. Concerts include a series of choral masterpieces at the Orpheum, a chamber music series at Ryerson United Church (45th and Yew) and Sunday-afternoon concerts in the Hotel Vancouver ballroom.

Vancouver New Music Society
606-6440

The New Music Society promotes contemporary classical music, such as concerts by the Philip Glass Ensemble and interdisciplinary performances incorporating dance, theatre or film. The society premieres works by Canadian composers and presents international composers and performers. The seven annual concerts are held at a variety of venues, including the Vancouver East Cultural Centre.

Vancouver Opera Association
682-2871

The VOA has been staging operas since 1960 and performs five major works a year, often with international stars.

The season runs from Oct to May or June at the Queen Elizabeth Theatre. Popular works such as *La Traviata, Carmen* or *Madama Butterfly* are balanced by more esoteric operas.

Vancouver Recital Society
602-0363

Two of the most successful concert series in Vancouver are offered by the Recital Society. The summertime Chamber Music Festival is held in a parklike setting, often at one of the private schools on the city's west side.

An optional dinner is served outdoors, or you are welcome to bring a picnic. Tickets are hard to come by, but some may be available at the door. If not, you could attend the half-hour pre-concert. Phone for information.

The main series (Sept to Apr) showcases internationally renowned musi-

cians, and the society has built a reputation for bringing some of the world's best performers—both aspiring new musicians and well-established talents—to Vancouver. The Vancouver Playhouse and the Orpheum are the venues for this series of concerts.

Early Music Vancouver
732-1610

The aim of the society is to promote medieval, Renaissance and baroque music using the instruments of the time.

Concerts are held at venues all over the city. Tickets are usually available at the door. The society also organizes an important summer festival of early music, held at UBC every July and Aug.

Vancouver Symphony Orchestra
684-9100

The VSO performs an eclectic mix of traditional symphonic works and pops. Guest soloists can range from Isaac Stern to Mel Torme. Most concerts are at the Orpheum; in summer the VSO also performs several free outdoor concerts, at local beaches or parks in the Lower Mainland. The culmination of the summer season is a mountain-top concert in the spectacular setting of Whistler Resort.

Dance

The **Dance Centre** is a nonprofit organization that provides information about dance activities in the city; call 606-6400.

Apart from the ones listed below, there are many resident companies that provide innovative dance performances, such as **Kokoro Dance, Mascall Dance, Judith Marcuse, the Goh Ballet** and **Kinesis Dance.** Companies that combine dance with theatre are **Jumpstart,**

Dancecorps, Battery Opera
Dance Company and **Vancouver
Moving Theatre**.

Ballet British Columbia
732-5003
Ballet B.C. is young, fresh and modern and constantly pushes the boundaries of modern ballet. Since its premiere in 1986, this highly acclaimed company has staged many well-received performances at the Queen Elizabeth Theatre (its regular venue) and throughout Canada. John Alleyne is the artistic director.

EDAM
876-9559
Experimental Dance and Music uses a multimedia presentation style. Productions are generally collaborations of choreographers, filmmakers, painters and musicians.

Karen Jamieson Dance Company
872-5658
Jamieson's award-winning choreography is bold, energetic and contemporary. The company makes a point of featuring Canadian composers, designers and artists and often presents cross-cultural collaborations—for example, incorporating Native themes.

Nightlife

Jazz 144

Rhythm and Blues 144

Comedy 144

Nice Quiet Bars 144

Lively Pubs and Bars 145

Nightclubs 146

Gay Clubs 147

Complete entertainment listings are in the *Georgia Straight*, Thursday's *Vancouver Sun* and Friday's *Province*.

Jazz

Call the 24-hour **Jazz Hotline** at 682-0706 for current and upcoming jazz events.

Alma Street Café
2505 Alma at Broadway
222-2244
Small groups perform mainstream jazz Wed to Sat in an informal restaurant with good food. $2 cover charge.

Carnegie's
1619 W Broadway at Fir
733-4141
Good mainstream jazz, solos and duos, Thurs to Sat. Minimum charge is $6.

Hot Jazz Society
2120 Main at 5th
873-4131
Dixieland, New Orleans and swing on Fri; occasionally big bands on Sun nights. Dance floor. $25 annual membership fee; then $6 for members, $10 for guests.

Glass Slipper
2714 Prince Edward at Kingsway
877-0066
Mainstream to contemporary jazz; open seven nights with live entertainment. Small artist-run space.

Rossini's Pasta Pallazo
1525 Yew at Cornwall
737-8080
Seven nights a week B.C. and some American talents perform; Sat afternoon jam session, 3:30–6:30, is a great time to stop by.

Rhythm and Blues

Yale Hotel
1300 Granville at Drake
681-9253
The home of R & B in Vancouver for many years. Very popular because of the talent the hotel lines up, local and imported, seven nights a week. Jam sessions Sat afternoon and Sun evenings.

Fairview Pub
898 Broadway at Oak
872-1262
Live performances seven nights a week; cover charge of around $5 for some big-name bands.

Comedy

Punchlines Comedy Theatre
684-3015
Standup comedy at 9, and also at 11 on Fri and Sat. (Club is cleared in between shows.) Closed Sun, Mon and Tues. Wed is an all-women show; Thurs is improv. Phone for new location.

Yuk Yuks
750 Pacific Blvd, foot of Robson
687-5233
Standup comedy. In summer, Thurs to Sat; shows at 9:30. In winter, Wed to Sat; shows at 9 Wed and Thurs, 9 and 11 on weekends. Wed is amateur night.

See also Entertainment and Culture (Back Alley Theatre).

Nice Quiet Bars

Bacchus Lounge
Wedgewood Hotel
845 Hornby near Robson
689-7777
A bright and airy lounge with a view of the street. Full of rather glamorous

The Four Seasons' Garden Lounge is rich in greenery. (Four Seasons)

people after work, but a pleasant, quiet bar later in the evening.

The Gallery
Hyatt Regency
655 Burrard at Melville
683-1234
An elegant private-club atmosphere.

Garden Lounge
Four Seasons Hotel
791 W Georgia at Howe
689-9333
Deluxe and expensive, with lots of greenery and deep lounge chairs.

Gérard Lounge
The Sutton Place Hotel
845 Burrard near Robson
682-5511
An elegant and comfortable gentlemen's-club atmosphere, complete with fireplace and unobtrusive

piano music from the adjoining Le Promenade. A favourite with the movie set.

The Park Royal Pub
Park Royal Hotel
540 Clyde, West Van
926-5511
The Tudor-style pub has quiet lounge atmosphere with a fireplace and background music.

Sylvia Hotel
1154 Gilford, west of Denman
681-9321
Spectacular view of English Bay from this nondescript but popular waterfront lounge.

Lively Pubs and Bars

Backstage Lounge
Arts Club
1585 Johnston, Granville Island
687-1354
A waterfront view. R & B on Thurs, Fri and Sat in summer and on weekends during winter. One of the best selections of scotch in town. Cover charge on weekends. Outdoor seating in fine weather. Great spot to mingle with the theatre set.

La Bodega
1277 Howe near Davie
684-8815
Spanish *tapas* bar with a very European atmosphere whose clientele ranges from the fashion crowd to flamenco guitarists. Very crowded on weekends; come before 8 PM. The food is good too.

Bridges
1696 Duranleau, Granville Island
687-4400
A lively, very casual Granville Island pub with a marine theme.

Joe Fortes
777 Thurlow near Robson
669-1940

The small bar and large restaurant are packed after work and on weekends with well-dressed young professional types. Piano player Tues to Sat.

Monterey Lounge & Grill
Pacific Palisades Hotel
1277 Robson at Jervis
684-1277

The Monterey's bright and airy lounge is comfy, a piano player provides light jazz Thurs, Fri and Sat evenings, and you can watch the Robson St crowd go by. On warm evenings there's some patio seating and a great variety of snacks available from the adjoining grill.

Unicorn Pub
770 Pacific Blvd, foot of Robson
683-4436

Live entertainment Wed to Sat (Irish Rovers' style as well as soft rock and top 40), British pub food and a large selection of ales create a lively, sing-along atmosphere.

The large outdoor patio is popular in the summer.

See also the Railway Club, below.

Nightclubs

Commodore Ballroom
870 Granville near Smithe
681-7838

The Commodore is probably the best mid-size venue in town. It holds about 1000 people; many big names have appeared here, and these days it often features rock stars. The 1929 building has a unique sprung dance floor. (The bounce comes from the railcar springs, rubber tires and horse-hair that support the wooden floor.) Once you start dancing, there's just no stopping.

Graceland
1250 Richards (alley entrance)
688-2648

The music is loud, the crowd is young, and the decor is concrete and steel. There's a different theme every night—Wed is reggae. A fringe club, probably the closest thing to a New York club. There are line-ups on weekends. Closed Tues.

Hungry Eye
23 W Cordova near Carrall
688-5351

A wild, really alternative club with a funky atmosphere. Bands are the up and coming on the alternative music scene. Live bands Wed to Sat; DJs spin music on Tues; closed Sun and Mon.

Luv-A-Fair
1275 Seymour at Drake
685-3288

Trendy young crowd. One of the most popular hangouts, it's best to arrive early. Open every night.

The Rage
750 Pacific Blvd, foot of Robson
685-5585

This progressive dance and concert club was formerly 86 Street Music Hall. The huge club still has the high-tech look and the 20–30s crowd. The music blares and large screens flash. Open Thurs to Sat, with some special events held during the week. Cover charge varies.

Railway Club
579 Dunsmuir at Seymour, upstairs
681-1625

One of Vancouver's best and smallest clubs. A pleasant place to have a drink or play some darts, the Railway also books some of the best bands in town. There's live music every night and a rock-a-billy jam session Sat, 3–7 PM, during winter. Sun is movie theme night; screenings start at 7.

Getting into the Railway can be a little complicated because technically it's a private club. What you do is arrive at the door and sign in as a guest. People have been doing this for years, and the club's so pleasant that it's worth the bother. Annual membership is $10, which gets you a card-key for the door and discounts on show admission.

The Red Lounge
818 Richards at Robson
688-2923
DJ music from jazz to easy listening. Formerly the Shaggy Horse, a gay club, now it's a mix of straight, gay and lesbian. Open Mon to Sat. Cover charge of $5.

Richard's on Richards
1036 Richards at Nelson
687-6794
The spot to see and be seen—some call it pretentious. Splashy interior, valet parking and long lines. Live and taped top 40 music. Dress code—no T-shirts or running shoes—Thurs to Sat. Open nightly.

The Roxy
932 Granville near Smithe
684-7699
House bands and canned music. A fun, clean club decorated like a big frat house party, which suits the largely student crowd.

Starfish Room
1055 Homer at Nelson
682-4171
Large club with a good setup to watch big-name locals and touring talent and some not-so-big names. Mainstream and alternative adult-oriented music. Closed Sun and Tue. Mon is DJ dance night; Wed to Sat there are live bands.

Town Pump
66 Water at Abbott
683-6695
Features original local and touring bands seven nights a week; music ranges from country and folk to alternative and funk. The club is popular, and the mixed crowd is pretty casual.

Twilight Zone
7 Alexander at Carrall
682-8550
College crowd, much less fashion conscious than at Graceland or Luv-A-Fair.

Nightclub Tour
Avoid line-ups and make an entrance by driving up in a white limo. Star Limousine Service (983-5577) has nightclub tours of the "in" spots.

Gay Clubs

Celebrities Night Club
1022 Davie near Burrard
689-3180
A large dance floor, long lines on weekends, cover charge Fri and Sat. Mixed crowd, principally gay. Open Tues to Sat.

Denman Station
860 Denman off Robson
669-3448
Friendly, subterranean neighbourhood bar. A social place with lots of activities, including darts and karaoke. Gay and lesbian crowd. Open seven nights; no cover charge.

Heritage House Hotel
455 Abbott at Pender
685-7777
There is the Lotus Club for dancing, Uncle Charlie's for an intimate drink or Chuck's Pub for darts, billiards and casual fare. Fri nights are "women only" in Lotus Club. Gay and lesbian crowd. Open seven nights; no cover charge.

Ms T's Cabaret
339 W Pender near Richards
682-8096
Occasional live music; Sat is country night. Mixed crowd—straight, gay and lesbian. Open Mon to Sat. No cover charge.

Numbers Cabaret
1042 Davie near Burrard
685-4077
Good dancing, movies, pool tables. Best club in town for cruising. Mostly gay crowd. Open seven nights. No cover charge.

The Odyssey
1251 Howe near Davie
689-5256
Clientele is young and stylish and predominantly gay. DJ, outdoor patio, pool table. Open seven nights. Cover charge Tues, Thurs, Fri and Sat. Mon night features strippers.

The Royal
Royal Hotel
1025 Granville at Nelson
685-5335
This friendly hotel bar is Vancouver's oldest gay bar. Live entertainment every night; very crowded. Wed is karaoke night. Mostly gay clientele. No cover charge.

Sports/Recreation

Auto Racing 150

Camping 150

Canoeing/Kayaking/Rowing 150
Routes, Rentals

Cruising 152
Routes, Rentals

Cycling 153
Routes, Rentals

Fishing 155
Charter Trips, Tackle Shops/Information/Licences, Fishing Gear,
Where to Fish

Golf 158
Public Courses, Private Clubs, Pitch and Putt

Hiking/Mountaineering/Indoor Climbing Walls 160

Horse Racing 160

In-Line Skating 160
Routes, Rentals

Jogging 161

Professional Sports 161
Tickets, Hockey, Football, Basketball, Baseball, Soccer

Rafting 162

Sailing 163
Cruise and Learn, Day Cruises, Charters

Scuba Diving 164
Where to Dive, Rentals

Skating 166

Skiing 166
Downhill, Cross-Country, Rentals

Swimming 171
At the Beach, Outdoor Saltwater Pools, Other Outdoor Pools,
Major Indoor Pools

Tennis 172
Outdoor Courts, Night Tennis, Indoor Courts, Rentals

Windsurfing 173

Without question, Vancouver is a sports-minded town and a perfect example of how geography and climate can shape people's lives. Is it any wonder that people are enticed outdoors by the balmy climate, the ocean and the mountains? Is it any wonder that people in central and eastern Canada—prisoners of freezing weather for six months of the year—think primarily of work? Vancouverites have other things on their minds.

Sport B.C. is an umbrella organization that can put you in touch with any sports association or give you up-to-the-minute information about any sport in B.C. The office is at 1367 W Broadway near Hemlock. Call 737-3000 during office hours.

Sports and recreational activities are listed here in alphabetical order.

Auto Racing

Indy Vancouver
Normally Pacific Blvd is a 50 km/h zone (30 mph), but during the Labour Day weekend you'll see maniacs whizzing by at 300 km/h (190 mph). In 1990 Vancouver became one of the 16 events on the Indy circuit. The downtown track is 2.7 km (1¾ miles) long, and cars do 103 laps. The final race, on Sunday afternoon, only takes two hours; practices and time trials are held for two days before.

Odds are grandstand tickets will be sold out, but standing-room tickets are usually available. Phone 684-4639.

Camping

For information about where to camp, see Where to Stay (Trailer Parks/Campgrounds).

When renting equipment, phone in advance to reserve equipment for summer weekends. Be prepared to leave a deposit.

Recreation Rentals
2560 Arbutus near W Broadway
733-7368
Everything from hiking boots to tents.

For information about renting camper vans and motor homes, check the *Yellow Pages* under Recreational Vehicles—Renting & Leasing. The vehicles can come equipped with linen, cooking and eating utensils and so on. Minimum rental period is usually a long weekend or one week.

Canoeing/Kayaking/ Rowing

Routes

False Creek
This trip is for the urban adventurer. Set off from Vanier Park, Sunset Beach or Granville Island and circumnavigate False Creek. From Sunset Beach, go under the Burrard, Granville and Cambie St Bridges and past the old Expo site and B.C. Place Stadium to the end of False Creek.

On the return trip, go along the south shore to pass by the waterfront community of False Creek. You could stop at the Riviera Café by the False Creek Marina to quench your thirst. Next is Granville Island and the public market, and then the commercial fishing docks between the Granville and Burrard St Bridges.

Now you are back where you started, having covered roughly 10 km (6 miles) in about three hours.

English Bay
The shores of English Bay, towards Stanley Park or by Kits Beach and Spanish Banks, are good paddling territory. *WARNING: Do not attempt to paddle under Lions Gate Bridge—the currents there are fierce.*

Vancouver's close-by mountain lakes and vistas please canoeists. (Judi Lees)

Deer Lake

Deer Lake is mostly a pastoral urban park, but 5 km (3 miles) of wooded shoreline and wilderness surround the lake. Burnaby Art Gallery, Shadbolt Centre for the Arts and Burnaby Village Museum, a reconstructed pioneer village, are within a short walk.

A great picnic place to take the children or spend a relaxing afternoon on the water.

Indian Arm

Indian Arm is a dramatically rugged inlet about 1.6 km (1 mile) wide and 30.5 km (19 miles) long, surrounded by 1200 m (4000-foot) mountains. Rent a boat at Deep Cove and paddle across Indian Arm to Jug Island, Combe Park or Belcarra Park. Or paddle south to Cates Park at the mouth of the inlet. A third alternative is to paddle all the way to the end of Indian Arm (four hours one way) for a good look at coastal wilderness.

East of Vancouver

If you'd rather paddle on a lake (and have a car and a day to spare), head east to Buntzen Lake, an hour's drive from downtown. Canoes and roof racks can be rented at the Anmore Grocery and Canoe Rentals, a short distance from the lake.

Rentals

Ecomarine Ocean Kayak

1668 Duranleau, Granville Island
689-7575
Double and single kayaks by the hour or day. A friendly crew will give you pointers if you're just beginning.

Adventure Fitness

1528 Duranleau, Granville Island
687-1528
Canoes, kayaks and power boats for rent. Handy to False Creek and English Bay.

Deer Lake Boat Rentals

Deer Lake
667-2628
On the east side of Deer Lake in Burnaby. Kayaks, canoes, rowboats, pedal boats and battery-powered boats for rent by the hour. Open weekends April-June; daily June-Sept.

Kayaking in Deep Cove is an excellent escape into nature. (L. Cumming)

It's a tricky entry to this lake. Go Canada Way to Burris; then right on Buckingham and left on Sperling.

Deep Cove Canoe and Kayak Rentals

Deep Cove
929-2268
Deep Cove is near the mouth of Indian Arm, a spectacular wilderness fiord in North Vancouver. Deep Cove Canoe Rentals is just south of the government wharf at the end of Gallant St. Canoes and kayaks for rent by the hour or the day.

Cruising

Routes

For a taped marine forecast, call 270-7411.

Howe Sound/Strait of Georgia

Howe Sound and the Strait of Georgia have some of the best cruising waters in the world and are the only protected saltwater cruising areas north of San Francisco. In addition, there are 28 marine parks between Vancouver Island and the mainland.

Howe Sound has many islands to explore, so bring a picnic lunch and find

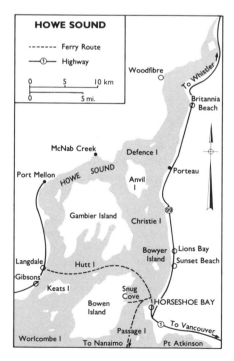

a secluded beach. Or cruise to Gibsons, where the CBC television series *The Beachcombers* used to be filmed.

If you want to meet other boaters, try lively Snug Cove on the east side of Bowen Island, a short distance from Horseshoe Bay. There is a sandy beach at Deep Bay, the next bay north of Snug Cove. Chinook salmon fishing is good here all year.

Regular bus service (#250 Horseshoe Bay) takes you from downtown Vancouver to Horseshoe Bay, where you can rent a boat. Supplies are available within easy walking distance.

Burrard Inlet

For a marine view of the city, cruise up Burrard Inlet into the beautiful natural setting of Vancouver Harbour. You'll see freighters, float planes and cruise ships from all over the world, engaged in the varied activities of the continent's second-largest port. Then there is a quick transition into a wilderness area, with good fishing at the east end of the inlet.

Rentals

Sewell's Landing Marina

6695 Nelson, Horseshoe Bay
921-3474

Motorboats by the hour, half-day or day; maps, fishing gear and licences also available here.

Cycling

A few words of advice about cycling in Vancouver. Wearing a helmet is mandatory in the city. Vancouver has few bike paths in the centre of the city, and riding on the sidewalks is illegal. Police do not hesitate to ticket cyclists for traffic violations. Bicycles are allowed on the SeaBus, the commuter ferry to the North Shore. The Aquabus transports cyclists and bikes

from the foot of Hornby, downtown, to Granville Island and False Creek (689-5858).

Cyclists are not allowed in the George Massey Tunnel under the Fraser River on Hwy 99 south of the city, but from May through Sept a shuttle service will take you and your bike through the tunnel at designated times. Call 271-0337 seven days a week.

If you are travelling by ferry with a bike, bus #404 Airport/Ladner Exchange has a bicycle rack. The #351 Crescent Beach/Vancouver and #601 South Delta/Vancouver buses also have bike racks.

Routes

There are many excellent cycling routes in and around the city.

Stanley Park

The seawall, a 9 km (5½-mile) paved path along the shore of Stanley Park, is a wonderful ride because of the spectacular views. The seawall is not a complete circle but connects with paths and roads. It is clearly divided in two: one side is for cyclists, the other for pedestrians. Cyclists must ride counterclockwise around the park and must dismount at a few designated busy spots. Start at the foot of Alberni or Georgia.

The seawall is a flat, easy ride that takes about an hour. If you must ride weekends, when the park is very busy, be patient and careful. During summer, members of the Bike Patrol (they wear bright yellow shirts) provide tourist information, give first aid and will even help fix a bike. They will warn fast cyclists as well.

There is also a perimeter road around the park, which is more challenging because of the hills. The one formidable hill, underneath the Lions Gate Bridge, can be avoided by riding down to the seawall just after Pipeline Rd.

Experience the variety and vastness of Stanley Park the easy way—by bicycle. (Rosamond Norbury)

The one-way road also goes counter-clockwise, so enter via Georgia and veer right. Except for this one hill, any road or bicycle path in the park is good for cycling. (See Stanley Park map.)

Port of Vancouver

This ride takes you past Bute Marina, Canada Place Pier, fish-packing plants, cargo docks and grain elevators. Start at the north end of Cardero, just east of the Bayshore Hotel, where an unnamed asphalt service road runs close to the water. (During the week there may be some construction in this section, so you may want to start farther east. On weekends, it's probably fine.) Ride east, picking your route carefully to stay close to the water; it is possible to ride almost to the Second Narrows Bridge.

The return trip is 15 km (9⅓ miles). The view is superb and the terrain flat, but watch for oblique railway tracks. You will have this road to yourself on weekends and evenings. Rentals are available nearby at Denman and Georgia.

Shaughnessy

An exclusive old neighbourhood with elegant mansions along quiet, tree-lined streets, this is a perfect area for meandering through on a bicycle. From downtown, take the Cambie St Bridge south to 16th Ave; then turn right and go along 16th until you reach Tecumseh. Pick up picnic supplies at Max's Deli at Oak and 15th and stop for a picnic at Crescent Park. Osler, Angus and the Crescent are the choice streets in Shaughnessy, but travel up the side streets as well. The Hycroft mansion at 1489 McRae has been restored to its 1912 style and is sometimes open to the public. Shaughnessy continues on the other side of Granville.

To return downtown, use the Burrard St Bridge; it's an easier ride and not as busy as the Granville St Bridge. Return trip is 13 km (8 miles).

Kitsilano Beaches

From downtown, cross the Burrard St Bridge and keep right onto Cornwall. Ahead a few blocks is lively Kits

Beach, with a huge, outdoor saltwater pool. Farther down Cornwall (it becomes Point Grey Rd) is Jericho Park, which is quieter, Locarno Beach and then Spanish Banks. Follow the beach path through Jericho Park or cycle along NW Marine. There are refreshment stands and washrooms at the beaches. The few hills on this route are not steep. Avoid rush hour.

The trip to Spanish Banks and back is 17 km (10½ miles).

University of British Columbia

The campus is separated from the city by the University Endowment Lands, a large wilderness area crisscrossed by hiking paths. Paved cycling paths run through the park alongside University Blvd, Chancellor Blvd and 16th Ave.

There is a very steep hill as you approach UBC, so use 8th Ave, which is the least arduous and from which you'll have one of the best views of the city (at 8th and Discovery). Tenth Ave would be a good return route.

The round trip from downtown with a short stop would take about three hours.

Southlands

This wonderful, oasislike spot (in the south end of the city beside the Point Grey Golf Course) resembles the English countryside. Southlands is the equestrian centre for the city, and you will encounter horses and riders on the bridle paths along the road. Southlands is a gem of a place, great for a picnic. There are no stores, however, so pack a lunch. A good spot to stop for your picnic is at the foot of Carrington. Go right along the trail for a view of the Fraser River.

There are hills on the route from downtown, 21 km (13 miles) return, but Southlands is as flat as can be. Taking the bus to Dunbar Cycles and renting a bike there would shorten the ride to 7 km (4⅓ miles) return.

Rentals

Robson Cycles
1463 Robson near Broughton
687-2777

Spokes Bicycle Rentals and Espresso Bar
1798 Georgia at Denman
688-5141

Bayshore Bicycles
745 Denman at Robson
688-2453

Recreation Rentals
2560 Arbutus near W Broadway
733-7368

Fishing

Charter Trips

You've come to B.C. and you want to catch a salmon, right? The sure way is to join a chartered fishing trip. The charter company looks after the details while you sit back and wait for the fish to bite. Charters are available by the half-day, day or week. Call any of these companies for more details:

Barbary Coast Yacht Basin
554 Cardero, north end of Bute
669-0088

Bayshore Yacht Charters
1601 W Georgia at Cardero
682-3377

Sewell's Landing Marina
6695 Nelson, Horseshoe Bay
921-3474
Reasonably priced four-hour group charters (skippered), with a reduced "sightseeing" rate (a real bargain at $19.95) for those who would rather enjoy the scenery than fish.

Fishing off the pier at Jericho Beach. (Rosamond Norbury)

Tackle Shops/ Information/Licences

If you'd rather go fishing on your own, you must find out about the local fishing restrictions. The tackle shops listed here are a good source of information. They will give you a current issue of the federal government's "B.C. Tidal Waters Sport Fishing Guide" and the provincial government's "B.C. Sport Fishing Regulations Synopsis for Non-tidal Waters." Any of these shops will sell you a saltwater or freshwater fishing licence and tell you where they're biting.

The Department of Fisheries runs an information service. By calling 666-6331 you can find out about restrictions, where and when to fish, and which lures to use.

The *B.C. Fishing Directory and Atlas*, available at most sporting goods stores, provides complete information about fishing locations.

Fishing Gear

Army and Navy
27 W Hastings near Carrall
682-6644

West Coast Fishing Tackle
2147 E Hastings near Victoria
254-0004

Three Vets
2200 Yukon at 6th
872-5475

Compleat Angler Tackle
4257 Fraser at 27th (rear)
879-8033

Ruddick's Fly Shop
3726 Canada Way, Burnaby
434-2420

Where to Fish

Burrard Inlet
Burrard Inlet is open all year. From July to Oct fish for coho along the north shore. Fish for chinook from Nov to Mar.

The Catch

Salmon

Chinook: 1.5 to 18 kg (3 to 40 pounds); record fish of 56 kg (123 pounds) have been caught
Coho: the most prized game fish in B.C.; 4.5 to 6.5 kg (10 to 14 pounds)
Chum: 3.5 to 4.5 kg (8 to 10 pounds)
Pink: 2 kg (4½ pounds)
Sockeye: 2 to 3 kg (4½ to 7 pounds)

Other Saltwater Fish

Abundant and easily caught delicacies include sole, flounder, red snapper, rock cod, ling cod, halibut and perch. Look for these white-fleshed fish around pilings, reefs and rocky areas. Use tiny shore crabs or mussels as bait.

Freshwater Fish

Steelhead trout: 2 to 11 kg (4½ to 24 pounds)
Cutthroat: 2 to 9 kg (4½ to 20 pounds)
Kokanee: 0.5 kg (1 pound); land-locked sockeye salmon with deep red flesh, considered the best food fish in B.C.

Shellfish

Crab, shrimp, prawns and bivalve mollusks such as clams, mussels, oysters and scallops all thrive on the Pacific coast. Bivalves found near populated areas, however, are undoubtedly contaminated. Ask the Dept of Fisheries about safe areas.

Warning: There is a natural phenomenon called "red tide," which is a bloom of reddish plankton in the ocean. Shellfish retain this plankton in their systems, where it does them no harm—but eating these shellfish can be deadly to humans. Call the Dept of Fisheries for up-to-date information on red tide.

Mussels and clams, the most common shellfish, are easily turned into lunch over an outdoor fire. Scrub the shells and throw them into a large pot with 2.5 to 5 cm (1 to 2 inches) of water or white wine. Cover and steam for a few minutes, just until they open. Eat them out of the shells with some butter, and don't forget the broth.

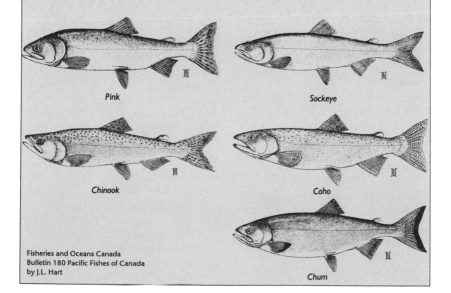

Pink

Sockeye

Chinook

Coho

Chum

Fisheries and Oceans Canada
Bulletin 180 Pacific Fishes of Canada
by J.L. Hart

Howe Sound/Horseshoe Bay

The Horseshoe Bay/Howe Sound area offers the best chance of catching chinook or coho. There are chinook all year in Howe Sound, peaking in Nov and Dec. Coho are available in summer and fall. This is one of the most popular fishing spots on the Pacific coast, and there are marinas all along the coast at Fisherman's Cove, Whytecliff, Horseshoe Bay, Sunset Beach and Lions Bay. Free boat launches in the area are at Fisherman's Cove and Porteau Beach.

Some of the best fishing spots in Howe Sound are Hole-in-Wall (on the mainland coast just north of the Horseshoe Bay ferry terminal), Queen Charlotte Passage (between Bowen Island and the mainland), Bowyer Island (off Sunset Beach), the Grebe Islets (near Fisherman's Cove), Bowen Island (south end) and Gambier Island (south end).

Sunshine Coast

Another hot spot for salmon fishing, especially from Secret Cove to Egmont. It is a three-hour trip from Horseshoe Bay to the Sunshine Coast, including a ferry ride from Horseshoe Bay to Langdale.

Boat rentals and charters are available at Secret Cove, Pender Harbour and Egmont.

Fraser River

A saltwater licence is needed below the town of Mission; above the town you must have a freshwater licence. Information about access to the many Fraser River sandbars is in the B.C. fishing guides mentioned earlier. Fish the mouth of the Fraser for sockeye during late summer; pink salmon are available in odd years.

Lakes and Rivers

For freshwater angling, try the Squamish–Cheakamus River system, the lakes near the Sunshine Coast, or Pitt,

Stave, Cultus and Harrison Lakes east of Vancouver. The Vedder–Chilliwack River is teeming with steelhead and coho. There is good fishing all year at Buntzen Lake, a popular canoeing lake where no power boats are allowed.

The Skagit River system, 160 km (100 miles) southeast of Vancouver, is the best for trout, especially fly-fishing.

On Vancouver's North Shore you can fish the Seymour River, the Capilano River and Lynn Creek, primarily for coho in late summer and early fall.

Golf

Golf is a popular year-round sport in Vancouver. Several large tournaments—both amateur and professional—are held annually. Call the **B.C. Golf Association** (294-1818) or **B.C. Professional Golfers Association** (274-7822) for details.

Public Courses

Several courses are close to the centre of the city. They are listed here in order of popularity and ease of play.

Fraserview Golf Course
7800 Vivian at 54th
280-8633
This most scenic of the municipal courses overlooks the Fraser River. Clubs and power carts for rent, cafeteria, bar, driving range. Fraserview is said to be the busiest course in the country. Par 71, 6346 yards.

University Golf Club
5185 University Blvd
University of British Columbia
224-1818
This popular public course is scenic and well kept and is the closest to the city centre. It is challenging but not punishing. The clubhouse has a din-

ing room and bar; clubs and pull and power carts can be rented. Par 72, 6157 yards.

Langara Golf Course
6706 Alberta near 49th
280-7888
Renovated in 1994, this is a new course with old-growth trees. Good intermediate golfing. It includes a clubhouse, a licensed restaurant and locker room facilities. You can walk or rent a pull cart. Particularly pretty course in fall. Par 71, 6100 yards.

There are about 20 other public courses just outside Vancouver. Some particularly good ones are:

Gleneagles Golf Course
6190 Marine, West Van
921-7353
Nine holes. Near Horseshoe Bay. Par 35, 2800 yards.

Mayfair Lakes
5460 No. 7 Rd, Richmond
276-0505
Beautifully laid-out, brand-new course. Water absolutely everywhere. Very good facilities and restaurant. Par 72, 6225 yards.

Peace Portal Golf Course
16900–4th Ave, Surrey
538-4818
Off Hwy 99 before the Canada–U.S. border, about an hour's drive from the city. Established in 1928. Heavily treed, undulating fairways. Nothing but raves about this course. Par 72, 6103 yards.

Private Clubs

Many private clubs accept guests accompanied by members. Most also have reciprocal privileges, whereby you will be admitted if you are a member of another bona fide club. You must have a membership card and/or a letter of introduction from your club pro. Phone first for confirmation. The best private courses are:

Capilano Golf and Country Club
420 Southborough, West Van
922-2442
Fairly rigorous course, with a breathtaking view. Par 72, 6221 yards.

Shaughnessy Golf and Country Club
4300 sw Marine at Kullahun
266-4141
Very prestigious and very busy. Must be with a member to play. Par 73, 6320 yards.

Point Grey Golf and Country Club
3350 sw Marine at Blenheim
261-3108
Par 72, 6279 yards.

Pitch and Putt

Eighteen holes of golf the quick way, with a short fairway. Three public pitch and putt courses are centrally located; all rent clubs.

Queen Elizabeth Pitch and Putt
Queen Elizabeth Park
Cambie at 33rd
874-8336
Open Feb to Nov.

Stanley Park Pitch and Putt
Stanley Park
681-8847
Open year-round.
Use the Beach Ave entrance.

Ambleside Pitch and Putt
1200 Marine, West Van
922-3818
Open Mar 1 to the end of Oct.

Central Park Pitch and Putt
Boundary and Kingsway, Burnaby
434-2727
Mar 1 to Oct 31
A short walk from the Patterson SkyTrain station.

The Cloverdale Rodeo

This event causes an explosion of excitement every May during the Victoria Day long weekend. It's the second-largest rodeo in Canada and among the top 15 in North America, with prize money big enough to attract the best cowboys from all over the continent. The events include calf roping, bronco riding, steer wrestling, wild-cow milking, street dances, parades, a casino, arts and crafts, pancake breakfasts, rides and a midway.

Hiking/Mountaineering/ Indoor Climbing Walls

The **Federation of Mountain Clubs of B.C.** offers courses in all levels of mountaineering and rock climbing and leads backpacking trips into the interior of B.C. If you're interested only in a day trip, the federation can provide you with a list of companies that offer shorter guided hikes. Call 737-3053.
See also Parks/Beaches/Gardens.

Cliffhanger Indoor Rock Climbing Centre

106 W 1st at Manitoba
874-2400
A climbing service for everyone from novice to expert. Children are welcome here.

Rock House Indoor Climbing Centre

520–3771 Jacombs near Bridgeport, Richmond
276-0012
Seventeen different walls, from low-angle for beginners to overhangs. Equipment and instruction provided.

Horse Racing

From Apr to Oct, thoroughbred races are run at **Hastings Park Racecourse**, at Hastings and Renfrew. Parade to post is 6:15 on Wed and Fri; 1:15 on Sat, Sun and holidays.
Brunch is served on Sun at noon in the clubhouse. To reserve a table on the clubhouse Table Terrace or in the dining room, phone 254-1631. Book well in advance for brunch or dinner. In the dining room you can view the races on closed-circuit television.
The rest of the year, from Sept to Apr, the action moves to the **Cloverdale Raceway** at 176th St and 60th Ave in Surrey for harness racing. Races are held at 7 PM on Wed and Fri and at 1:15 PM on Sat and Sun. Call 576-9141 for more information.

In-Line Skating

Vancouver's mild climate is ideal for this fast-growing sport. Officially, it is not allowed on sidewalks or streets, but the rule of thumb seems to be that as long as skaters are courteous and safety-conscious, authorities don't clamp down. Check with local skaters and those who work in the skate shops for the latest word. Here are some routes that locals enjoy.

Routes

Seymour Demonstration Forest
A sanctioned 11 km (7-mile) route in North Vancouver. Not for novices, since there are some steep sections.
See Sightseeing (Special Interest Tours).

Stanley Park Seawall
Only about 1.5 km (1 mile)is an approved area for skaters, but in-liners share the bicycle path with cyclists and there doesn't seem to be a prob-

lem. During summer, the seawall is patrolled by park employees on bicycles. Fast skating is frowned on. The seawall is crowded on weekends.

False Creek/Granville Island/ Vanier Park

This is a popular route shared with cyclists. Start at the bottom of Denman and Beach and go east; the route goes around False Creek to Vanier Park. In a few places you are on the road, and near Granville Island there's a cobblestone section that's tricky. Or you can start just west of Granville Island and enjoy the route along Vanier Park to Kits Beach.

See Sports/Recreation (Cycling).

Rentals

Alley Cat Rentals
1779 Robson near Denman
684-5117

Jogging

Seawall, Stanley Park
The flat asphalt path along the seawall has stunning scenery to keep you going for all 10 km (6 miles).

Lost Lagoon, Stanley Park
The path that circles the lagoon is accessible from the foot of Alberni. It is a level gravel pathway, about 1.6 km (1 mile) long, excellent for an easy run.

Seawall, False Creek
The seawall starts at Fisherman's Wharf by the Burrard St Bridge and runs past Granville Island and the community of False Creek to the Cambie St Bridge. The trip is 5 km (3 miles) return. If you need sustenance, stop at Isadora's on the edge of Granville Island near the seawall; see Restaurants (Breakfast).

English Bay
A level pathway starts behind the

Vancouver Aquatic Centre and follows the water's edge to Stanley Park, 2 km (1¼ miles) one way.

Kits Beach/Vanier Park
A series of asphalt and dirt paths starts at Vanier Park on the Kitsilano side of the Burrard St Bridge. The paths follow the water around Kits Point, past the Vancouver Museum, the planetarium, the Maritime Museum, Kits Beach and the Kitsilano Yacht Club. The return trip is about 5 km (3 miles) and is fairly flat.

Ambleside Seawall to Centennial Seawalk
The paths in Ambleside Park start at the east side and follow the water for the length of the park. You then have to pick your way along the beach and the road for a short distance until the beginning of the Centennial Seawalk. This 1.6 km (1-mile) path is asphalt and completely flat. The views are wonderful—the city, Lions Gate Bridge, Stanley Park and the marine traffic.

Professional Sports

Vancouver residents are too busy jogging, skiing or sailing to spend time cooped up in an enclosed stadium, and so professional sports sometimes end up being victims of low attendance. But there are some diehard fans out there.

Tickets

Tickets for professional football, hockey and other sports events can be purchased from Ticketmaster outlets, which have branches at all Eaton's stores and at the information booths of major malls. Or you can order your tickets by phone (280-4444) and charge them to Visa, MasterCard or American Express.

Hockey

In 1968 Vancouver entered the National Hockey League. The Vancouver Canucks played their first season two years later to near-sellout crowds. They lost more games than they won for the first 12 years, but the fans were always there.

Recently the Canucks made a quantum leap to respectability, winning the Smythe Division in 1992 and taking the 1995 Stanley Cup Finals to seven games against New York in 1995. Even though they lost the final game, the fans still loved them. Russian star Pavel Bure has become a local hero. In 1995 Bure and his teammates moved to General Motors Place, a new, 20,000-seat sports and entertainment stadium close to the centre of the city. For information about the Canucks, call 899-7400.

Football

The B.C. Lions have had a rocky history. They finished the first season in 1954 with only one win. After eight more tough years they finally made it to the Grey Cup and then won it in 1964. The glory was short-lived: by the end of the next season they were in last place again. It wasn't until 1994 that they won the Grey Cup again, beating Baltimore in the last few seconds of the game. The Lions play all their games in the B.C. Place Stadium downtown; their season starts in June and runs until late Oct. For information about the Lions, call 583-7747.

Basketball

Basketball fans welcomed the news in February 1994 that the city had been granted an NBA franchise. By the time the newly formed Vancouver Grizzlies hit the courts in November 1995, GM Place had been built and over 13,000 season tickets sold. This is the first NBA team to call Vancouver home. The season runs Nov to Apr, and the Grizzlies play 44 home games and travel to 28 North American cities on road trips. For information about the Grizzlies, call 899-7400.

Baseball

Do you have fond memories of sunshine, hot dogs and Sunday afternoon baseball? Catch the Vancouver Canadians of the Pacific Coast League at grand old Nat Bailey Stadium from Apr to Sept. The highly popular Canadians are a cult in Vancouver and their games often sell out, so arrive early. Tickets are available at the door. The stadium is at Ontario and 29th, on the east side of Queen Elizabeth Park. Phone 872-5232 for times or check the newspapers.

Soccer

The Vancouver 86ers play in the American Professional Soccer League (known as the A League). Exhibition games may see them hosting teams from Italy, England or Portugal. They play in the recently renovated Swangard Stadium in Burnaby; their season is May to Oct. Phone 299-0086 for information and tickets.

Rafting

If the daredevil in you wants to try whitewater rafting, companies in Vancouver organize trips that will take you through Hell's Gate, the Washing Machine, Devil's Cauldron or the Jaws of Death. The Thompson and Chilliwack Rivers are known for frothing white water and the Fraser for whirlpools and waves. Fraser River trips are also more historical, and most are on motorized rafts. Taking

Old-time baseball at Nat Bailey Stadium with the Vancouver Canadians. (Fred Skolovy)

part in the paddling is the more exciting trip.

Some companies transport you from the city to the interior of B.C., or you can drive yourself to a meeting place in the area, a one- to three-hour trip from Vancouver. Rain suits are provided, but it's a good idea to bring a change of clothes.

In addition to the excitement of white water, overnight trips usually include camping under the stars, swimming, fishing, bonfires and salmon barbecues.

It is also possible to raft rivers in the Squamish and Whistler areas—within a one- to two-hour drive from the city. Although these rivers do not have the white water found in the interior rivers, these are fun trips. In winter one of these trips can be combined with eagle watching in the Squamish region.

There are many companies offering rafting trips.

Hyak Wilderness Adventures
734-8622
Offers paddling trips of one, two and six days on the Thompson, Chilliwack or Chilko rivers. This company picks up from hotels and transports you to the rafting destinations.

Canadian River Expeditions
1-604-938-6651
Specializes in scenic float trips with no white water.

Rivers & Oceans
1-800-360-7238
Float trips on the lower Squamish and Cheakamus and whitewater rafting on the Elaho–Squamish, Chilko, Chilcotin and Fraser. (A float on the Cheakamus can be combined with eagle watching in Dec or Jan.)

Sailing

Cruise and Learn

If you don't sail but would like to, you can learn while visiting Vancouver. Several sailing schools offer a cruise-and-learn vacation, a five-day trip around the Gulf Islands on boats that are 9 to 12 m (30 to 40 feet) long. For

Setting sail off Jericho Beach into the waters of English Bay. (Rosamond Norbury)

about $750 you get sailing instruction, food and a berth. Trips run regularly from May to Oct with four students and an instructor. An advanced version is also offered. Considering the amount you could spend on hotels, restaurants and entertainment, this course offers a unique combination of sun, salt water, new territory and new skills. The bonus is finishing with a Canadian Yachting Association certificate.

Cooper Boating Centre
1620 Duranleau, Granville Island
687-4110

Sea Wing Sailing School and Yacht Charters
1818 Maritime Mews, Granville Island
669-0840

Day Cruises

During the summer, Cooper Boating Centre (see above) has three-hour cruises in English Bay on 6 to 12 m (20- to 40-foot) yachts. They leave from Granville Island; cost is $25 a person with a minimum of four people.

Charters

If you are an experienced sailor you can rent a sailboat for an evening, half-day, day or longer. Blue Pacific (below), Sea Wing or Cooper will arrange charters, with or without a skipper.

Please note that in False Creek sails are prohibited and the maximum speed is five knots.

Blue Pacific Yacht Charters
1519 Foreshore Walk, Granville Island
682-2161

Scuba Diving

Divers in British Columbia encounter an incredible range of marine life: sea stars, anemones, coral, seals, sea lions, killer whales, the largest octopus species in the world, wolf eels, crabs, abalone, snails, prawns, 180 varieties of sponges and over 325 kinds of fish.

Around Vancouver most scuba diving is done in Howe Sound and Indian Arm. Both are steep-sided inlets formed by glacial activity. Indian Arm is at the east end of Burrard Inlet, and Howe Sound is the Horseshoe Bay region and beyond.

No diving is allowed in Vancouver Harbour between Lions Gate Bridge and Second Narrows Bridge. To dive in the outer harbour, advise the Vancouver Port Corporation at 666-2405.

If you plan to dive a lot in British Columbia, buy the book *141 Dives in the Protected Waters of Washington and British Columbia* at one of the major dive shops (see Rentals at the end of this section).

Where to Dive

If you wish to dive with your own group, following are some suggestions for day trips. Because of the rugged, vertical shores, access is a problem. All the spots listed here have shore access and are rated for beginners as well as advanced divers, except where indicated.

Whytecliff Park

This West Vancouver park has the province's only "Marine Protected Area." In fact it's the only one in Canada. You may get lucky and spot a resident octopus. The best visibility is from Oct to Apr.

Follow signs to the park from Horseshoe Bay.

Lighthouse Park

This West Vancouver park is about 9.7 km (6 miles) past Park Royal Shopping Centre, and the entrance is off Marine Dr. A half-hour walk takes you from the parking lot to the shore. Lighthouse Park has been described as the "richest" dive in Vancouver. For intermediate and advanced divers.

Porteau Cove

This popular spot is a good place to meet other divers around a beach fire

Scuba diving is a year-round activity. (Gary Mallander)

at the end of the day. On Hwy 99, 24 km (15 miles) past Horseshoe Bay, you will see an arched sign over the road saying Porteau Camp. About 1.6 km (1 mile) ahead is parking and beach access. Porteau Cove is a provincial marine park and has an artificial reef made from old ships' hulls, a wreck of a minesweeper, a campground, showers and a boat launch.

Cates Park

This park is at the mouth of Indian Arm. Access is via the Dollarton Highway, 5 km (3 miles) past the Second Narrows Bridge, very close to the city. Telephone the Vancouver Port Corporation (666-2405) if you intend to dive here. Park near the dock west of Roche Point and dive about 180 m (200 yards) to a rocky reef. For intermediate and advanced divers.

Gulf Islands

If you are willing to travel farther, diving in the Gulf Islands is spectacular.

Try Beaver Point on Saltspring. Take the ferry from Tsawwassen to Long Harbour on Saltspring. Follow the signs to Fulford Harbour. Just before the town, take Beaver Point Rd for 9.7 km (6 miles) to Ruckle Park. Park at the end of the road and walk 800 m (875 yards) to the shore. Dive in the bay if you are a beginner or at the point if you are experienced.

Rentals

These stores all rent equipment by the day, and some even rent personal gear such as fins and masks to divers from out of town.

You will need a 6 mm (¼-inch) neoprene wet suit in B.C. waters. The dive shops frequently organize trips for the day, the weekend or longer, as well as night dives. Occasionally, boat charters are available. For visitors, the stores will arrange whatever is necessary—air, transportation or diving partners. Most trips are geared to beginners and intermediate divers. Proof of diving certification and tank inspection is necessary to obtain air.

Diver's World
1817 W 4th at Burrard
732-1344

Diving Locker
2745 W 4th near Macdonald
736-2681

Adrenalin Sports
1630 W 5th at Fir
734-3483

Skating

You can skate outdoors on the lower level of **Robson Square** from Nov until early Mar; bring your own skates.

The rink at the **West End Community Centre** (Denman and Nelson) is open Oct through Mar, evenings and weekends, and rents skates. Phone 257-8333.

At **Britannia Community Centre** (Napier off Commercial), the rink stays open all year and will also rent skates. Phone 253-4391 for public skating times.

Skiing

You name it, Vancouver's got it! There's handy, effortless skiing at Grouse, Seymour and Cypress, about a half-hour drive from downtown, and world-class skiing in the Whistler-Blackcomb area, a couple of hours away. Take your pick.

Downhill

Whistler

Vertical drop: 1530 m (5020 feet)
Base elevation: 652 m (2140 feet)
Lifts: 4 quad expresses, 3 triple and 1 double chairlifts, 2 T-bars, 1 gondola. Capacity 23,000 people an hour
Runs: over 100; longest 11 km (7 miles)
Terrain: 25% novice, 55% intermediate, 20% expert
Average snowfall: 907 cm (357 inches)
Snow reports: Vancouver 687-6761, Whistler 932-4191
Facilities: A whole village supplies anything a skier could want: instruction, helicopter skiing, cross-country (rentals, instruction, unlimited terrain), paragliding, snowmobiling and two mountain-top restaurants. Recently a half-pipe and "terrain garden" were added for snowboarders. Dual-lift tickets may be purchased for access to both Whistler and Blackcomb lifts.

Book accommodation through the Whistler Resort Association (Vancouver 664-5625, Whistler 932-4222 or toll free from the U.S. or Canada 1-800-944-7853).
Getting there: Whistler is 120 km

(75 miles) north of Vancouver on Hwy 99, a spectacular but sometimes hazardous road—keep your wits about you. Chains are often mandatory.

There is daily train and bus service to Whistler from Vancouver. (Whistler/Blackcomb bus 662-8051)

Comments: Whistler, along with neighbouring Blackcomb (following), can only be described in superlatives: the largest ski area in North America, the longest ski season in western Canada, and so on. Not just the best skiing in this area, Whistler resort has been voted the number one ski destination in North America by several top ski magazines. The season runs from late Nov to April.

See also Excursions from Vancouver (Whistler).

Blackcomb

Vertical drop: 1609 m (5280 feet)
Base elevation: 675 m (2215 feet)
Lifts: 6 quad expresses, 3 triple chairlifts, 2 T-bars, 1 handle tow, 1 platter, 1 gondola. Capacity 27,000 people an hour.
Runs: 100 plus; longest 11 km (7 miles)
Terrain: 20% novice, 55% intermediate, 25% expert

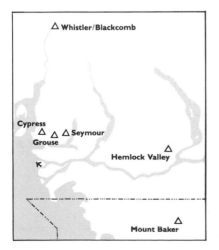

Average snowfall: 838 cm (330 inches)
Snow reports: Vancouver 687-7507, Whistler 932-4211
Facilities: Instruction, rental and repairs, three restaurants, plus all the facilities in neighbouring Whistler Village. A favourite with snowboarders, with two half-pipes and a snowboard park.

Dual-lift tickets available for access to both Blackcomb and Whistler. Unlimited cross-country.
Getting there: Same as Whistler.
Comments: The highest lift-serviced vertical drop in North America and the largest summer glacier-skiing operation.

No other resort on the continent offers skiing on two superb mountains beside each other, and most skiers are hard-pressed to say which mountain they prefer; both have thousands of enthusiastic fans. Winter season and hours are the same as Whistler. Blackcomb also offers summer skiing, 12–3:30 daily, on the Horstman Glacier, serviced by a T-bar.

See also Excursions from Vancouver (Whistler).

Grouse Mountain

Vertical drop: 365 m (1200 feet)
Base elevation: 885 m (2900 feet)
Lifts: 2 aerial trams to ski area, 4 double chairs, 1 T-bar, 2 rope tows
Runs: 13; longest 2.4 km (1.5 miles)
Terrain: 30% novice, 50% intermediate, 20% expert
Average snowfall: 488 cm (192 inches) with snow-making equipment
Snow reports: Vancouver 986-6262
Facilities: Rentals, instruction, cafeteria, dining room, night skiing until 11, ski check.
Getting there: Grouse is 12 km (7.5 miles) north of Vancouver, a 20-minute drive from downtown via Lions Gate Bridge and Capilano Rd.

Public transit goes to Grouse from

Grouse Mountain

Grouse Mountain offers skiing half an hour away from downtown Vancouver.

downtown. On Georgia catch the #246 Highland bus westbound, and at Edgemont and Ridgewood transfer to the #232 Grouse.

Comments: Grouse is most often used by people who want to learn to ski after work, and there are many ski school programs.

The brilliant chain of lights to the north of the city that can be seen year-round is the arc lighting on the ski runs. It's worth a trip up the mountain to ski—day or night—since the view from the Cut is spectacular.

Mount Seymour Provincial Park

Vertical drop: 365 m (1200 feet)
Base elevation: 1010 m (3314 feet)
Lifts: 4 double chairlifts, 1 double rope tow
Runs: 25; longest 2.4 km (1.5 miles)
Terrain: 40% novice, 40% intermediate, 20% expert
Average snowfall: 255–305 cm (100–120 inches)
Snow reports: Vancouver 879-3999
Facilities: Instruction, rentals, day lodge, cafeteria, night skiing until 10,

snowshoe and cross-country rentals and instruction. No accommodation in park.

Getting there: Mount Seymour is 16 km (10 miles) north of Vancouver. Take the right-hand turnoff after Second Narrows Bridge and follow the signs. Accessible by car only.

Comments: A family and learn-to-ski area. Beginner's cross-country trails are marked but not groomed.

Cypress Bowl

Vertical drop: 533 m (1750 feet)
Base elevation: 980 m (3215 feet)
Lifts: 4 double chairlifts, 2 rope tows; capacity 3600 people an hour
Runs: 25; longest 3.2 km (2 miles)
Terrain: 20% novice, 40% intermediate, 40% expert
Average snowfall: 355 cm (140 inches)
Snow reports: Vancouver 926-6007
Facilities: Day lodge, cafeteria, 26 km (16 miles) of cross-country trails, rentals, instruction, lounge. No accommodation.

Getting there: Cypress is a 30-minute drive from downtown Vancouver,

16 km (10 miles) away. Go over the Lions Gate Bridge and take the Upper Levels Hwy west.
Comments: The snow may be wet and heavy.

Hemlock Valley

Vertical drop: 348 m (1142 feet)
Base elevation: 1006 m (3300 feet)
Lifts: 1 triple and 2 double chairlifts, 1 tow; capacity 4200 people an hour
Runs: 19; longest 1.6 km (1 mile)
Terrain: 30% novice, 45% intermediate; 25% expert
Average snowfall: 500 cm (197 inches)
Snow reports: Vancouver 1-604-918 0002
Facilities: Rentals, instruction, day lodge with cafeteria, restaurant, night skiing on Sat, accommodation at Hemlock Resort (1-604-797-4444) near lifts, 30 km (19 miles) of cross-country.
Getting there: Hemlock is 125 km (78 miles) east of Vancouver, 27 km (17 miles) off Hwy 7 near Harrison Hot Springs. Take chains.
For bus information call Hemlock Resort.
Comments: Not a huge mountain but has good dry powder. Season is from mid-Dec to mid-Apr.

Mount Baker (In the U.S.A.)

Vertical drop: 457 m (1500 feet)
Base elevation: 1310 m (4300 feet)
Lifts: 2 fixed quads, 6 double chairlifts, 2 rope tows; capacity 8000 people an hour
Runs: 48; longest 3.2 km (2 miles)
Terrain: 30% novice, 42% intermediate; 28% expert
Average snowfall: 1905 cm (750 inches)
Snow reports: Vancouver 688-1595
Facilities: Instruction, rentals, cafeteria, daycare. No accommodation on mountain.
Getting there: Mount Baker is 120 km (75 miles) south of Vancouver, a two-hour drive. Take Hwy 99 south to Hwy 542; then go east. Or take Hwy 1 east to the Sumas exit; then go south. Take chains. Car access only.
Comments: Although Mount Baker is in the United States, it is a popular destination for skiers from Vancouver.

Of the mountains close to Vancouver, Baker receives the heaviest snowfall. The season is long, usually until mid-May. Baker is popular with snowboarders and has a half-pipe. Baker is run by the U.S. Forest Service and is not a resort, so amenities are few. Accommodation is limited; book well in advance or go for the day. Sometimes closed midweek; phone for dates.

Cross-Country

There are some cross-country ski areas within reach of Vancouver in the Lower Mainland. Cypress, Whistler and Manning are well groomed and well marked and provide the best skiing.

The season for cross-country skiing generally runs from the beginning of Dec until the end of Mar.

Cypress Bowl
The closest to Vancouver, Cypress's Hollyburn Ridge on the North Shore has 16 km (10 miles) of groomed and track-set trails, of which 5 km (3 miles) are lit for evening skiing. Hot food is available at Hollyburn Lodge. There are lessons in classical and skate skiing. For information: 922-0825. Cypress is busy on weekends because it is so close to the city. For a snow report, call Vancouver 925-2704.

Whistler
There are two cross-country areas adjacent to Whistler Village. The best is

the Lost Lake network, 22 km (13½ miles) of set trails. A day pass lets you take advantage of warming huts, trail maps and meticulously groomed trails. A 4 km (2½-mile) section is lit for night skiing. A free and more informal cross-country area is the golf course, which occasionally has about 6 km (3¾ miles) of set trails. These areas would appeal to beginners or those interested in a workout rather than a wilderness experience.

For back-country skiing try Cheakamus Lake Trail (a flat logging road not far from Whistler Village), the 14 km (8¾-mile) Singing Pass Trail, and Callaghan/Madeley Lake. For information or a cross-country snow report, call 932-6436 (seasonal).

Manning Park

The best cross-country area in the Lower Mainland is at Manning, where conditions compare favourably to those in Scandinavia. Back-country terrain trails total 190 km (118 miles), and 30 km (18½ miles) of trails are groomed for track and skating technique. There's a full range of lessons available. The inland location means drier snow and plenty of sunshine. For snow information, call 689-7669 in Vancouver; after hours call 1-604-869-2911.

The park is a three-hour drive east of Vancouver, via the Trans-Canada Hwy to Hope, then Hwy 3 to Manning Park. Accommodation is available in cabins, in chalets and at Manning Park Lodge, which has a café, dining room and pub. Phone 840-8822 for accommodation.

Rentals

Carleton Cycle and Outdoor Recreation
3201 Kingsway near Rupert
438-6371
Cross-country only. Closed Sun.

Destination Ski Rentals
1550 Marine near McGowan, North Van
984-4394
Downhill and cross-country.

Sigge's Sport Villa
2077 W 4th at Arbutus
731-8818
Cross-country only.

Grouse Mountain Ski Shop
6400 Nancy Greene Way, North Van
984-0661
Downhill only. Open days and evenings.

Hollyburn Ski Lodge
Hollyburn Ridge, North Van
922-0825
Cross-country only.

Mount Seymour Ski Shop
1700 Mt Seymour Rd, North Van
986-2261
Downhill only.

Secondhand Equipment

Cheapskates
3644 W 16th near Dunbar
222-1125
Cheapskates has five locations, all within a few blocks of each other and each carrying gear for particular sports. Apart from the things you would expect, like secondhand bikes and skis, you'll also come across Gore-Tex jackets, picnic coolers, goalie pads and rowing machines—all at less than half of the price that you'd pay for new equipment.

Sports Junkies Consignors
600 W 6th near Cambie
879-0666
This store takes in and sells secondhand sporting goods, clothing and equipment for all sports except hunting.

Recreation Rentals
2560 Arbutus at Broadway
733-7368
Downhill and cross-country.

The Board Room
1911 Pine at 4th
734-7669
Snowboards only.

Swimming

At the Beach

The city has 11 sandy beaches good for swimming. The water temperature is refreshing, peaking at 21°C (70°F) in the summer. The following beaches have lifeguards on duty from the Victoria Day weekend through Labour Day:

Second Beach in Stanley Park
English Bay
Sunset Beach
Kits Beach
Jericho Beach
Locarno Beach
Spanish Banks

Outdoor Saltwater Pools

Vancouver has two outdoor saltwater pools overlooking English Bay: at Kits Beach and in Stanley Park at Second Beach.

Kitsilano Pool
Kitsilano Beach
731-0011
The Kits Pool is gargantuan, modern and heated to 26°C (79°F). Both small children and serious swimmers use this pool because its depth is graduated and because it is so large. Open from Victoria Day (May 24) to Labour Day, Mon to Fri, 7 AM–8:45 PM (7–9 AM adult swim); Sat and Sun, 10–8:45.

Adults $3.55, with discounts for seniors and children.

Second Beach Pool
Second Beach, Stanley Park
Located beside the seawall, this freshwater pool was upgraded and reopened in the summer of 1995. It's plenty large for a good workout, and there are three lanes designated for swimming laps. With a beach next door, this pool has always been a favourite with youngsters, and now there are three small waterslides. There is a lifeguard on duty, and there are children's lessons and aqua-fit classes for adults during July. Open May-Sept; hours 10–8:45; some mornings there are early bird swims. Cost is $3.55 for adults, with discounts for seniors and children. Call 257-8371.

Other Outdoor Pools

Kerrisdale Centre
5851 West Blvd at 42nd
257-8105

Mount Pleasant Centre
3161 Ontario at 16th
874-8165

New Brighton
North foot of Windermere
298-0222

Oak Park
990 W 59th at Oak
321-2818

Sunset Centre
404 E 51st off Main
321-1616

Major Indoor Pools

The two best indoor swimming facilities are the Vancouver Aquatic Centre in the West End and the University of British Columbia (UBC) Aquatic Centre. Both are Olympic-size pools with diving tanks, saunas, whirlpools and exercise gyms. Both facilities are open late in the evening.

There are also two smaller indoor pools downtown operated by the YMCA and the YWCA.

UBC Aquatic Centre
University of British Columbia
822-4521
During the school year, there is public swimming on evenings and weekends. The pool is also open to the public during the day in June, July and Aug. Phone to check times.

Vancouver Aquatic Centre
1050 Beach, south end of Thurlow
665-3424
On the shore of English Bay. Closed annually for maintenance the last two weeks of Aug and the first week of Sept. Public swim times vary, so phone ahead.

YMCA
955 Burrard at Barclay
681-0221
Open to men and women at co-ed swim times; there are some men-only swim times. Out-of-town YMCA memberships are honoured. Day passes for nonmembers are available and allow full use of all facilities, including the pool, sauna, massage, drop-in fitness classes, weight room and racquetball, handball and squash courts.

YWCA
535 Hornby near Dunsmuir
895-5800
Open to men and women. Out-of-town memberships honoured, or you can purchase a day pass for access to the pool, sauna, whirlpool or weight room or any of the exercise or dance-fit classes.

Tennis

Vancouver is Tennis Town. The outdoor season runs from Mar to Oct, with the odd lucky day in the winter. Even 180 public courts are not enough, and you will probably have to wait on summer weekends.

Outdoor Courts

With one exception, all public courts are outdoors, are free and operate on a first come, first served basis. You'll find the most courts at:

Stanley Park
Twenty-one courts (17 by the Beach Ave entrance, and 4 by Lost Lagoon at the foot of Robson). From Apr to Sept, 9 of the 17 courts at the Beach Ave location can be reserved for a small fee. Call 488-0767.

Andy Livingston Park
Pacific and Carrall
The newest addition is two courts at this recreational park close to the centre of the city.

Queen Elizabeth Park
33rd at Cambie
Twenty courts.

Kitsilano Beach Park
Ten courts.

Jericho Beach Park
Five courts behind Jericho Sailing Centre.

Other public courts in pleasant surroundings are:

False Creek Community Centre
Granville Island
Three courts.

False Creek (residential area)
North of 2nd, foot of Heather
Five courts with a view from the top of a parkade.

Dunbar Community Centre
4747 Dunbar at 33rd
Six courts.

Rupert Park
Rupert at 1st Ave
Four courts.

Almond Park
12th at Dunbar
Two courts.

Elm Park
41st at Larch
Two courts.

Tatlow Park
2nd at Macdonald
Three courts.

Night Tennis

The only lit public courts are on the Langara Campus of Vancouver Community College, on 49th between Cambie and Main.

Indoor Courts

Most indoor courts are at private clubs, but here are a couple where you can play on a rainy day.

University of B.C. Tennis Club
6184 Thunderbird Blvd at East Mall
822-2505
Four indoor courts (should book ahead) and 10 outdoors. Pay as you play.

Delta Pacific Resort & Conference Centre
10251 St Edwards off Bridgeport, Richmond
276-1140
Book same day for indoor courts.

Rentals

Recreation Rentals
2560 Arbutus at Broadway
733-7368

Windsurfing

Windsurfing schools operate at various beaches in town and will supply everything you need: instruction, board, wet suit and life jacket. The introductory rental/instruction packages vary from one to six hours, depending on the school. If you know anything about surfing or sailing, you are one step ahead; if not, the uninitiated can become competent after a few hours.

No sailboards are allowed at the mouth of False Creek between the Granville and Burrard St Bridges.

Windmaster
Denman and Pacific
(English Bay Beach House)
685-7245
Three levels of windsurfing instruction (including beginner courses) are offered in English Bay.

Windsure Windsurfing School
1300 Discovery
224-0615
Lessons and rentals at Jericho Beach.

Shopping

Shopping Areas 176
Robson Street, Granville Island, West 4th Avenue, Yaletown, West Broadway, Chinatown, South Granville, Kerrisdale, Gastown, West 10th Avenue, Shopping Centres

Accessories and Extras 178

Art Supplies 178

Auctions/Antiques/Oriental Rugs 178

Books and Magazines 179

Books (Used) 182

Clothing 182
For Men and Women, For Women, Maternity Wear, For Men, Vintage and Consignment

Home Furnishings 184

Kitchenware 186

Outdoors Equipment 186

Photo Supplies/Film Processing 187

Recorded Music 187

Shoes (Men's and Women's) 188

Souvenirs 188

Specialty Food Stores 189
Bakeries, Cheese, Coffee and Tea, Delis and Gourmet Take-Out, Ethnic Foods, Fish/Shellfish, Ice Cream

The public market and waterfront restaurants of Granville Island. (Bob Herger, Photo/Graphics)

Shopping Areas

Robson Street

Robson is always bustling. The street is exactly what pedestrians relate to: sidewalk cafés, trees and small stores all wedged together. The sidewalk restaurants entice you to have a cappuccino in the sun and watch the crowds.

Granville Island

Don't miss Granville Island for the dockside outdoor restaurants, the Granville Island ferry, the Net Loft, the Kids Only Market and, most of all, the public market. It's a real success story for Vancouver. If you detest crowds, don't go near the place on weekends.

See Sightseeing for more details.

West 4th Avenue

The W 4th Ave storefronts stretch from Burrard to Alma and offer a mix of shops for personal and home needs. There's a variety of record, book and clothing stores, and for your home, there are shops selling glass, kitchenware, linens and everything for the bathroom. You can eat sushi or Thai noodles, or drink espresso.

Because Kitsilano is very much a young, with-it neighbourhood, there are lots of sporting goods stores to outfit you with the perfect hiking boots, the fitness solution to your life, swim goggles, the latest Japanese bicycle or the gaudiest pair of jams.

Yaletown

Once a rowdy warehouse region—it boasted more saloons per hectare than anywhere else in the world during the late 1800s!—now Yaletown is hip. Architects and designers occupy loft apartments, brick heritage buildings house classy furniture shops, brightly coloured awnings pretty up storefronts, and doctors and lawyers reside in posh high-rises. Fashion and furniture are found here, as well as some galleries. When you tire of shopping, *the* place to plop is the Yaletown Brewing Co on Mainland. A super selection of micro-brewery suds, pizza and pasta, billiards and a large outdoor patio. The business crowd frequents Yaletown, so it can be busy.

West Broadway

From Trafalgar to Waterloo, W Broadway is a thriving neighbourhood shopping area, once the heart of the Greek community. There's not too much of it left now, but you will see Greek restaurants and food stores. One of the city's best men's wear stores, Mark James, is in this area.

Chinatown

Pender St for two blocks east and west of Main is the centre of Chinatown, the second largest in North America. Keefer, east of Main, is lively as well. Don't miss *dim sum*—see Restaurants (Chinese). Also see Sightseeing (The Sights) under Chinatown.

South Granville

The shopping area on south Granville St stretches from W 7th to 16th Ave, offering lots of Persian carpets, antiques, clothing and food stores and a good number of excellent galleries. South Granville used to be an enclave of older and wealthier residents but has become much trendier, as you can tell from some of the dramatic storefronts.

Kerrisdale

Shop in Kerrisdale on W 41st from Maple to Balsam, where you'll run into well-heeled matrons in pearls. The area can be exclusive and expensive but has stores worth going out of your way for, such as Hager Books, Forster's Cheeses and Windmill Toys.

Good bakeries and florists and a camera store.

Gastown

Gastown, the oldest part of Vancouver, has been quite touristy for the last 20 years, but on weekdays around lunch hour it is also abuzz with members of the local design community, who have their offices there. Water St from Richards to Main is the heart of Gastown, and most stores are open Sundays in the warmer months.

West 10th Avenue

This shopping area on W 10th at Trimble is near the University of British Columbia campus and has some first-rate stores: several women's clothing stores, Duthie Books, furniture and lots to eat.

Shopping Centres

Two shopping centres a bit different from most are **Oakridge** (at Cambie and 41st) and **Park Royal** (on the North Shore just west of Lions Gate Bridge). The completely renovated Oakridge has primarily up-scale shops, such as Bally Shoes and Birks Jewellers. Park Royal, North and South, has two department stores, Eaton's and the Bay. Both malls also have independent stores that are more exclusive than those in the average shopping centre.

Pacific Centre and **Vancouver Centre** are two downtown underground malls that join Eaton's and the Bay at Granville and Georgia. Pretty well everything you need is in this mall, including a Holt Renfrew.

Metrotown, in Burnaby, actually comprises three major centres complete with 12 movie theatres, a Holiday Inn, and many restaurants and megastores, making it the largest mall in B.C. Eatons, Sears, the Bay and Future Shop are a few of the many stores. It is conveniently reached by the SkyTrain.

Accessories and Extras

Beadworks
1666 Johnston, Granville Island
682-2323
One of the most unusual stores in the city. Hundreds of varieties of beads (bone, wood, ceramic, amber, silver, glass, etc.) with all the fasteners, wire, thread and helpful information you need to make any piece of jewellery. There's even a craft table; you can borrow tools and set to work on your own creation. The store has lots of finished pieces around for inspiration.

Gulliver's Travel Accessory Store
Arbutus Shopping Centre
4255 Arbutus near King Edward
733-0111
If you have a secret passion for poking around hardware or stationery stores, you'll love Gulliver's. There are hundreds of quirky little gadgets, all to make the life of a weary traveller a touch easier. Also in Park Royal North, Richmond and Langley.

Martha Sturdy
3039 Granville near 14th
737-0037
775 Burrard near Robson
685-7751
Bold and dramatic jewellery, all designed by Martha Sturdy.

La Jolie Madame Lingerie
Pacific Centre, upper level
669-1831
Very feminine and pretty underclothes, lots of French lace and silk.

Satchel Shop
Pacific Centre, lower level
669-2923
1024 Robson at Burrard

662-3424
Superlative bags, small leather goods and luggage.

Zig Zag
4424 W 10th
224-2421
This sassy store sells pop fashion accessories.

Art Supplies

Behnsen Graphic Supplies
1016 Richards at Nelson
681-7351
Large, modern graphic supply store with the largest selection in the city.

Maxwell's Artists Materials
206 Cambie at Water
683-8607
The largest art supply store in town. Particularly good range of papers and how-to art books, as well as graphic supplies. In the SeaBus terminal.

Opus Framing/Artist Resource Centre
1360 Johnston, Granville Island
736-7028
Painting, drawing and print-making supplies—everything for the artist who works on paper, canvas or linen.

Auctions/Antiques/ Oriental Rugs

Main from 20th to 35th Ave has many antique stores, generally with furniture from Britain. Near the corner of 10th and Alma are a few stores specializing in Canadiana. For Oriental rugs, go along Granville from 7th to 14th Ave.

Maynard's Auctioneers
415 W 2nd at Cambie
876-6787
Home furnishings auctions on Wed at 7 PM. Phone for times of the art and

antique auctions that are held periodically.

Love's Auctioneers
1635 W Broadway near Fir
733-1157
Auctions are held on Wed at noon and 7 PM.

Three Centuries Shop
321 Water, Gastown
685-8808
Precious and rare antiques from the 18th, 19th and 20th centuries.

Folkart Interiors
3715 W 10th near Alma
228-1011
Specializes in folk art and Canadiana furnishings as well as locally made reproductions.

Old Country Mouse Factory
3720 W 10th near Alma
224-8664
Refinished European pine antiques and reproductions.

Canada West
3607 W Broadway near Alma
733-3212
Specializes in antique pine furniture.

Peter Tolliday Oriental Carpets
2312 Granville at 8th
733-4811
The leading dealer in Oriental carpets, particularly old and antique carpets.

Persian Arts and Crafts
692 Seymour near Georgia
681-4639
The name is misleading, since the selection goes far beyond arts and crafts; the store has items like hand-carved tables and impressive 100 per cent silk Persian rugs. The one-of-a-kind rugs are labelled with the maker's wax identity seal, a sign of quality.

Books and Magazines

Banyen Books
2671 W Broadway near Macdonald
732-7912
Alternative lifestyles, eastern religion, yoga, recovery, nutrition, gardening—you name it. A good place to browse and buy.

Blackberry Books
1663 Duranleau, Granville Island
685-4113
This Granville Island store is packed on weekends, partly an overflow of the hordes at the public market but also because it's a darn good bookstore.

Bollum's Books
650 W Georgia at Granville
689-1802
This new kid on the book block is pretty impressive, containing more than 250,000 books shelved in the lovely old Birks Jewellery building. Plan a long stay. Classical music or jazz provides a soothing background, there are comfy chairs and handy stools for sitting, and books are everywhere. You can check the top 10 bestseller lists for London, New York and Hong Kong as well as for Canada. Bollum's is possibly the best place in town for computer and business books. You may wander into a reading or a signing in the Last Word Café. Fri evening and Sat afternoon there's live music in this small, deli-style café downstairs. Open till 10 Sun to Thurs and midnight Fri and Sat.

Book Warehouse
632 W Broadway near Heather
872-5711
1150 Robson near Thurlow
685-5711
2388 W 4th near Balsam
733-5721
Discounted best sellers and a huge selection of bargain books. Hours vary,

but the stores are open until 9 or 10 nightly.

Chapters
4700 Kingsway
Metrotown
431-0463
Created by the merger of SmithBooks and Coles Book Stores, the Canadian-owned Chapters opened in this Burnaby location in late 1995. This mega-bookstore stocks around 100,000 titles, as well as an extensive selection of magazines, CD-ROMs and other multimedia products. Visitors can enjoy readings, cooking and craft demonstrations, and autographing sessions and then pop into the in-store Starbucks for a java break.

Chief's Mask
73 Water near Abbott
687-4100
Books by or about North American Native peoples.

The Comicshop
2089 W 4th near Arbutus
738-8122
New and used comics and sci-fi, probably the best this side of Toronto.

Duthie Books
919 Robson at Hornby
684-4496
345 Robson near Hamilton
602-0610
2239 W 4th near Vine
732-5344
4444 W 10th near Trimble
224-7012
Arbutus Shopping Centre
4255 Arbutus near King Edward
738-1833
The Duthie's stores on Robson and W 4th have an excellent selection and helpful staff. The W 10th branch is more academic. The newest one is at Library Square. All are open Mon to Sat, 9–9. The stores on Robson and W 10th are open Sun, 12–5; the store on W 4th is open Sun, 10–5.

Granville Book Company
850 Granville near Robson
687-2213
Lots of traffic means things are often in disarray, but this store does have books that other stores don't. Excellent computer and sci-fi selection. Good place to kill time waiting for a movie to start. Open until midnight every night except Fri and Sat, when it's open until 1 AM.

Hager Books
2176 W 41st near Yew
263-9412
One of the best neighbourhood bookstores around.

Manhattan Books and Magazines
1089 Robson near Thurlow
681-9074
Excellent choice of discount books as well as imported and domestic magazines. One of the few places to get the *Village Voice*. Large selection of books and magazines in French. Open seven days a week.

Mayfair News
1535 W Broadway off Granville
738-8951
If you're looking for out-of-town newspapers, this is the place. Also an

The Comicshop caters to kids, collectors and nostalgia-seekers. (Rosamond Norbury)

excellent magazine selection. Open until 10:30 every evening.

Mystery Merchant
1952 W 4th near Cypress
739-4311
A bit of Olde England, with dark wood shelves and a sliding ladder. What would be too precious under other circumstances works perfectly in a mystery bookstore—it makes you want to hang around on a rainy afternoon. Both new and used books.

Pink Peppercorn
2686 W Broadway near Stephens
736-4213
Cookbooks galore! Also cooking videos.

Sportsbook Plus
2100 W 4th at Arbutus
733-7323
Books, magazines and videos on every kind of sport.

Travel Bug
2667 W Broadway near Trafalgar
737-1122
Dwight and the crew at the Travel Bug add to the thrill of an upcoming trip with their enthusiasm and helpful tips. Travel accessories and maps round out the excellent selection of books.

University Bookstore
6200 University Blvd
University of British Columbia
822-2665
One of the largest bookstores in Canada, this is more like a department store—the space is shared with jogging gear and notebooks. Textbooks and trade books.

Vancouver Art Gallery Giftshop
750 Hornby at Robson
682-2765
Best spot for art books and magazines. Also cards, prints and design-oriented gifts.

Wanderlust
1929 W 4th near Burrard
739-2182
Kitsilano has been blessed with two superb travel bookstores. If you're nutty about travel books, walking into Wanderlust will give you that died-and-gone-to-heaven kind of feeling.

White Dwarf Books/Dead Write
4374 W 10th near Trimble
228-8223
Sci-fi and fantasy on one side, mystery on the other.

Wilkinson's Automobilia
2531 Ontario off W Broadway
873-6242
Wilkinson's sells automotive and motorcycle books, shop manuals and other collectible items.

William McCarley's
213 Carrall at Water
683-5003
Books on architecture, design and graphic arts.

Women in Print
3566 W 4th near Dunbar
732-4128
Fiction and nonfiction for and about women. Excellent selection on women's health issues. Open daily.

World Wide Books and Maps
736 Granville near Georgia, basement
687-3320
Maps and travel books, as well as government publications. The place to go if you need a topographical map for hiking anywhere in B.C.

See also Vancouver Kidsbooks in With the Kids (Shopping).

Books (Used)

If you like touring secondhand bookstores, pick up a brochure called "Guide to the Secondhand & Antiquarian Bookstores of Greater Vancouver." It's available in secondhand bookstores.

Antiquarius
341 W Pender near Homer
669-7288
Vintage magazines, posters, photos, sheet music, books and a collection of other fascinating odds and ends.

Ashley's Books
3754 W 10th at Alma
228-1180
Particularly good for art and fiction.

Lawrence Books
3591 W 41st at Dunbar
261-3812
May be the best used-book store in town; worth going out of your way for. Specialties include Canadiana, children's books and military history.

MacLeod's Books
455 W Pender at Richards
681-7654
Very good general stock with specialties including western Canadiana, literature and antiquarian books.

Clothing

For Men and Women

A•Wear
350 Howe at Hastings (street level)
685-9327
A branch of the up-scale Leone's that carries only Canadian-designed A•Wear. There's a large selection of both men's and women's casual, sports, business and evening attire, all moderately priced.

Boboli
2776 Granville near 12th
736-3458
Hard to believe that clothes can be *this* expensive. Smashing storefront.

Club Monaco
1153 Robson near Thurlow
687-8618
The preppy look of these clothes can be enticing simply because they are so well made and so reasonably priced. There's half a dozen other outlets, including one in Pacific Centre.

E. A. Lee
466 Howe near Pender
683-2457
Classic and traditional; plenty of navy blazers and grey flannel. Also men's shoes and some tailored women's fashions.

Holt Renfrew
Pacific Centre
681-3121
The upper level of this elegant department store houses sportswear, shoes and exclusive classic designs. Canada's version of Saks Fifth Ave. It is also the only Canadian outlet for Vancouver designer Catherine Regehr's glitzy evening wear.

Knitwear Architects
City Square, 12th at Cambie
879-7010
A unique concept, not really a wool store, but certainly one for people who knit. The store has about 25 sweaters on display, all its own designs. First you pick a style and then you select the yarn from a sample chart, and out comes the kit, ready to go. Styles (mostly for women, a few for men and children) are more up to date than at other wool stores. Yarns are cotton, wool, silk or mohair. If you're from out of town, get on the mailing list—the store has a wonderful catalogue.

Leone
Sinclair Centre
757 W Hastings at Howe
683-1133
It's impossible to talk about the clothes without mentioning the store. Leone is the most avant-garde (in the well-designed Italian way) retail space in town. It should be—they poured $4 million into building it. Small, ultra-high-fashion boutiques for men and women.

For Women

Bacci Design
2788 Granville near 12th
733-4933
Casual European designer clothes and Italian shoes for the ultra fashionable. Very expensive.

Enda B.
4346 W 10th near Discovery
228-1214
Started out as a natural fibre/designer label store, and although there is still a large stock of *au naturale,* there is also a wealth of designer labels here. Plan hours for this spree; the store includes a children's play area and a cappuccino bar.

Laura Ashley
1171 Robson near Bute
688-8729
This British chain sells small floral print fabrics and romantic country-look fashions for you and your home.

LeslieJane
1480 Marine Dr at 14th, West Van
922-8612
This store has achieved more atmosphere than any other we know of in town. The clothes are romantic and folksy, made of natural fibres, corresponding with the friendly, neighbourhood feel of the place.

Margareta
5591 West Blvd

266-6211
1441 Bellevue, West Van
926-2113
Besides their own popular label, Margareta's has Regina Porter, Votre Nom and other favourite designers.
   Also stores in Richmond and Surrey.

Vis-À-Vis Clothing
3109 Granville at 15th
730-5603
Opened in the fall of 1995, this store features some unknown Canadian designers as well as established labels like Limbo of Vancouver and Loucas of Toronto. There's an excellent selection of everything from sports to evening wear in the middle price range.

Wear Else?
2360 W 4th near Balsam
732-3521
789 W Pender near Granville
662-7890
4401 W 10th at Trimble
221-7755
Oakridge Centre, Cambie at 41st
266-3613
Park Royal Shopping Centre, West Van
925-0058
High-calibre store for the working woman, with sportswear, office clothes, evening wear and accessories. Prices medium to high.

Maternity Wear

Hazel & Co Maternity & Kids
2209 W 4th near Yew
730-8689
Hazel & Co. maternity clothing is designed and manufactured in Vancouver. Knitwear, suits, festive—it's all here. Also children's wear, sizes 0–10.

For Men

Edward Chapman
833 W Pender near Howe
685-6207

Long-standing retail business dating back to 1890. Conservative selection of quality clothing, accessories and gifts. Specializes in British woollens.

Finn's Clothing
3031 W Broadway near Macdonald
732-3831
2159 W 41st near West Blvd
266-8358
Large selection, with emphasis on quality dresswear. The store on 41st also sells women's clothing.

Mark James
2941 W Broadway at Bayswater
734-2381
Business and fun clothes for young professional men. American and European imports at medium to high prices. Good range of accessories.

S. Lampman
2126 W 41st near West Blvd
261-2750
Preppy sportswear and dresswear.

Harry Rosen
Pacific Centre, upper level
683-6861
Oakridge Centre, Cambie at 41st
266-1172
Ivy League designer fashions: Calvin Klein, Armani and the like. Sportswear and dress-for-success clothes.

See also Clothing for Men and Women, above.

Vintage and Consignment

Ex-Toggery
6055 West Blvd near 45th
266-6744
Quality secondhand store in this upscale neighbourhood spells bargains. Not high fashion, but some good basics. Also has samples.

Second Suit for Men & Women
2036 W 4th near Arbutus
732-0338

Up-to-date used clothing, discounted samples and some new fashions for men and women. Traditional to trendy.

Turnabout
3121 Granville near 15th
732-8115
3060 W Broadway near Carnarvon
731-7762
One of the better used-clothing stores, with current fashions and higher prices.

Value Village
1820 E Hastings, near Victoria
254-4282
6415 Victoria at 39th
327-4434
Value Village is a department store full of secondhand merchandise. Some things can be quite junky, but the store is particularly good for children's clothing. Very cheap. In other locations as well.

Home Furnishings

Yaletown is one of the prime areas for interior designers and furniture stores. Check out Mainland, Homer and Hamilton Streets from Davie to Smithe.

Chintz and Company
901 Homer at Smithe
689-2022
A cornucopia of design ideas—a unique candelabrum, a batik cushion, some funky folk art—it's all here along with a vast selection of fabrics. This place is a maze of rooms—there are also dishes, glassware, tables, sofas and other furnishings. Chintz and Company specializes in complete design services.

Country Furniture
3097 Granville at 15th
738-6411
Heavy pine furniture, rocking chairs and four-poster beds with country-

look accessories. Prices are good and the quality excellent.

Form and Function
4357 W 10th near Trimble
222-1317
Contemporary furniture with a clean, uncluttered Shaker look: beds, tables, sideboards and cabinets, all made from solid wood. The store does custom design and also stocks glass tables and rattan pieces inspired by antiques.

Ikea
3200 Sweden Way, south end of Knight St Bridge, Richmond
273-2051
Ikea attempts to provide low-cost furniture by getting you to pick items out of the warehouse and assemble them at home.

The look is Scandinavian, modern and clean. The store also has a good range of household accessories: sheets, fabrics, kitchenware, kids' furniture, rugs and lamps. In Ikea's famous ball room (literally filled with soft plastic balls), your children can romp and tumble while you shop. Family refreshments in the in-store Scandinavian cafeteria.

Industrial Revolution
2306 Granville at 7th
734-4395
A great selection of designer products for the home. Noted for their storage systems, patio furniture and halogen lighting fixtures. Furniture is modern and stylish.

Inform Interiors
97 Water St at Abbott
682-3868
Whatever the latest is in ultramodern furniture design, you'll find it at Inform first, and most of it is designed by the owner. There are also home and office accessories and a good selection of imported light fixtures.

Jordans Interiors
1470 W Broadway near Granville
733-1174
This is the best store if you are looking for that "polished designer look" in fine furniture and quality workmanship. Note the finely lacquered furniture and use of nail-free joinery. Interior design services as well as furnishings and floorings. Several locations.

Livingspace
1550 Marine Dr near Bowser, North Van
987-2253
Lots of very modern Italian lighting fixtures and leather sofas.

Metropolitan Home
353 W Pender at Homer
681-2313
Specializes in '50s furniture such as turquoise-blue, kidney-shaped coffee tables and Naugahyde bar stools.

New Look Interiors
1275 W 6th near Hemlock
738-4414
Good for traditional-looking furniture, mostly teak and rosewood. Large showroom with modern sofas, carpets, lamps, console units and children's furniture at good prices.

Roche-Bobois
1010 Mainland at Nelson
669-5443
If you fantasize about glove leather and down-filled sofas, go to Roche-Bobois, one of a worldwide French chain of elegant, modern furniture stores. All the furniture is European and very expensive but of true quality.

Sofas à la Carte
909 W Broadway near Oak
731-9020
A new concept in furniture buying: the large, well-organized showroom has a dozen styles of sofas and armchairs and hundreds of large samples

of price-coded fabric. You make your choice, and in a few weeks your locally made, custom-crafted sofa is ready.

Yaletown Interiors
1004 Hamilton at Nelson
669-7544
You'll find good service and a good selection of contemporary styles from North American manufacturers.

Kitchenware

Basic Stock Cookware
2294 W 4th near Vine
736-1412
Large kitchenware store with complete selection, including major sections devoted to table-top and coffee paraphernalia.

Casa
420 Howe near Pender
681-5884
If you're looking for a brightly flowered pasta dish, this is the place. Casa specializes in Majolica dinnerware, made and hand-painted in a small town in Italy. Some patterns found here cannot be purchased anywhere else in Canada. You can pay in the $500 range for one item, but it will be unique. There's also glassware, stainless steel flatwear and linens—if you wish to grace your table with real French linen, you can find it here.

Market Kitchen
1666 Johnston, Granville Island
681-7399
Small but very well-stocked kitchenware store across from the market.

Ming Wo
23 E Pender at Carrall
683-7268
2170 W 4th near Yew
737-2624
A large old cookware store in China-

town, jammed full of much more than woks and cleavers—you'll find tortilla presses, pasta machines, soufflé dishes and more. There are many outlets, all owned by the Wong family, which began the business in 1917. This 4th Ave store has all the basic kitchen needs; the one a block east has basics as well as high-end kitchen goodies.

Tools and Techniques
250–16th near Marine, West Van
925-1835
Big, bright and well stocked, with a full range of cooking utensils, coffee beans and a demonstration kitchen.

Outdoors Equipment

Coast Mountain Sports
2201 W 4th at Yew
731-6181
Serious outdoors equipment and lots of outdoors clothes, all top of the line—the L. L. Bean of Vancouver. In general, more high end than their main competitor, Mountain Equipment Co-op. Open daily.

Mountain Equipment Co-op
130 W Broadway at Columbia
872-7858
This huge, busy and rather chaotic store sells equipment for wilderness-oriented recreation. This is a non-profit business owned and directed by its membership, meaning substantially lower prices. Membership is only $5 and is necessary if you're making a purchase. Members get beefy spring and fall catalogues. Closed Sun.

See also Sports/Recreation.

Photo Supplies/Film Processing

ABC Photocolour
1618 W 4th at Fir
736-7017
Best colour processing.

Kerrisdale Cameras
2170 W 41st near Yew
263-3221
Local chain, but the main store has the largest selection and is the most service oriented. New equipment, trade-ins and rentals, with a separate store (a couple of doors down) for darkroom supplies. Several other locations.

Lens and Shutter
2912 W Broadway at Bayswater
736-3461
Excellent sales staff in this huge store. Like most camera stores in town, it will match competitors' prices.

London Drugs
540 Granville near Dunsmuir
685-0105
1187 Robson near Bute
669-8533
The London Drugs camera department is the best for everyday low prices and sales. No darkroom supplies. One-hour photo finishing.

You can also get film processed quickly at the following locations:

CP Foto
551 Howe near Dunsmuir
681-7025

1 Hour Photo
Pacific Centre, lower level
681-2511

Recorded Music

A & B Sound
556 Seymour near Dunsmuir
687-5837

A high-volume chain with a more daring selection than others. Often has loss-leaders on the current hits. Don't miss the extensive jazz and classical sections upstairs.

Banyen Sound
2669 W Broadway near Trafalgar
737-8858
New age cassette tapes and CDs. Also talking tapes on topics such as relaxation techniques and listening copies of music.

Black Swan
3209 W Broadway near Trutch
734-2828
Specializes in jazz, blues, folk and some rock. Domestics and imports.

D & G Collectors Records
3580 E Hastings near Boundary
294-5737
Best place for vintage 45s (special orders taken). Heavy on rockabilly and country. New and used.

Highlife Records and Music
1317 Commercial near Charles
251-6964
Specializes in reggae, African, Caribbean and jazz, but you'll also find rock, folk, blues, pop and country. A discriminating though not large selection. New and used.

HMV
1160 Robson near Thurlow
685-9203
CDs and tapes cover the spectrum from alternative to blues, jazz to classical. The best selection, though, is in the pop and rock sections. Also stores in Park Royal and Metrotown.

Magic Flute Record Shop
2203 W 4th at Yew
736-2727
A well-stocked store selling classical CDs as well as jazz and world music. A friendly staff is happy to help you.

Odyssey Imports
534 Seymour near Dunsmuir
669-6644
Almost exclusively high-priced British, Japanese and European imports, especially the latest British dance music. Lots of T-shirts, books and posters.

Sikora's Classical Records
432 W Hastings near Richards
685-0625
The classical music specialists; new and used records and CDs.

Zulu Records
1869 W 4th at Burrard
738-3232
Best independent rock record store in the city. Lots of imports and used records, CDs and tapes. Owned and operated by one of the friendliest guys around.

Shoes (Men's and Women's)

Aldo
1018 Robson near Burrard
683-2443
Part of a Montreal chain; street-fashion shoes for men and women.

Dack's Shoes
1055 W Georgia, Royal Centre
687-0918
High-quality traditional men's shoes. Also in Metrotown.

Ferragamo
918 Robson at Hornby
669-4495
Very expensive and very classic men's and women's Italian shoes.

Freedman Shoes
2867 Granville near 13th
731-0448
One of the largest shoe stores in town and one of the best. Fashionable shoes in the medium price range for men and women. Good leather bags.

Ingledew's
535 Granville near Pender
687-8606
A full range of conservative, quality shoes for men and women in the medium price range. Also in Park Royal, Oakridge and Metrotown.

Pegabo
1137 Robson near Thurlow
688-7877
Pacific Centre
683-3381 (main level)
688-0266 (level two)
Trendy quality shoes for men and women, mostly from Italy.

Roots
Pacific Centre, upper level
683-5465
Shoes, bags, belts and leather jackets in the Roots no-frills style, which somehow always remains fashionable. Quality Canadian-made leather goods for men and women.

Sheppard Shoes
852 W Hastings near Granville
685-0734
Name brands of quality men's shoes.

Stephane de Raucourt
1067 Robson near Burrard
681-8814
European shoes and accessories for women, high quality and fashionable.

Walk with Ronsons
Pacific Centre, main level
682-0795
Comfort is the key to walking shoes here—Rockports, Birkenstocks, Mephisto and comfy dress shoes. Several locations.

Souvenirs

Where to find a memento of Vancouver or a present to take home that is not trashy or cheaply made? Try the museum gift shops.

Museum of Anthropology
6393 NW Marine, UBC Campus
822-3440
It is difficult to call the objects in the Museum of Anthropology gift store souvenirs. What you'll find here are exquisite crafts from Pacific Northwest Native groups and the best choice of books on the subject.

Science World
1455 Quebec, near Terminal and Main
443-7440
This gift shop for kids is full of curious toys and gadgets, mostly with a scientific bent. There are inexpensive pocket telescopes, skeletons that glow in the dark, computer books, and many other weird and wonderful gifts.

Vancouver Aquarium
Stanley Park
685-5911
The ClamShell, the gift store beside the Vancouver Aquarium, has the largest assortment of quality souvenirs. A huge selection of West Coast nature books for children and adults, lots of toys, jewellery, Indian and Eskimo art, and the best Vancouver T-shirts.

Specialty Food Stores

Bakeries

La Baguette et L'Échalote
1680 Johnston, Granville Island
684-1351
This French bakery and gourmet take-out sells baguettes, croissants, fancy cakes and more. Try the store's healthy Peasant Farmer bread—there's no yeast, fat or sugar added, and it comes in a variety of flavours, from rye to fruit. Across from the public market. Very busy on weekends. Also a location at Lonsdale Quay.

Bombay Sweets
6556 Main near 50th

321-1414
A sleek sweet shop that makes traditional Indian sweets from almonds, carrots, pistachios, coconut, and so on. The carrot halvah demands a return visit.

Bon Ton
874 Granville near Smithe
681-3058
This European-style pâtisserie and tearoom has been around since 1931 and is famed for the most decadent cakes in town. The Diplomat, for example, is multiple layers of butter cream, pastry and rum-soaked cake slathered in more butter cream and nuts.

Ecco Il Pane
See Restaurants (Bakery Cafés).

Elsie's Bakery
1555 Yew near Cornwall
731-7017
One of the best all-round neighbourhood bakeries. Handy to Kits Beach. Great care with ingredients and preparation puts Elsie's a step above. The coffee cake and bran muffins get our highest recommendation.

Keefer Chinese Bakery
251 E Georgia near Main
685-2117
Being a fan of barbecued pork buns (slightly sweet buns with barbecued pork baked inside), one day one of us bought a sample from each Chinese bakery in Chinatown and tried them all. The Keefer Bakery won. Only 80¢ for this scrumptious snack. The coconut buns and tarts are delicious as well. The three other Chinese bakeries in this same block are also good.

MacKinnon's Bakery
2715 Granville at 11th
738-2442
A wide range of bread, cookies, squares and gooey cakes. We dare you to walk by the window without stopping.

Pâtisserie Bordeaux
3675 W 10th near Alma
731-6551
Excellent croissants, but it's really the gâteaux and tarts that win us over. They look fabulous and taste even better. Reasonably priced, open Sun. Haven't had a thing we didn't like. Very French.

Siegel's Bagels
1883 Cornwall at Cypress
737-8151
Apparently Vancouver did not know what a real bagel tasted like until Siegel's came along. Its tasty treats— 14 varieties of bagels, some sweet— are often steaming hot from the brick oven.

Terra Breads
See Restaurants (Bakery Cafés).

Uprising Breads
1697 Venables near Commercial
254-5635
A healthy, East End bakery run by a workers' co-operative. Probably the best whole-grain breads, and great scones, cakes and muffins too.

Cheese

Dussa's Ham & Cheese
Granville Island Public Market
688-8881
Everything from fine French goat cheeses to hearty Canadian Rat Trap cheddar.

Forster's Fine Cheeses
2104 W 41st, near East Blvd
261-5813
Small store with an enormous array of quality cheeses you won't find elsewhere, and you can count on freshness. Also cheese accompaniments like pâtés and lox.

Coffee and Tea

Basic Stock
2294 W 4th at Vine

736-1412
Fresh, quality coffee, an extensive selection of coffee-brewing equipment, especially espresso machines, and a small espresso bar.

Continental Coffee
1806 Commercial at 2nd
255-0712
A "Little Italy" coffee store where Anita will fix you up with a dark-roast Italian coffee. Cappuccino to go.

Starbucks
See Restaurants (Espresso Bars).

Torrefazione Coloiera
2206 Commercial at 7th
254-3723
Spartan, East End Italian coffee store with some of the best coffee around.

Delis and Gourmet Take-Out

La Baguette et L'Échalote
1680 Johnston, Granville Island
684-1351
You will find everything for an elegant picnic except the bottle of Nuits St-Georges. There are mousses, pâtés, quality cheeses, stuffed croissants and brioches, breads, pastries, cakes and chocolates.

Bread Garden
812 Bute at Robson
688-3213
1880 W 1st at Cypress
738-6684
1040 Denman at Comox
685-2996
2996 Granville at 14th Ave
736-6465
A wide selection of desserts, healthy salads and entrées such as chicken pie, vegetable torte or frittata. Eat in or take out.

Dussa Delicatessen
4125 Main near 25th
874-8610

Easily the best European-style deli in town; too bad it's not in a handier location. Still, it isn't that far away, and you know it's worth it as soon as you walk through the door. The store offers several fine homemade salads, lots of sausages and cheeses at low prices, and some pastries.

Dussa is in the middle of a row of secondhand furniture and antique stores running from about 20th to 30th. You could start at 20th and browse through antique stores, pick up a picnic lunch at Dussa, continue antique shopping up to 30th, and then walk west a couple of blocks to Queen Elizabeth Park for lunch.

Lazy Gourmet
1596 W 6th at Fir
734-2507
We never get past the counter with the mocha cheesecake, toffee bars, dream bars, pumpkin and cranberry muffins, sticky buns and the like. So we often miss the seafood quiche, the spinach-and-feta pie and the chicken pesto—and end up with two desserts. There may be a seat by the window if you're lucky.

Leslie Stowe Fine Foods
1780 W 3rd at Burrard
731-3663
This topnotch caterer has opened a retail food store selling exquisitely prepared take-out dishes (crabcakes with a variety of special sauces, for example) and specialty packaged foods.

Que Pasa Mexican Foods
3315 Cambie at 17th
737-7659
Que Pasa not only makes the best tortillas in town (eight types) but also has molés and salsas by the pound, a complete Mexican cookbook reference shelf and a few take-out dishes—in short, absolutely anything you would need for a Mexican feast.

Stock Market
Granville Island Public Market
687-2433
A brilliant concept carried out perfectly. Originally the idea was to sell soup stocks by the litre (beef, chicken, fish, vegetarian, Chinese, duck, etc.). Then came sauces—satay, black bean, fruit, béarnaise and more—followed by a dozen different salad dressings, pasta sauces, vinegars, salsas, mustards, jams, jellies and chutneys. The Stock Market offers three different soups every day to be taken home or eaten there. The thing that we find so amazing is that *everything* is produced out of a 28 m^2 (300-square foot) stall at the market. The place is truly a wonder. (Oh, we should mention the breakfasts. This may not appeal to everyone, but check it out if you're attracted to Sunny Boy Cereal—a hot seven-grain cereal—topped with chunky homemade applesauce or maple syrup and surrounded by cream.)

Ethnic Foods

Asian (Chinese, Indonesian, Japanese and Thai)
Excellent selection of seasonings, spices, sauces, cookbooks, fresh noodles and produce at the South China Seas Trading Company stall, Granville Island Public Market.

Chinese
In Chinatown, shop on Pender and Keefer, one block east of Main. In Richmond there is a smaller "Chinatown" in the Aberdeen mall at 4400 Hazelbridge Way, near the corner of Cambie and No. 3 Rd.

East Indian
Shop on Main from 48th to 51st Ave and at Patel's on Commercial at 6th Ave. Patel's has food from 24 countries.

Granville Island Public Market

The public market is the most popular spot to buy specialty foods, and for good reason. There is a huge array of quality foods that most merchants take great care to display well (they make even raw squid look irresistible). It amazes us when we see people, obviously out for a Sunday jaunt, leave empty-handed. When we go to pick up a dozen oysters, we end up with a shopping bag full of other delectable things we couldn't say no to.

The market is in a huge building at the northwest corner of the island, and just outside the market building are two excellent food stores: a French bakery and charcuterie called La Baguette et L'Échalote, and a shellfish store, the Lobster Man.

Crowds are thick and traffic is heavy on Sat and Sun on the small island. Parking can be a gruesome experience.

Market hours in the winter are Tues to Sat, 9–6. On holidays, open Mon, closed Tues. In the summer from Victoria Day (May 24) to Labour Day, open every day.

Greek
On W Broadway from Macdonald to Trutch, especially Parthenon Foods.

Italian
On Commercial a few blocks north and south of 1st Ave.

Japanese
Powell from Jackson to Gore, and Kobayashi-Shoten Asian Grocery Store at 1518 Robson near Nicola.

Kosher
Small selection at Kaplan's near 42nd on Oak, and Leon's at Oak and 21st.

Mexican
The only store that sells exclusively Mexican food products is Que Pasa on Cambie near 17th.

Middle Eastern
North Vancouver has a few Middle Eastern shops such as the Iransuper Market at 989 Marine Dr near Lloyd, and Pars Bakery and Deli at 1643 Lonsdale at 16th.

Fish/Shellfish

Fujiya Fish and Japanese Foods
912 Clark at Venables
251-3711

Lobster Man
1807 Mast Tower, Granville Island
687-4531

Longliner Sea Foods
Granville Island Public Market
681-9016

Salmon Shop
Granville Island Public Market
669-3474

Seven Seas
2344 W 4th near Vine
732-8608

Ice Cream

La Casa Gelato
1033 Venables at Glen Dr
251-3211
No. 3 Rd at Cambie, Richmond
270-1453
Every ice cream flavour you can imagine—Vince Misceo makes 150 flavours; 60 are here to taste—and some you can't imagine. Ginger, garlic, edible flowers, red bean, wasabi, passion fruit (Vince's favourite), even the smelly, exotic durian fruit is in this parlour, where you are encouraged to taste before you buy. Said to have the

A Few Market Tips

- Shop weekdays instead of weekends.
- If you must shop on weekends, go between 9 and 10 AM or between 5 and 6 PM. Otherwise, grin and bear it.
- Once you are on the island, don't waste time looking for a parking spot close to the market—just take the first one you see. You will be at most a five-minute walk away.
- On weekends you can avoid the whole congestion problem by parking on 1st, 2nd or 3rd Ave. just east of Burrard. It's then a 10-minute walk.

A Sampling of Favourite Market Foods

- **Duso's** Sauce, a decadently rich cheese, cream and herb sauce for pasta.
- Freshly squeezed juice from the **Fraser Valley Juice & Salad Bar**: carrot, watermelon, hot apple-ginger, etc. Also the best salads.
- Fresh goat cheeses from **Dussa's Ham & Cheese**.
- Coffee roasted on the spot at the **Coffee Roaster**.
- A litre of freshly made fish stock from the **Stock Market**.
- The freshest Fraser Valley produce—whatever's in season, whether it's raspberries or tiny new potatoes.
- Golden mantle oysters from the **Salmon Shop**.
- **Stuart's** 40 varieties of breads.
- Chocolate fudge from **Olde World Fudge**.
- The stunning display of pastries, breads, chocolates and take-out foods at **La Baguette**, just outside the market building.

For information about the rest of Granville Island, see Sightseeing.

A cheerful produce merchant at the Granville Island Public Market. (Rosamond Norbury)

best chocolate in town. The ice cream is *the* best—made with cream, eggs, freshly squeezed fruit and little sugar. There are sorbettos for the health-conscious.

Local Seafood

You've got your flatfish—sole or flounder, a delicate white fish served in thin fillets.

Ling cod, which comes in fillets or steaks, is available any time of the year but is best in the winter.

Lean firm halibut steaks are best from May to Sept.

Thick red snapper fillets are around all the time.

You've also got a choice of five kinds of salmon: sockeye (which usually ends up in a tin), pink, chum, or the prized chinook and coho. Big salmon harvests are in the summer and fall.

Pacific mackerel is an oily fish with a distinctive flavour.

Steelhead trout, similar in taste to salmon, is best in winter.

Clams harvested locally are either littleneck or butter.

Mussels are becoming respectable and often wind up steamed in restaurants.

Dungeness crab, usually weighing only half a kilogram or so (a pound or two), stalk the local waters year-round.

Alaskan king crab, with legs 60 cm (2 feet) long, is brought in fresh, Aug to Nov, from the Queen Charlotte Islands on the northern B.C. coast.

Shrimp and prawns, 5 to 20 cm (2 to 8 inches) long, are in season year-round.

Sea scallops from the north coast are available all year, and tiny, delicate bay scallops are fresh in winter.

The large Pacific oyster, which was imported from Japan in 1912, is now the most popular commercial oyster. You'll be offered them raw, stewed, baked, barbecued, smoked, pan-fried and deep-fried.

With the Kids

Kids and Animals 196

Day Trips 197

Other Outings 200

Museums 201

Babysitting 202

Entertainment 202

Restaurants 202

Shopping 204
Books, Clothing and Shoes, Consignment Shops, Furniture, Toys

Many of these activities are not just for kids and so are described in more detail in other sections. Also check the What's On section of Thursday's *Vancouver Sun* under Families and under Children for the week's special events.

Kids and Animals

Maplewood Children's Farm
405 Seymour River Pl, North Van
929-5610
Maplewood is a 2 ha (5-acre) petting farm of barnyard animals run by the North Van Parks Department. The original farm dates back to the early 1900s. Complete with a barn, over 200 animals and birds, small pastures and a creek, it is an ideal getaway for city kids.

Visitors can pet a rabbit, feed guinea pigs and waterfowl, and check out horses, cows, donkeys and pigs. The favourite spot seems to be Goathill, where the younger set cavort with frisky goats that love to nibble shoelaces and other clothing. A milking display is held daily at 1:15.

Parents can relax in a covered picnic area. Special events and children's programs are held throughout the year.

Open Tues to Sun, 10–4. Closed Mon except on holidays. Admission is $1.25 for children, $1.75 for adults and $5.50 for families.

Drive over the Second Narrows Bridge to North Van and take the Deep Cove/Mount Seymour exit; turn left at Seymour River Place. Two B.C. Transit bus routes go right by the farm: #212 Deep Cove and #211 Seymour.

Richmond Nature Park
11851 Westminster Hwy, Richmond
273-7015
Richmond Nature Park is 40 ha (100 acres) of shrubbery and peat bog,

with paths leading you on a nature expedition. The boardwalk around the pond—where you may spot ducks, herons, turtles and dragonflies, depending on the season—is accessible to strollers and wheelchairs. There's a bird-watching tower near here, and longer trails wind through the bush. Each section of the bog is home to a different colony of creatures, so this walk is an adventure. Wear boots if it's been wet.

The Nature House is full of games and displays on natural history, as well as live animals like snakes, frogs and salamanders. The Nature House is open every day, 9–5. Admission is free.

Drive south on Hwy 99 and take the Shell Rd exit; then go left onto Westminster Hwy. There is public transit to the park, but it is long and involved (call 521-0400).

George C. Reifel Migratory Bird Sanctuary
Some of the Canada geese, ducks and swans at the entrance to the refuge are quite tame—some were injured, have been rehabilitated and have decided to stick around—and are a particular delight to young children. Bird feed can be purchased in the shop. Children particularly enjoy hiding in the wooden shelters to peek out at waterfowl and climbing the four-storey observation tower. See Parks/Beaches/Gardens for more information.

Horse Shows
Southlands Riding Club (263-4817) at 7025 Macdonald off 53rd holds hunter/jumper and dressage shows from spring to fall. Call to find out about events.

Vancouver Aquarium
If you don't have time for a complete visit, the beluga and harbour seal pools on the west side of the aquarium were built to be viewed from

Beluga pool at the Vancouver Aquarium.

both outside and inside the complex. So there is no admission charge for this preview. See Parks/Beaches/Gardens for more information.

Stanley Park

For animals, visit the Children's Farmyard, where children can mingle with pigs, cattle, chickens and the like. There are also pony rides. Lost Lagoon and Beaver Lake have lots of ducks, geese and swans, but please don't feed them bread—it's very bad for them. Bring lettuce or buy bird seed at the Lost Lagoon concession. Also, there are brazen little squirrels all over the park that are used to being fed by hand.

Day Trips

Granville Island

Take the bathtub-sized Granville Island ferries from the Aquatic Centre for a five-minute trip to the island and visit the Kids Only Market, the impromptu performers around the public market, the water park, glass blowers (1440 Old Bridge), wooden boat builders (1247 Cartwright) and the adventure playground.

The Kids Only Market is in a refurbished two-storey building at the entrance to Granville Island. It is jam-packed with over 24 colourful, vibrant stores as well as a lunch spot geared to those under 14. Books, kites, puppets, arts and crafts, clothing and any toy or gizmo that a child would fancy are all found in the shops. The Kids Only Market is busy on weekends and often quiet during the week. Every Sat in summer there are free events for the whole family— during special events, clowns, magicians and face painters wander the Market. Open daily year-round.

The water park and the adventure playground near the False Creek Community Centre are supervised daily, 10–6. The water park is a riot. It's a huge wading pool, at the centre of which are a revolving fire hydrant and hoses that kids can use to douse anyone in reach. The adventure playground has innumerable rope and log configurations and a water slide.

See Sightseeing (Granville Island) for other ideas.

Stanley Park
Besides the animals and aquarium listed above, there is a miniature train ride, pitch and putt golf, tennis courts, several playgrounds—one with an old fire engine—picnic spots, totem poles and Native dugout canoes, a traffic school for kids aged 5 to 8, bicycle paths (bicycle and stroller rentals are just outside the park), beaches and swimming pools. If it's warm, stop by the water adventure playground across from Lumbermen's Arch. Also, Second Beach Pool has waterslides and a lifeguard; there's a sandy beach beside it and an adventure playground close by.

See Parks/Beaches/Gardens (Stanley Park) for more details; also Sports/Recreation (Swimming).

The water park provides hours of entertainment for kids; parents can keep a watchful eye from the patio of Isadora's Restaurant next door. (Rosamond Norbury)

Chinatown
Older kids might enjoy a trip to Chinatown to shop for inexpensive gifts and souvenirs: paper kites, Chinese tops, chopsticks to try out at lunch. Also see Sightseeing (Chinatown) and Restaurants (Chinese).

Children and ducks at Lost Lagoon in Stanley Park. (Rosamond Norbury)

Kits Beach/Kits Pool

At the beach, the water's a bit chilly for real swimming, but it's fine for wading and a lifeguard is on duty all summer. There are grassy areas all around the beach, as well as swings and monkey bars and a concession stand.

The heated outdoor pool at Kits Beach sits right at the water's edge. An enormous pool with lanes marked off for serious swimmers, it also has a long and gradual slope at one side that is perfect for young children. The pool gets congested on sunny weekend afternoons, but mornings are fairly quiet.

Kits Beach and Pool are adjacent to the Maritime Museum and handy to downtown.

Royal Hudson

Ride a vintage steam locomotive up the coast. See Sightseeing (Royal Hudson/MV *Britannia*).

Pedal Boats on Deer Lake
667-2628

Deer Lake is in Burnaby, a 30-minute drive from downtown. At the east end of the lake are boat rentals with pedal boats, canoes, rowboats and kayaks, as well as picnic tables, a sandy beach and a lifeguard. The only access to the east side of the lake is via Canada Way, Burris or Buckingham St. Even though it is a small, urban lake, it is citified only at one end; most of the shoreline is wooded and good for exploring by water. Avoid weekends if possible.

Canoeing at Deep Cove
929-2268

Deep Cove is a small community on a deep inlet of the North Shore and is accessible from downtown by public transit. Deep Cove Canoe Rentals will supply a canoe so that you can paddle to the nearby islands and parks. Since you're in this area, stop at Honey Doughnuts and Goodies at 4373 Gal-

lant. The kids will love the luscious doughnuts, and the adults will savour the gourmet coffee. See Sports/Recreation (Canoeing/Kayaking/Rowing).

Grouse Mountain Skyride/Mount Seymour Chairlift

See Parks/Beaches/Gardens/(Grouse Mountain).

Seymour Demonstration Forest

See Sightseeing (Special Interest Tours).

Queen Elizabeth Park/Bloedel Conservatory

Things of interest at the park are the duck pond; the Bloedel Conservatory, with its tropical plants and birds under a geodesic dome; and the giant Henry Moore sculptures (great to climb on).

Cycling Barnston Island

You pedal quiet country roads on this small island in the Fraser River. After a short, free ferry ride, you can cycle a 10 km (6-mile) circle route where you encounter little traffic. Pack a picnic in your backpack and have lunch overlooking the Fraser from a grassy knoll; there are a few places you can get right down near the water. Head east on Hwy 1 to 176th St and then go north; then go east on 104th Ave. There's parking, and the ferry runs continuously.

Berry Picking

The U-pick raspberry, blueberry and black currant season runs roughly from mid-June to late July, depending on the weather. Call Bissett Farms at 946-7139 for more information.

The farm is just before the entrance to the George C. Reifel Migratory Bird Sanctuary at 2170 Westham Island Rd. Take the Ladner exit from Hwy 99.

Stern-Wheeler Ride up Burrard Inlet

For this Harbour Ferries tour, see Sightseeing (Touring Vancouver).

University of British Columbia/ Pacific Spirit Regional Park

Walk through the forest in the park, swim in the pool at the Aquatic Centre, or see the dinosaur skeleton and fabulous gems in the geology museum. Older children keen on science will enjoy the cyclotron at TRIUMF; see Sightseeing (Other Tours).

Also see Parks/Beaches/Gardens (Pacific Spirit Regional Park), Sports/ Recreation (Swimming) and Sightseeing (Special Interest Tours).

West Van Playgrounds

Two of the best playgrounds in town are in West Vancouver, at Ambleside Park (see Parks/Beaches/Gardens), off Marine Dr at 13th, and at John Lawson Park, at the foot of 16th St. Both parks are beside the ocean, and John Lawson has a beach, pier, toy train, two odd little cement igloos and a wading pool. You can walk along the seawall from John Lawson to feed the ducks and swans at Ambleside.

Lynn Canyon Park

Visit the ecology centre, go hiking and picnicking, and walk across the suspension bridge 73 m (240 feet) above the rapids.

Lynn Canyon is accessible from downtown by public transit via the SeaBus and the #229 Phibbs Exchange/Westlynn bus. Everything in the park is free.

Lighthouse Park

A good place for kids to get a taste of the wilderness. They'll love running along the wooded trails and scrambling on the rocks near the lighthouse. See Parks/Beaches/Gardens.

Newton Wave Pool

13730–72nd Ave near King George Hwy
594-7873

Body surfing in Vancouver?! Besides the wave pool with metre-high (3-foot) waves, there are waterslides, a wading pool, an exercise room, a whirlpool, a steam room, babysitting and a coffee shop. You can also rent inner tubes, air mattresses and kick boards. Well worth the drive. Phone for directions.

Skiing

Preschool ski lessons are given at Grouse Mountain (downhill) and at Cypress (cross-country); you must register in advance. Drop-in ski lessons for juniors are held on Grouse weekends and holidays. Call the Grouse Mountain Ski School (980-9311) for particulars.

Splashdown Park

943-2251
Twisting waterslides—120 m (400 feet) of them—are the main attraction, but there are also hot tubs, patios for tanning, lawns for picnics, a snack bar, a video arcade, volleyball, basketball, smaller slides for little kids and a toddlers' pool. The water is heated. (Even if the weather is marginal in town, it is always sunny in Tsawwassen.) Located on Hwy 17 just before the Tsawwassen ferry terminal. Admission is $14.95 for 11 and older, with discounts for younger children and half-days.

Other Outings

Cliffhanger Indoor Rock Climbing Centre

Ideal for youngsters who love to climb. There is special equipment for the younger set. See Sports/Recreation (Hiking/Mountaineering).

Playland

Exhibition Park
E Hastings near Renfrew
255-5161

The rides and miniature golf are open weekends in the spring and every day in the summer. Hours vary; call ahead. Day passes are $18 for those over 120 cm (4 feet) tall and $14 for those under that height. Prices are higher during the Pacific National Exhibition.

Power Plant

750 Pacific Blvd, foot of Robson
682-8770

Make your own cassette recording! Sing along with pre-recorded music in small studios that hold up to 10 people. You can choose from top 40, classic rock or country. Cost is $20 for 30 minutes and includes the cassette. During summer there are group rates for children.

Richmond Go-Kart Track

6631 Sidaway, Richmond
278-6184

An 800 m (½-mile) asphalt track with lots of curves. Cost is $7.50 for 10 minutes. To ride solo, children must be 10 years of age or over 137 cm (4 foot, 6 inches); others must ride with an adult. Open every day from noon to dusk.

Drive south on Hwy 99, take the No. 4 Rd exit, go east on Westminster Hwy, and turn right on Sidaway.

Sunday Afternoon Baseball

Combine a picnic in Queen Elizabeth Park with a Vancouver Canadians game at neighbouring Nat Bailey Stadium. Games start at 1:30 on weekends and at 12:15 during the week. Watch for Autograph Day, when kids can go an hour before game time and meet their favourite players. There's also between-inning fun contests (children are chosen at random to take part). The $5.50 tickets are re-

There are many hands-on experiences at Science World. (Science World)

duced to $3.25 for kids 14 and under. Call 872-5232 for the schedule.

VanDusen Garden

Kids will be kept busy winding their way out of the Elizabethan maze, which is 1.5 m (5 feet) high and is planted with a thousand cedars. Steps are placed throughout so that younger children can get their bearings, and parents can keep track of progress from the grassy hill beside the maze.

Museums

Science World is Vancouver's only museum expressly for children. Kids also love walking on board the *St Roch* (a restored two-masted schooner) and the tugboat wheelhouse, both in the **Maritime Museum**. Another favourite is the **B.C. Sports Hall of Fame and Museum**; kids love the action in the Participation Gallery. And don't forget the special events

The Maritime Museum is a favourite with the younger set. (Kevin Miller)

that regularly take place at the **Burnaby Village Museum**. For more details about these and other museums, see Museums/Art Galleries.

Babysitting

See Essential Information (Babysitting).

Entertainment

CN Imax Theatre
Canada Place
682-4629 (info)
280-4444 (tickets)
A huge, five-storey screen shows edge-of-your-seat films: ride the Colorado River through the Grand Canyon, or explore the mysteries of flight, speed, space or some such delight. Reserved seats.

Museum of Anthropology
6393 NW Marine, UBC Campus
822-5087
Family events (often related to Native culture) are periodically scheduled on Sun afternoons.

Restaurants

Chinese restaurants cater to families, and so mess and noise are not usually a problem. Bite-sized *dim sum* is served in small portions. See Restaurants (Chinese).

Simpatico Ristorante
See Restaurants (Greek).

Vancouver International Folk Music Festival

The Little Folks Festival is the children's component of the annual three-day folk festival (602-9798). One of the six stages is geared especially to family entertainment, and there are also kids' activity areas, but the entire festival could be a family event. Children's day passes are $5 on Sat and Sun; kids are admitted free on Fri night. The festival takes place in mid-July at Jericho Park.

Vancouver Children's Festival

With luck, you'll be in town with kids for the Vancouver Children's Festival, held in May at Vanier Park. If so, take advantage of the top-notch local and international actors, mimes, musicians, clowns, storytellers, jugglers and puppeteers gathered solely to entertain young people.

Huge, colourful tents are set up at Vanier Park on the shores of Burrard Inlet, and events are staged for a whole week. About 200 entertainers come from all over B.C. and as far away as New York, Portugal and Japan. An excellent detailed program, available at ticket outlets, describes the performances and the ages they appeal to.

Outside the performance tents, there is free entertainment—strolling musicians, mimes, jugglers and the clowns who delight in painting small faces. Activity tents are set up for storytelling, games, kite-making, dance and toddlers' activities, and one holds a Goliath-size sandbox.

Although the festival is well attended, some tickets are available the week of the festival. Tickets go on sale in March at Ticketmaster outlets. Once the festival starts, tickets are available on site.

If you can't get tickets for the event you have your heart set on, go anyway for the free on-site entertainment and activities. For more information, call 687-7697.

Face painting, music and good times at the annual Children's Festival. (May Henderson)

Sophie's Cosmic Café
2095 W 4th at Arbutus
732-6810
Sophie's is a hip diner, jammed with '50s and '60s kitsch, that welcomes children. The food is well-prepared up-scale diner fare but is not as cheap as you'd like it to be. Come early or wait in line on weekends. Open for breakfast, lunch and dinner.

Topanga Café
See Restaurants (Mexican).

Isadora's
1540 Old Bridge, Granville Island
681-8816
Play area for kids inside the restaurant and out. See Restaurants (Breakfast/Brunch).

Old Spaghetti Factory
53 Water near Abbott, Gastown
684-1288
Old-time paraphernalia, a vintage streetcar and silent movies. Children's portions available.

Tomahawk Barbecue
1550 Philip near Marine, North Van
988-2612
Mostly burgers (named after local Native chiefs), hot dogs, sandwiches and big breakfasts—very good quality and reasonably priced. Full of Native memorabilia, and kids are given an Indian headdress. Open every day for breakfast, lunch and dinner. See Restaurants (Breakfast/Brunch).

Shopping

Books

Vancouver Kidsbooks
3083 W Broadway at Balaclava
738-5335
Run by a former librarian and current mom. The best assortment of children's books, as well as an excellent selection of board books for ba-

bies. Also carries CDs and tapes. Good selection of French titles.

Clothing and Shoes

Absolutely Diapers
2050 W 4th near Arbutus
737-0603
A cute little store with clothes for newborn to three years and, yes, a variety of cloth diapers. There are also toys, books, stuffed animals and other paraphernalia for children. Closed Mon.

Angels on Bellevue
1463 Bellevue near 15th, West Van
926-8737
Down the block from Bears Toy Store. Angels carries a number of Vancouver designers' lines, including 100 per cent cotton playwear by Bravo. Sizes range from one year to eight.

Bratz
2828 Granville near W 12th
734-4344
Looking for designer clothes for kids? This is the place. The European clothing is lovely and incredibly expensive. Also shoes and gifts. Sizes are for newborn to junior adult. Kids' hair salon in the store.

Isola Bella
5692 Yew near 41st
266-8808
All clothing and shoes sold here are made in Europe. For 3 months to 16 years.

Kiddie Kobbler Children's Shoes
Park Royal South, West Van
926-1616
Good selection of quality children's shoes. Knowledgeable staff makes sure you get the right fit.

Peppermintree Children's Wear
4243 Dunbar near 27th
228-9815
One of the best kids' stores in Vancouver. Fashionable, quality clothes, shoes and accessories in the

The Kids Only Market on Granville Island has dozens of shops just for kids. (Rosamond Norbury)

medium price range, mainly Canadian labels. Sizes are from newborn to 16. The friendly staff are experienced moms with helpful suggestions. Kids' play area. Open every day.

Please Mum
2951 W Broadway near Bayswater
732-4574
2041 W 41st
264-0366
(also at Oakridge and Metrotown)
Clothing for newborns to 10 years that is 100 per cent cotton, all designed and manufactured in Vancouver.

Consignment Shops

Nipper's
3712 W 10th near Alma
222-4035
Consignment clothes, infant to size 10, at medium prices. Some shoes and infant equipment.

See also Shopping (Clothing), under Vintage and Consignment, for Value Village.

Furniture

Ikea
3200 Sweden Way, south end of Knight St Bridge, Richmond
273-2051
Vast selection of colourful contemporary furniture and accessories for the whole family, generally at low prices. Ikea's famous ball room has hundreds of soft plastic balls to jump on, throw and bury yourself in. It's for kids 3 to 7 and is supervised. An outdoor playground has tire rides, a suspension bridge and all sorts of climbing contrivances. The cafeteria has kid-size furniture and a children's menu, including baby food.

Kids Furniture World
12680 Bridgeport near Knight, Richmond
278-7654
Specializes in pine, maple and oak children's furniture. Near Ikea.

TJ's Kiddies Korner
3331 Jacombs (behind Ikea), Richmond
270-8830

This one-of-a-kind store will buy back what your child outgrows. Consequently, it sells new and used articles. Best selection and prices on items like Evenflo carseats and Perego strollers. TJ's also does repair work, sells parts and rents infant equipment.

Friendly Bears
4411 No. 3 Rd near Cambie, Richmond
276-8278
Largest selection of kids' furniture with prices that are moderate to high.

Toys

B.C. Playthings
1065 Marine near Lloyd, North Van
986-4111
This toy store definitely warrants a detour. It has educational and creative toys at good prices, including art supplies, preschool supplies, climbing equipment, puppets, puzzles, games and an excellent selection of CDs and tapes. Wonderful wagons and face-colouring crayons. Catalogue is available. Call the above number or 1-800-663-4477 to order.

Bears Toy Store
1459 Bellevue and 15th, West Van
926-2327
This store is so delightful that you won't be able to tear yourself away. It is the home of more than 1000 teddy bears but has all kinds of other toys too, many European, and a very good choice of imported dolls. All the toys on display are meant to be touched. Open daily.

3-H Society Boutique
2112 W 4th at Arbutus
736-2113
All the toys here are handmade, often by the homebound or handicapped, and they will custom-make toys according to your wants. Their Raggedy Ann and Andy dolls are magical.

Opus Framing/Artist Resource Centre
1360 Johnston, Granville Island
736-7028
This frame shop, across from the city's largest art school, carries a large selection of art supplies. Parents come for the paints, pencils and pastels containing nontoxic, nonpolluting pigments. They also have the best selection of 3-D materials for sculpting and the broadest colour range of inexpensive pens and pencils. Open daily.

The Toybox
3002 W Broadway at Carnarvon
738-4322
A neighbourhood toy store with an excellent range of toys for newborns up to 10-year-olds. Good selection of board books and cassettes.

The Zoo Wildlife Boutique
Park Royal North
926-5616
This is a great place to buy children's gifts. There is some clothing but mostly stuffed toys and all sorts of fun paraphernalia. Also in several malls.

See also Sightseeing (Granville Island) for Kids Only Market.

Excursions from Vancouver

Gulf Islands 208
Getting There, Services, Accommodation, Island Hopping

Galiano Island 209
Tourist Information, Where to Stay, Other Lodging, Restaurants,
Sports and Recreation, Scenic Spots, Special Events, The Arts

Mayne Island 214
Tourist Information, Services, Where to Stay, Restaurants, Sports and
Recreation, Scenic Spots, Special Events, The Arts

Saltspring Island 217
Tourist Information, Where to Stay, Other Lodging, Restaurants,
Sports and Recreation, Scenic Spots, The Arts, Special Events

Whistler 221
Getting There, Tourist Information, Where to Stay, Restaurants,
Sports and Recreation

Gulf Islands

The Gulf Islands form a cluster between the mainland and the south end of Vancouver Island. The southern Gulf Islands are Galiano, Mayne, Saturna, North and South Pender, and Saltspring. Spanish place names come from Captain Dionisio Galiano, who was the first European to explore the area in 1792.

Because the only public access is by ferry, the islands are fairly undeveloped. In the '50s and '60s they were a community of artists, writers, retired people and others looking for an alternative style of living. Now, with increased ferry service, there are also many weekend cottagers.

The climate of the islands, which is sunnier and drier than Vancouver's, has always been an attraction—resorts were built on the islands as early as the late 1800s.

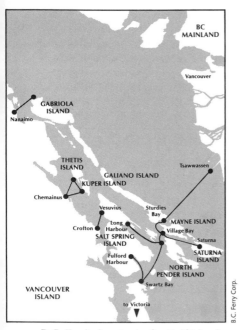

B.C. Ferries' routes in the Gulf Islands.

Getting There

B.C. Ferries travel to all the Gulf Islands. Most trips are milk runs, stopping at each island. The two islands closest to Vancouver, Galiano and Mayne, have the shortest ferry trips—50 to 90 minutes. Ferry service runs from Tsawwassen one to three times a day.

The Gulf Islands route is one of the few on which you can make a car reservation, an absolute necessity for summer weekends and holiday weekends. Phone **B.C. Ferries** in Vancouver at 277-0277 for the schedule and at 669-1211 for reservations. See also Getting Around (Ferries).

The Gulf Islands are serviced by air from Vancouver with **Hanna Air** (1-800-665-2359) and **Harbour Air** (1-800-665-0212).

Services

There are no banks or bank machines on Galiano or Mayne, but on each you will find a post office, gas station, liquor store, bakery, and deli and small grocery stores. Saltspring is much more developed, and in the town of Ganges you'll find a supermarket, a small shopping centre and branches of the Canadian Imperial Bank of Commerce and Bank of Montreal.

Accommodation

Accommodation on the islands is limited; don't count on finding a place to stay without a reservation, particularly on summer and holiday weekends. The **Gulf Islands Bed and Breakfast Registry** (539-5390) will book accommodation on any of the Gulf Islands. Many places will pick you up from the ferry if you are coming without a car. Request this when making your reservation. Prices for high season average $85–120 for B&B

A quiet cove in the Gulf Islands where you'll find playful harbour seals. (Dick Tipple)

accommodation and start around $75 for cabins. Inns range from $95 to $295.

You will find a choice of accommodation, including rooms in private homes (an informal bed and breakfast), bed and breakfast in large Victorian houses that cater to several guests, rustic cabins, modern rumpus room-style cabins and elegant inns.

Island Hopping

Whether it's a case of the grass being greener or packing as much as possible into your holiday, you will probably want to visit other islands. You can take inter-island hops with B.C. Ferries. Enthusiastic cyclists enjoy exploring different islands. (Cost for an island-hop is $2.75 one way.)

Galiano Island

Galiano, a skinny island that is 26 km (16 miles) long, is the first ferry stop. Year-round residents number about 900, most of whom live at the south end. The logging giant MacMillan Bloedel owns about half of the island.

You will find a post office at the market and a gas station (539-5500) in Sturdies Bay. The liquor store is at the Corner Store (539-2986). The excellent Trincomali Bakery and Deli (539-2004) is one block from the ferry terminal on Sturdies Bay Rd.

Tourist Information

A tourist booth, at Sturdies Bay near the ferry dock, keeps irregular hours but is generally open in the summer when the ferry lands. Throughout the year you can write to the **Galiano Island Visitors Association**, Box 73, Galiano, BC V0N 1P0. Or phone 539-2233.

Where to Stay

Woodstone Country Inn
Georgeson Bay Rd
539-2022

Accommodation on Galiano tends towards the rustic except for the Woodstone Inn, which is best described as rural sophistication. The inn is a large, two-storey clapboard building on 3 ha (7½ acres), overlooking farm land. The 12 guest rooms are furnished with antiques and wicker. All have bathrooms and half have patios. Request a room with a valley view.

The living room has a huge stone fireplace and chintz-covered wingbacked chairs. There is a meeting room available. The somewhat formal dining room has fixed-price, three-course dinners. A hearty breakfast (eggs from free-range chickens) and afternoon tea are included with your room.

A stroll away from the inn is a marsh teeming with bird life. The inn provides gum boots, binoculars and bird books for bird watchers. The Woodstone is a non-smoking, adult-oriented establishment. Doubles $95–145.

Country lanes through thick coastal rain forest on Galiano Island. (Heather Frankson)

Sutil Lodge Heritage Guest House
Southwind Dr, Montague Harbour
539-2930
Sutil Lodge is more like a deluxe summer camp than an intimate weekend getaway. Built as a fishing lodge in 1928, it has a fabulous location on Montague Harbour. The rooms are charming (brass beds and original fir panelling) but tiny, and you won't want to lounge around in them. Much more comfortable are the sitting room and the old-style dining hall, both with fireplaces. You'll find your gregarious hosts, Tom and Ann Hennessy, chatting about Galiano's history or organizing such activities as the daily picnic supper cruise or a kayaking trip on their catamaran (see Sports and Recreation, below). Breakfast is a hot entrée with baked goods and freshly made jam. Four of the eight rooms have views; all share bathrooms. Seven rustic sleeping cabins are a few steps from the water. Sutil Lodge is good family accommodation. No smoking. Doubles $85 with a view, $75 without; cabins $50. Breakfast included.

Driftwood Village Resort
Bluff Rd
539-5457
These 10 cottages, some new, some old, sit on a lightly treed lot about five minutes from the beach. Some are small studios and others are larger one- and two-bedrooms. All have a rustic feel, even though they are well equipped with kitchens, electric heat, TVs and private patios. Most have fireplaces, and wood is provided. The cottages are built around a lovely landscaped area that has a badminton net, sandbox, barbecue pit, picnic tables and fruit trees. Some cabins now have skylights and Jacuzzi tubs; there's an outdoor hot tub. Pets are

welcome. Easily accessible for cyclists. Doubles $80–120.

Madrona Lodge
Porlier Pass at Cook Rd
539-2926

The Madrona is an old-style resort with seven Panabode cabins, each with a sun deck and fire pit. They are classic West Coast cottages with chipboard flooring and seashell and driftwood decorations. Fresh flowers welcome you to the spotless cabins.

Families dominate in the summer and you need to book several months in advance. Owner Gill Allen, a painter, conducts art classes for children in July and Aug while her husband putters around with his vintage car collection. Old bicycles, rowboats, badminton equipment, a treehouse and a playground are available.

In the winter the Madrona is popular with scuba divers. Pets are welcome. Three other units, quite separate from the cabins, are in the woods across the road, overlooking the water. Doubles $65–75.

Laidlaws' Bed and Breakfast
539-5341

The Laidlaws' property is on a high cliff over Trincomali Channel, amid arbutus trees and salal. There are three guest units—one is in the house, the other two are small cottages. Guests staying in the main house are especially catered to with a fine, full breakfast. This gracious room has a fireplace, private bath and French doors opening onto a terrace.

One of the cottages is a converted greenhouse with the lower walls in stone and clapboard now replacing the glass. It sleeps two in a queen-size bed downstairs and two more in a sleeping loft. A little fireplace, kitchen nook and clawfoot bathtub add to the comfort. The other cottage is cozy and bright, with French doors

opening onto a large deck with an ocean view. There are beds downstairs and up, as well as a kitchen, a washing machine and a wood stove for heat. In both cottages, a continental breakfast is brought to your door.

Because of the cliff, Laidlaws' is adult-oriented accommodation. Smokers are requested to smoke outside. Doubles $125.

Bodega Lodge Resort
Cook Rd at Porlier Pass Dr
539-2677

The resort has 10 ha (25 acres) at the north end of the island. The six log cabins each have three bedrooms, two bathrooms, three decks, a kitchen and a fireplace. The main lodge also has two bed/sitting rooms, a suite, a lounge and a meeting room. A big attraction at Bodega is the horses—this is the only place on the island to go on guided trail rides. There are 40 km (25 miles) of trails for horses or hikers. Guests can fish at a stocked trout pond. Doubles $60–80.

Other Lodging

Other B&Bs to consider: **Lion's Gate Guest House** (formerly Holloway House) (539-3225), **Shelter Bay B&B** (539-2994) and **Moonshadows Guest House** (539-5544). The **Bellhouse Inn** (539-5667 or 1-800-970-7464) has some cottages ideal for families.

Restaurants

La Berengerie   **$$**
Montague Harbour Rd
539-5392

La Berengerie has a warm and cozy country-style dining room. The fixed-price, four-course menu varies but leans towards continental. You'll generally find regional specialties such as salmon and local produce. Arrive early for an apéritif on the porch. Fre-

Montague Harbour on Galiano Island. (Heather Frankson)

quent live dinner music such as classical guitar. Must book in advance. (See also Where to Stay, above.)

Woodstone Country Inn   **$$$**
Georgeson Bay Rd
539-2022
The Woodstone is open to nonguests for dinner. The dining room is the most formal on Galiano. Request a table by the window looking out on a lovely pastoral scene. The fixed-price, three-course menu with several entrée choices changes every day. Entrée choices one night were rosemary and garlic roasted lamb loin, fresh grilled swordfish with caperberry butter, macadamia nut chicken with orange and ginger sauce, roast duck with plum sauce and poached salmon with shrimp Pernod butter. Reservations a must. (See Where to Stay, above.)

Hummingbird Inn   **$**
Sturdies Bay Rd at Porlier Pass Rd
539-5472
Generally known as the Pub, the Hummingbird serves simple food: burgers, chowder, fish and chips.

Often crowded in the evenings. Open every day for lunch and dinner. Occasional live entertainment, usually a local guitarist.

The Hummingbird operates a bus, the only one on the island, that goes from Montague Harbour (for campers and boaters) to the Pub. During the summer it leaves Montague Harbour on the hour, starting at 6 PM.

Sports and Recreation

Cycling on Galiano requires stamina; the island is long and hilly, and you may find yourself walking up some hills. The narrow winding roads have no paved shoulders, so it is imperative to ride single file. Bikes can be rented at **Gulf Island Kayaking** (539-2442), **Ben's Bikes, Sea Kayak and Canoe Rentals** (539-2442), and **Galiano Bicycle** (539-2806).

No experience is necessary for year-round guided kayak trips, also offered by Gulf Island Kayaking (see above). Trips range from three hours to five days, and longer ones combine kayaking with camping or stays at bed and breakfasts. They also offer kayak and canoe rentals. Other rentals and guided trips are available from Ben's (see above) and **Canadian Gulf Islands Sea Kayaking** (539-5390)— see below for catamaran trips.

Two campgrounds with a total of 39 sites are located in **Montague Harbour Provincial Park**. You must hike to one of them; the other is accessible by car. It is first come, first served, and finding a spot can be difficult during the summer or on long weekends. There are no RV hookups on the island. In Canada the beach below the high tide line is public property. Because tides are much lower in the summer, it is possible to camp on the beach. Summertime campfires are prohibited.

Fishing gear and bait are available at **Sturdies Bay Gas and Groceries** (539-5500) in Sturdies Bay. For fishing charters call **Mel-N-I Charters** (539-3171).

The pretty nine-hole **Galiano Golf Course** (539-5533) was established in 1975 and has a licensed clubhouse that serves lunch and dinner.

Bodega Resort (539-2677) offers guided trail rides on 40 km (25 miles) of scenic trails with 360° views.

Daily during the summer, Tom Hennessy of **Canadian Gulf Island Catamaran Cruises** (539-2930) sets sail on his 14 m (46-foot) catamaran for a four-hour cruise. Catamarans are fast and smooth and have plenty of flat deck space, so they are safe for children. You will sail to Seal Rocks, a bird sanctuary, and stop at a sandy beach on Saltspring Island for a picnic supper. Cost is a reasonable $35.

The Gulf Islands are probably the most popular diving destination in southwestern B.C. Air is available at **Madrona Lodge** (539-2926), at the north end of the island, near excellent diving spots at Virago Point and Alcala Point. **Galiano Dive Services** (539-3109) also provides air, instruction and charters.

If you want to swim, keep in mind that water on the east side of the island is warmer than on the west. Beaches with public access are at Coon Bay in **Dionisio Point Provincial Park** at the north end of the island. There are shell and pebble beaches on both sides of the peninsula at Montague Harbour Park.

There is one tennis court at **Galiano Golf and Country Club**.

Scenic Spots

By Galiano standards it's a long drive to the northern tip of the island at Coon Bay, but the beaches here are perhaps the best on the island: sand or smoothly sloped sandstone rock.

Montague Harbour Provincial Park is the site of 3000-year-old Aboriginal middens that are still visible in the cliffs by the shore. An island/peninsula juts out of the park into the harbour; at low tide you can walk around on the beach, and at high tide you can take the path up above.

Galiano Bluffs Park was bequeathed to the people of Galiano. You can drive via Burrill Rd and Bluff Rd to the top of the bluffs through stands of old-growth fir and cedar and arrive at views of Victoria and the American San Juan Islands. There are also hiking trails in the park.

Bellhouse Park, also a legacy to islanders, is a good picnic spot. It has picnic tables and good views of Active Pass and the Mayne Island lighthouse. Access is by Burrill Rd and Jack Rd.

Special Events

An island-wide fire sale is held at the fire-hall on the Victoria Day weekend. On the July 1 long weekend the Jamboree, a family event, is held at North End Hall. The Fiesta, on the Aug 1 long weekend, includes a parade, salmon barbecue, homemade pies, pony rides and games of chance. Dances are held at the community hall near the Pub on Saturday nights of long weekends.

The Arts

The **Dandelion Gallery** (539-5622) in Sturdies Bay exhibits local painting, sculpture, glass, jewellery and photographs and sells books written by Galiano Islanders. Open every day in the summer and every weekend the rest of the year.

Check at the Travel Infocentre for amateur theatre productions, which are held occasionally. Most summer weekends there are special events, from art shows to visiting novelists who give readings.

Mayne Island

Compared to long, narrow Galiano, Mayne, the second ferry stop, is small and compact—you can drive anywhere in about 10 minutes. Whereas Galiano is covered with forest, Mayne is more pastoral. It has a population of about 830 and even fewer tourist amenities than Galiano. Don't expect much choice in restaurants or accommodation; the charm of these islands lies in the beaches and tidal pools, the birds, seals and sea lions, the coastal forests and the slower pace of life.

Tourist Information

Pick up the indispensable map produced by the islanders, which is available free on the ferry and at any store on Mayne. Not only will it help you get around but it also lists all the services and attractions on the island. In high season, tourist information is available at the museum in Miners Bay. During the year write to **Mayne Island Chamber of Commerce**, Box 160, Mayne Island, BC V0N 2J0.

Services

There's no bank here, but you will find the **Miners Bay Trading Post** (539-2214), which is a grocery store/liquor store, as well as a service station, and a bakery/espresso bar at Miners Bay. At Fernhill Centre, **Mayne Open Market** (539-5024) has fresh and natural foods, snack food, housewares, gifts, stationery; the post office is here along with fax service.

Where to Stay

Fernhill Lodge
Fernhill Rd
539-2544
Along with the historical dinners served at Fernhill Lodge, you have a choice of themed rooms: 18th-century French, Canadiana, farmhouse, Jacobean, East Indian, Moroccan or Oriental. The Jacobean Room, for example, has Tudor panelling and a four-poster bed that you have to jump up into. All rooms have private baths, and the lodge has an inviting library and sun room. The guests also have the use of a piano, outdoor sauna and hot tub. Doubles $90–139.

Oceanwood Country Inn
Dinner Bay Rd
539-5074
Eleven of the 12 deluxe rooms at the Oceanwood have a view of Navy Channel, which separates Mayne from North Pender. All have bathrooms, and most have whirlpools, French doors, fireplaces or terraces. Each room is decorated differently, with Canadiana pine, Victorian mahogany and romantic chintzes.

The inn sits on 4 ha (10 acres) of wooded waterfront property. It has a lawn for croquet, a sauna and an outdoor hot tub. The small conference room, living room, library (chock-a-block with books and magazines) and games room with bridge tables (where afternoon tea is served) are all for the use of guests. Breakfast and afternoon tea are included. No children, no pets. During the winter, theme weekends are built around wine tastings, nature outings, murder mysteries and the like. Doubles $130–295. See also Restaurants, below.

Blue Vista Resort
Arbutus Rd
539-2463

Oceanwood Country Inn sits on the waterfront of Mayne Island.

The Blue Vista is a good bet for family accommodation. Eight fully equipped cabins sit in a parklike setting, close to Bennett Bay, and are within walking distance of the best beach on the island. There are one- and two-bedroom cabins, which are more modern than rustic, but some have fireplaces and all have decks. Barbecues and bicycles are available. Pets welcome in off season. Doubles $50–70.

Root Seller Inn
Miners Bay
539-2621
This warm and friendly country-style bed and breakfast has four rooms. The location is popular with hikers and cyclists because it is in the heart of activity at Miners Bay—within walking distance of stores and the pub. All rooms share baths. Doubles $65–75.

A few other B&Bs to consider: **Bayview B&B** (539-2924), **Tinkers B&B** (539-2280) and **Wilde-flower Inn B&B** (539-2327). For families, try **Mayne Cliff** (529-2236).

Restaurants

Fernhill Lodge $$
Fernhill Rd
539-2544
Fernhill Lodge has built its reputation on historical dinners. One night dinner may be inspired by Chaucer; the next, by Cleopatra or the Romans. The Crumblehumes research these historical meals, make a few adaptions for the 20th century and serve dishes like red snapper with plums, coriander and wine (apparently a favourite of Cleopatra's), leek and walnut soup or a Chaucerian salmon with thyme sauce. Themed meals are available on request; otherwise there is a contemporary farmhouse menu. Reservations a must.

Oceanwood Country Inn $$$
Dinner Bay Rd
539-5074
The Oceanwood is open to nonguests

for dinner, a fixed-price meal that is seasonal and focusses on local produce. Recent renovations changed the location of the dining room; it now takes advantage of the lovely oceanfront setting. One fall menu offered Roma tomato soup with basil oil, marinated young potato and peppered shrimp salad, seared curried Pacific halibut on apple cilantro brown rice and chili chocolate mousse parfait. All wines are from the West Coast. Book in advance.

Springwater Lodge $
Miners Bay
539-5521
Strictly pub food—burgers, sandwiches, and fish and chips—but it's well done, and when you eat in the sun on the deck overlooking Miners Bay, it's even better.

Sports and Recreation

Although Mayne is not flat, it is one of the easier islands to bicycle around. The island is compact and roads form convenient loops. Rentals are available at **Tinkerer's Retreat** (539-2280).

Bait and licences are available at **Active Pass Auto Marine** (539-5411) in Miners Bay. The best spot for summer salmon fishing around the islands is in Active Pass, the body of water separating Mayne and Galiano. **Active Pass B&B Charters** (539-2262) have guided, fully equipped fishing charters.

Eagle Spirit Charters (539-5540) offers fishing and sightseeing trips; gear and bait provided.

Island Charters (539-5040) will arrange charters on a Saturna 33 sailboat for a half day, a day or overnight. The company will pick you up or drop you off at one of the other Gulf Islands.

Mayne Island Kayak and Canoe Rentals (539-2667) rents by the hour or by the day; they will pick up at the ferry and have a variety of put-in areas around Mayne.

The best swimming beaches are the long, wide, sandy beach at Bennett Bay and the protected Campbell Bay beach, known for its warm waters. Dinner Bay Community Park with beach, barbecues, playground and playing fields is ideal for families.

A public tennis court is behind the fire-hall on Felix Jack Rd off Fernhill Rd.

There are two private campgrounds on Mayne—**Fern Hollow Campground** (539-5253) and **Journey's End Farm** (539-2411).

Scenic Spots

It is about a 45-minute to an hour's walk to Helen Point; access is off Village Bay Rd. This walk starts with a steep downhill, but it isn't difficult after that. Designated an Indian Reserve in 1877, the point has no residents today. Two wooded trails lead to a mossy bank above the entrance to Active Pass. Ideal for a picnic, with views of the ferries, and you often have eagles soaring overhead.

Mount Parke is a 12 ha (30-acre) wilderness park and the highest point on the island. Access is off Fernhill Rd via Montrose Rd, and you can drive part way up the mountain. Views of Vancouver, Active Pass and Vancouver Island are almost 360°. The unmanned satellite radar station on the mountain top monitors ship traffic in Active Pass.

St Mary Magdalene Church, built in 1898, is one of many fine Victorian buildings on Mayne. Stately old houses of the same era are in Miners Bay and on Georgina Point Rd. You can glean a little of the history of the island from the old cemetery beside the church. Across the street is a stairway leading down to the beach.

The **Active Pass Lighthouse**, built in 1885, at Georgina Point is open to the public every afternoon, 1-3. The grassy grounds are perfect for a picnic. This is a good bird-watching spot, particularly in winter, and there are many tidal pools along the sandstone shore.

The beach at **Bennett Bay** is very popular and is the warmest for swimming because it is so shallow. On a clear day, Mount Baker in Washington State is visible in the distance.

Special Events

The Fall Fair is held on the third weekend in August, the same time as the Springwater Salmon Derby, and the Salmon Bake is on the Sunday before Labour Day.

The Arts

Several artists and craftspeople open their studios to the public daily in the

The shoreline of much of the Gulf Islands is either steep cliffs or this smooth sandstone. Odd formations have been sculpted by thousands of years of hammering by the sea. (Dick Tipple)

summer and on weekends during the rest of the year. Check the map published by the islanders for locations and times.

Mayne Island Little Theatre stages amateur productions in spring and fall; watch for posters.

Saltspring Island

Saltspring is very different from the other Gulf Islands. It is the largest, most populous (10,000 residents) and most developed. Unlike the others, Saltspring has a real town, even a shopping centre, 100 B&Bs and more real estate agents than you'd care to see in one place. Other singular features are the several small lakes, which provide warm swimming spots, and the 14 briny springs at the north end of the island that gave the island its name.

Ferries from Tsawwassen arrive at Long Harbour. There are regularly scheduled float plane flights from Vancouver Harbour and Vancouver Airport to Ganges Harbour. (Harbour Air 537-5525 or 1-800-665-0212.)

It would be difficult to visit Saltspring without a car, but some B&B

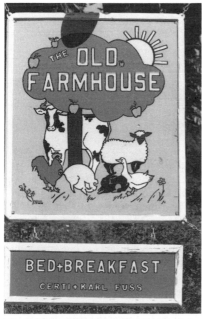

The Old Farmhouse is one of Saltspring Island's 100 B&Bs. (Judi Lees)

At Saltspring's Lakeside B&B days begin with fresh fruit platters served on the deck. (Judi Lees)

hosts may be willing to pick you up at the ferry terminal or from Ganges Harbour. Check when making a reservation.

The first settlers on Saltspring were black Americans fleeing slavery in 1857. The island started and developed as an agricultural community and is now famous for its Saltspring Island lamb and its hospitality—during summer it can be packed with tourists.

Tourist Information

Tourist information is available year-round at the Travel Infocentre (537-5252) at 121 Lower Ganges Rd in Ganges: July and Aug, 8 AM–6 PM; rest of the year, 10 AM–4 PM. You can write to the **Saltspring Island Chamber of Commerce**, 121 Lower Ganges Rd, Ganges, BC V8K 2T1.

Where to Stay

Of the many B&Bs on Saltspring, here is a sampling:

The Old Farmhouse
1077 North End Rd
(537-4113)
You drive up a long driveway, through enviable flower gardens and into a parklike setting of large trees, a hammock and swinging benches, a gazebo and everywhere flowers. To add to the picture-perfect setting is the old farmhouse. Gerti and Karl Fuss have enhanced the charm of this 1890s farmhouse by adding space and amenities without losing the wonderful hominess of this heritage building. The four guest rooms are cozy with floral wallpapering, comfy furnishings and private baths. The two downstairs rooms have private patios, and the upstairs ones have small balconies that overlook the grounds—it's not unusual to see deer wandering by. There are nice touches like fresh flowers and sherry in each room. The sitting room has a welcoming bay window sofa. You feel as though you have stepped back in time—television and telephones are brought out only on request. Guests prefer to wander the grounds or curl up with a book and escape the 20th century.

Each day Gerti bakes cinnamon buns, croissants and muffins, fresh fruit often includes raspberries from the garden, and she's known for her specialties such as smoked salmon soufflé and cheese blintzes. Doubles $125–150.

Lakeside B&B
118 Natalie Lane
537-2571
End your day with a peaceful paddle on a mirror-calm lake and awaken the next morning to the tap-tap of a pileated woodpecker adorning a stump outside your bedroom window. Lakeside B&B is hidden away on the shores of Cusheon Lake. It offers the best of both worlds, since you can

The Gulf Islands are one of the best sailing areas in the world. (Dick Tipple)

enjoy water activities such as swimming, fishing, canoeing or kayaking and mix with the friendly family (Candace Snow and Jack Rosen have two small sons), or you can retreat to your room and enjoy the privacy of this home surrounded by trees and overlooking the lake. The Blue Room has a private entrance, Jacuzzi tub and some Asian touches from the owners' travels. The Cedar Room has the option of a king-size or twin beds and is adorned with Native art.

Lakeside B&B welcomes families, but this is a quiet home where couples are equally comfortable. There are thoughtful extras, such as the array of bath products, fruit basket and tea tray left out for you to help yourself.

On warm days, breakfast is served on the deck. The setting and the food are memorable. As the sun sparkles off the lake, you enjoy fresh fruit,

spinach quiche, healthy breads and "breakfast dessert," a wonderful berry crumble. You won't need lunch.

Doubles $80–95.

Weston Lake Inn
813 Beaver Point Rd
653-4311

"A small piece of heaven" is one of many plaudits in the guest book at Weston Lake Inn, and it does have a heavenly quality about it. High on a hill, where wind whispers through the Douglas fir, the large home has decks, a hot tub area and exquisite gardens overlooking Weston Lake. Wilson, the world's friendliest English sheepdog, welcomes you. Susan Evans and Ted Harrison have honed B&B hosting to a fine art. They provide robes that so you can wander down to the hot tub, there's a large entertainment lounge with fireplace, and the house and three guest rooms are beautifully furnished, complete with original art. All rooms have private baths; one has a queen-size and twin bed. It's adult oriented but children over 14 are welcome. Susan makes her own granola, the blended juices are freshly squeezed, the eggs are from the couple's free-range chickens, and Susan has a wide repertoire of breakfast menus; the three-cheese scones are one of many favourites with repeat guests. Susan's also a whiz with low-fat sauces such as the one on her poached eggs with smoked salmon. Ted offers sailing charters on the 10 m (36-foot) sloop *Malaika*. Doubles $105–110.

Other Lodging

A few other recommended B&Bs are **Beddis House** (537-1028), **Green Rose Farm and Guest House** (537-9927), and **San Michele by the Sea B&B** (537-5514). Besides **Lakeside B&B**, check with **Applecroft Family Farm** (537-5311) and **Cottage Resort** (537- 2214) for family accommodation.

Cabins can be rented on the sea or by a lake at **Salty Spring Seaside Resort** (537-4111), **Spindrift Resort** (537-5311), and **Cusheon Lake Resort** (537-9629).

The most deluxe and expensive lodging is at **Hastings House** (537-2362), an elegant and gracious 12 ha (30-acre) estate. Five beautifully restored buildings house 11 guest accommodations.

Rates for B&Bs during summer range from about $60 to $195, cabins are in the $75–150 range, and Hastings House rates range from $310 to $440 for double.

Restaurants

Our favourite place to eat is the **Vesuvius Inn** (537-2312), both for the good pub food and the spectacular

setting on Vesuvius Bay. The **Bouzouki Greek Café**, owned by Steve and Georgia Asproloupos, has authentic Greek dishes and super desserts (537-4181). Other recommended restaurants are **House Piccolo** (537-1844), **Moby's Marine Pub** (537-5559) and the **Tides Inn** (537-1470).

Hastings House has a formal dining room with a traditional menu— you can try local seafood or the island's famous lamb.

Sports and Recreation

Rent bicycles at **Island Spoke Folk** (537-4664) in Ganges. Keep in mind that the north end of the island is flatter. Canoes, kayaks and small power boats as well as scooters are for rent at the **Salt Spring Marina**. The marina also has a full- service scuba shop and will arrange fishing and sailing charters. Fishing licences can be purchased here or at **Mouat's Hardware**.

Island Escapades (537-2537) offers kayaking, sailing, hiking and climbing day trips and instruction as well as longer expeditions. The Gulf Island Explorer is for two, three or four days of kayaking.

Arrange horseback riding through **Salt Spring Guided Rides** (537-5761).

Four public tennis courts are located on Vesuvius Rd near North End Rd, next door to the new outdoor pool and across from the **Salt Spring Island Golf and Country Club** (537-2121). This nine-hole, par-72 course is open to visitors all year.

Scenic Spots

Beaver Point in **Ruckle Provincial Park** is an exquisite picnic and hiking spot: smooth rocks sloping into the water, arbutus trees on the point and small pebble coves for beachcombing. Trails are suitable for family hiking. Ruckle Park is also a historic site. The Ruckles were one of Saltspring's first farming families; their farmhouse and outbuildings still stand in the park and are identified by plaques.

On the way to Ruckle Provincial Park stop at **Everlasting Summer** (653-9418), a lovely herb and flower garden open daily March to Dec.

Mount Maxwell is not the highest point on the island, but it has a viewpoint that you can drive to and a network of easy trails. It's a great place to view a sunset.

Beddis Beach at the end of Beddis Rd is wide and sandy and is good for sun-bathing, bird-watching and beachcombing. It is best at low tide. Other beaches are at Beachside Dr on Long Harbour, **Booth Bay** (access is via Baker Rd) and **Drummond Park** at Fulford Harbour.

The Arts

During the summer artists sell their work daily at **Artcraft** in Mahon Hall in Ganges. The **Saltspring Festival of the Arts** offers music, theatre and dance in July. Watch for posters or inquire at the Travel Infocentre.

Volume II (537-9223) is a small but first-rate bookstore in Mouat's Mall in Ganges. (While you are in the mall stop at fragrant **Salt Spring Soapworks**; all the soaps are handmade using natural products.) Also at the mall is the **Pegasus Gallery of Canadian Art** (537-2421). There are many galleries and artists' studios on Saltspring. Two other notable galleries are **Ewart Gallery of Fine Arts** (537-2313) and **Stone Walrus Gallery** (537-9896). At the Travel Infocentre there is a map of artists' studios, and you can do a self-guided tour every Sun from Apr to Oct.

Special Events

There is a Saturday market in the centre of Ganges from Apr to Oct that features everything grown or crafted on the island.

The fall fair—a real country fair with animals, games and midway—is held the third weekend in Sept.

Whistler

The face of Whistler changes constantly. Some of us recall the days when skiing at Whistler Mountain cost $7 and when the Whistler Village site was a garbage dump.

Today both Whistler and Blackcomb Mountains are well developed, and the resort is recognized as one of the world's best ski destinations. And, in just over a decade, it has become a major draw in summer, with dozens of outdoor activities as well as a repertoire of summer festivals. There's Mozart, jazz, country and blues, Vancouver Symphony Orchestra concerts and daily street entertainment.

The resort can be confusing for a first-time visitor, since it's made up of several villages with sprawling residential neighbourhoods stretching along the road and up the mountainsides. The hub is Whistler Village. Its award-winning compact layout is a pedestrian area with everything— from a grocery store and a pharmacy to classy restaurants—no more than a five-minute walk away, including the ski runs.

In winter the village is festive in a dressing of snow and lights; in summer the maze of streets is alive with entertainment, people eating outdoors and smiling shoppers. Most of the hotels are on the perimeter of the village and have underground parking. If you're visiting for the day, use the large free lots nearby.

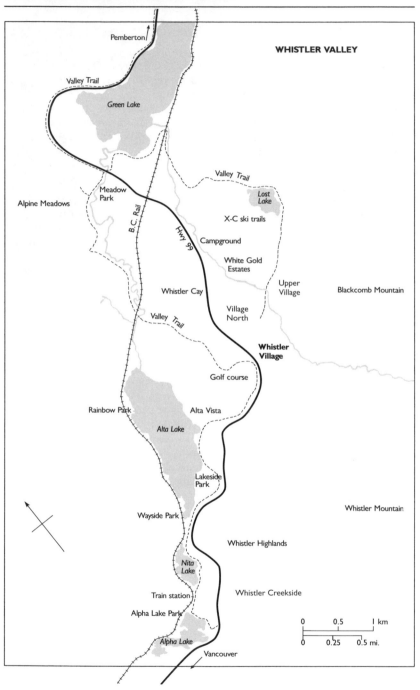

WHISTLER VALLEY

Pemberton

Valley Trail

Green Lake

Valley Trail

Meadow
Park

Alpine Meadows

Lost
Lake

X-C ski trails

B.C. Rail

Hwy 99

Campground

White Gold
Estates

Upper
Village

Blackcomb Mountain

Whistler Cay

Village
North

Valley Trail

**Whistler
Village**

Golf course

Rainbow Park

Alta Vista

Alta Lake

Lakeside
Park

Whistler Mountain

Wayside Park

Whistler Highlands

Nita
Lake

Train station

Whistler Creekside

Alpha Lake Park

Alpha Lake

Vancouver

0	0.5	1 km
0	0.25	0.5 mi.

Whistler Village hums with activity in summer as well as winter. (Leanna Rathkelly)

A 10-minute walk or short drive uphill is the Upper Village, which has several large hotels and condominium complexes, shops, restaurants and mountain access. The heart of the Upper Village is Chateau Whistler. In summer, in particular, many people enjoy this area for a quieter stay and the posh surroundings of the Chateau. In winter, lift lines are less crowded here and there are several good pubs for après-ski—one with a large outdoor deck that's popular on sunny spring days.

A footbridge over Village Gate Blvd links Whistler Village to the new Village North. When completed, Village North will comprise a plaza, a condominium complex above retail and restaurant space and underground parking. Already in place is the Marketplace, which has more of a shopping mall feel to it, since it is not a "pedestrian only" complex. It is primarily retail space and has some amenities for locals, such as an insurance office, real estate offices, dry cleaners and a bank.

Whistler Creek, about 3 km (2 miles) south of Whistler Village, was the original development in the sixties. Today there is a gondola and chairlift to Whistler Mountain as well as a ski and rental shop, small retail mall, and several pubs and delis popular with the locals. There are plans for a major development of Whistler Creekside.

Getting There

Whistler is 120 km (75 miles) north of Vancouver on Hwy 99, a 90-minute drive. The winding mountain road can be dangerous in the winter. Snow tires are mandatory and chains are sometimes necessary. Call the **Department of Highways** (1-900-451-4997) for road conditions. Car rentals are available at Whistler through ABC Rent-A-Car (938-4343), **Budget** (932-1236) and **Thrifty** (938-0302).

Throughout the year you can travel by train from Vancouver to Whistler (**B.C. Rail**, 984-5246). It is a scenic trip, but the schedule lacks flexibil-

Whistler Resort is among the top ski destinations in North America. (Whistler Resort Association)

ity—there is only one train daily. The station is closest to Whistler Creekside; a free shuttle bus transports train passengers to the village.

There are over half a dozen bus and coach services; **Maverick Coach Lines** (662-8051) departs from Vancouver Bus Depot and drops off at a variety of points throughout Whistler, and **Perimeter Transportation** (261-2299) runs daily trips between Whistler and Vancouver International Airport.

There is no scheduled air service to Whistler, but **North Vancouver Airlines** (278-1608 or 1-800-228-6608) flies from Vancouver to Pemberton, 35 km (22 miles) north of Whistler.

There are a number of charter services, including **Helijet Airways** (938-1878 or 273-4688) and **Whistler Air** (932-6615).

Tourist Information

A tourist information booth (932-5528) is on the highway at Lake Placid Road, 3 km (2 miles) south of Whistler Village. Another booth is at the front door of the Conference Centre in the village. You can also call the **Whistler Resort Association**. To book accommodation call 932-4222 in Whistler or toll free in the U.S. and Canada (except Vancouver) at 1-800-944-7853. For other information, call the association's activity line at 932-2394.

Where to Stay

Accommodation at Whistler falls into four groups: high-priced luxury hotels, mid-range condominium hotels, pensions, and a few hostels and B&Bs. Off-season rates generally apply Nov, Dec and Apr (also Jan at some places). During high season, minimum stays of three nights are required when you make a reservation. The Whistler Resort Association (see above) will book accommodation for you.

The best hotels, the **Chateau Whistler** (938-8000), the **Delta Whistler Resort** (932-1982), **Whistler Fairways** (932-2522) and the Radisson's **Le Chamois** (932-2882) will cost you an arm and a leg (nothing is cheap at Whistler) unless it's off season. Wherever you stay, visit the Chateau. The lobby is fabulous: huge fireplaces, stone pillars, comfy overstuffed wingbacked sofas, handmade Mennonite rugs, antique pine furniture and Canadiana folk art. Stop for a drink in the Mallard Bar and visit the shops. The Chateau has a health club for guests as well as a spa where treatments can be booked by guests and nonguests. There is everything from aromatherapy to a range of massages. There are plans to expand the Chateau with another 200 rooms. During high season, room prices start around $200 for doubles.

Many of the mid-range hotels were built in the late seventies and have been refurbished. Most have been planned for skiers and have kitchen facilities and sleep at least four people. There is a wide variety of condominium complexes throughout Whistler. A standard two-bedroom, two-bathroom suite with a pull-out couch in the living room will be a tight squeeze for two families or three couples, but it is one way to keep the cost down.

The third group, the pensions, are chalet style and are usually run by Austrian, German or Swiss Canadians. They are in large houses with half a dozen guest rooms and private family quarters. The pensions are in residential areas rather than in the village, though many are only a 15-minute walk away. If you are coming without a car, the innkeepers will drive you to and from the ski lifts. In the evening you could walk or take a cab to a restaurant. Hearty breakfasts are included, and many rooms have private baths. Pension rates are about $115 for two in high season and $80 during the rest of the year.

Pensions are a great deal because, along with comfortable accommodation, you get affable and informative hosts and interesting breakfast companions, perhaps from Boston or Berlin. The pensions are **Edelweiss** (932-3641), **Lorimer Ridge** (938-9722), **Chalet Luise** (932-4187), **Durlacher Hof** (932-1924), Alta Vista (932-4900) and **Carney's Cottage** (938-8007).

In the budget category, there are four dormitory-style hostels (some have private rooms as well) with rates in the $20 a night range. **Whistler Hostel** (932-5492) is a member of Hostelling International and has a

Whistler's wooded paths and mountain trails make it ideal for mountain biking. (Leanna Ruthkelly)

beautiful setting on the shore of Alta Lake. There are ten small lodges and B&Bs, which cost about $90 a night—for example, **Stancliff House** (932-2393) and **Idylwood B&B** (932-4582). These can be booked through Whistler Resort Association.

Restaurants

There are many expensive restaurants in Whistler; you'll spend $100 for two with no problem. If you want a good meal on a weekend during ski season, make a reservation a few weeks in advance.

Umberto Menghi operates two Italian restaurants here: **Il Caminetto**

Snowmobiling offers quick access to backcountry in the Whistler area. (Eric Sinclair)

(932-4442) and **Trattoria di Umberto** (932-5858) in the village. Another favourite for pasta is **Araxi Ristorante** (932-4540) in the centre of the village.

The **Rim Rock Café & Oyster Bar** (932-5565) at Whistler Creekside has a big reputation for seafood. **Val d'Isère** (932-4666), which is a little cheaper than the others, serves classic French food and is in the village.

Both restaurants in the Chateau Whistler are very good. The **Wildflower** (938-2033) is charmingly decorated in rich colours and displays an assortment of old wooden birdhouses. It offers lavish buffets for breakfast, lunch and dinner or a menu featuring foods of the Pacific Northwest. It has Heart Smart menu selections. **La Fiesta** (938-2040) is a fun restaurant that serves Spanish *tapas*, Mexican entrées and hot rock cooking. It's livelier than the Wildflower.

There are two topnotch Japanese restaurants, **Sushi Village** (932-3330) and **Irori** (932-2221), in the village. For Thai cuisine, there's Thai One On (932-4822) in the Upper Village.

If all you want is a decent burger, try **Jimmy D's Roadhouse** (932-4451) or go to **Cinnamon Bear Bar** in the Delta and have a dual mountain burger. **Citta** (932-4177) offers pub fare and is a popular hangout for young people. For families, try the **Old Spaghetti Factory** (938-1081). If you like Greek, **Zeuski's Taverna** (932-6009) is a bargain. Another bargain for take-outs (there are a few seats) is **Ingrid's Village Café** (932-7000).

Sports and Recreation

For specific information, call the **Whistler Resort Association** activity line at 932-2394. If you want more detailed information about hiking and mountain bike trails or canoe routes, you may want to purchase a copy of *The Whistler Outdoors Guide,* which is available from bookstores in Vancouver and Whistler.

The **Whistler Outdoor Experience Company** (932-3389) in the bottom level of the Chateau books a wide variety of outdoor activities.

For skiing in winter, see Sports/Recreation (Skiing). In addition, you can try snowmobiling, which gets you into the backcountry; call **Blackcomb Snowmobile** (932-8484) or **Whistler Snowmobile Guided Tours** (932-4086). There's ice skating at **Meadow Park Sports Centre** (938-3133) and snowshoeing with **Canadian Snowshoeing Services** (932-7877). Backcountry ski touring and ice climbing is available with **Whistler Alpine Guides** (938-9242). For sleigh rides, contact **Whistler Outdoor Experience** (932-3389).

Winter or summer, visit the **Whistler Museum** (932-2019) or take a tour of **Whistler Brewery** (932-6185). Also in both seasons, the very adventuresome can experience paragliding; call **Parawest Paragliding** (932-7052).

Summertime can be action-packed, if you wish. You can rent mountain bikes and either set off on your own or join a group. Trails lead from the village to Lost Lake; you can get there and back in an hour. The Valley Trail, a 42 km (26-mile) cycling and hiking trail, will take most of the day. Some of the trail is paved and flat; north towards Lost Lake it is a bit more of a challenge.

Bikes can't be reserved, so get there early in the day.

Mountain Riders (932-3659) and **Whistler Backroads** (932-3111) are both in the village and have rentals.

Another option is to join a bike tour. Tours can last two hours, all day or several days. Itineraries are geared to different levels of ability. A popular guided ride is the Descent, where you take your bike up Blackcomb or Whistler Mountain on the gondola or chair and ride back down. Call **Whistler Outdoor Experience** (932-3389) or **Whistler Backroads** (932-3111). Whistler Backroads will arrange a heli-biking trip, in which you are transported to some remote destination with mountain bikes and a guide.

In-line skating rentals are available from **High Performance Shop** (938-7726) and **Whistler Blades** (932-9669), among others. The Valley Trail, also used by cyclists and walkers, is excellent for in-line skating.

Five lakes are within 5 km (3 miles) of the village. **Whistler Outdoor Experience** (932-3389) rents canoes, windsurfing boards and Laser sailboats at Edgewater Outdoor Centre on Green Lake. The company also offers windsurfing lessons and short canoe trips. For a four-hour pedal-paddle trip, you are provided with a bicycle to pedal to Green Lake. There you can paddle the canoe that's waiting for you and then cycle back.

The **Whistler Campground** (932-5181) is the closest to the village, 1.6 km (1 mile) north. Whistler is near the edge of **Garibaldi Provincial Park** (898-3678) and a few kilometres north of **Brandywine Falls Provincial Park**; both have campgrounds.

Fishing attracted people to Whistler for decades before anyone thought of skiing there. The five lakes and many rivers and streams surrounding Whistler still provide great trout fishing. Go to **Whistler Backcountry Adventures** (938-1410) for tackle, licences and guided trips. There is catch and release fly-fishing available. Also call **Whistler Fishing Guides** (932-4267).

Golf is available May to Oct. Whistler boasts three courses. Arnold Palmer designed the **Whistler Golf**

Course (932-4544), an 18-hole championship course (6100 yards, par 72) adjacent to the village. The **Chateau Whistler Golf Course** (6635 yards, par 72; 938-2092) was designed by Robert Trent Jones. The most recent addition is the **Nicklaus North Course** (938-9898) with 6925 yards (par 71).

Hikers love these mountains. For a challenging hike, the favourite is Singing Pass and Russett Lake (about eight hours return trip); it's hard work, but the reward is lovely alpine meadows. Try to get a ride to the trail head.

You can take a lift up Blackcomb or Whistler, where there are several trails for hiking on your own. Or join a group for a free guided mountain-top hike. Call **Whistler Mountain** (932-3434) or **Blackcomb Mountain** (932-3141). The Valley Trail, which leads in several directions from the village out to the five lakes, is good for family hiking. For organized group trips, call **Whistler Outdoor Experience** (932-3389) or **Backroads Mountain Bike Adventures** (932-3111).

Horseback riding is available (also in winter); call **Western Adventures on Horseback** (894-6155) or **Pemberton Stables** (894-6615).

Climbing specialists at **The Escape Route** (938-3338) will arrange equip-ment rental, instruction or guided trips if you wish to learn about rock climbing and mountaineering techniques.

The area offers both scenic rafting and whitewater trips, which vary from two hours to full days. Wet suits are included in the whitewater excursions—a perfect thing to do if it's raining. Call **Whistler River Adventures** (932-3532) or **Wedge Rafting** (932-7171).

Summer glacier skiing on Black-comb (932-3141) usually lasts until mid-Aug. There is also a selection of ski clinics and camps. If you are an experienced skier, you could try a day of heli-skiing: four glacier runs on fresh powder—3660 vertical meters (12,000 feet), **Tyax Heli-Skiing** (932-7007) or **Whistler Heli-Skiing** (932-4105).

Four outdoor tennis courts are available at **Myrtle Philip Elementary School** at the village. Courts are also located at **Alpha Lake Park, Meadow Lake Park** and **Emerald Park**. If you're serious about the game, **Chateau Whistler** has excellent tennis clinics. The Chateau, as well as the **Delta Whistler Resort** and **Tantalus Lodge**, have pay-as-you-play courts. Recently the **Whistler Racquet and Golf Resort** added 10 courts; 3 are covered for year-round use.

Index

Accessories stores, 178
The Accord restaurant, 47
Active Pass Lighthouse, 217
Air B.C., 80
Aircraft: airshows, 100; emergencies, 12; museums, 131–32; tours, 93–94, 117
Airport, Bellingham, 71
Airport, Seattle (SeaTac), 71
Airport, Vancouver International, 3, 77–80; accommodation near, 29; bank machines, 79; getting to, 71, 78
Airport, Victoria, 80
Airporter bus, 71
Airshow, Abbotsford, 100
Alcohol. *See* Breweries; Liquor stores; Wine
Alcoholics Anonymous, 12
Ambleside Park, 159, 161, 200
Ambulance service, 12
Amtrak, 73
Anthropology, ubc Museum of, 82, 124–25, 202
Antiques, 178–79
Aquabus Ferries, 86
Aquarium, Vancouver, 111, 196–97
Aquatic Centre: ubc, 171, 172; Vancouver, 172
Architecture, 97
Archives, City of Vancouver, 128
Arriva restaurant, 58–59
Art galleries, 83, 85, 132–34
Arts Club Theatre, 86, 136–37
Art supply stores, 86, 178
Auctions, 178–79
Auto clubs, 13
Automobiles. *See* Cars
Auto racing, 100, 150

Babysitters, 16, 95
Bacchus Ristorante, 44
Bakeries, 43–44, 60, 189–90
Banking, 14, 208
Bard on the Beach Shakespeare festival, 100, 137
Barnston Island, 199
Bars, 24, 71, 94, 144–46. *See also* Clubs; Lounges
Baseball, 162, 201
Basketball, 3, 8, 162
Bayshore Hotel, 26–27
Beaches: Ambleside, 159, 161; English Bay, 108, 171; Gulf Islands, 213, 217, 221; Jericho, 82, 103–4, 171, 172; Kitsilano, 93, 154–55, 161, 171, 172, 199; Locarno, 103–4, 155, 171; Second, 109–10, 171; Spanish Banks, 82, 103–4, 155, 171; Sunset, 150, 171; Third, 109; Wreck, 103–4
Beer. *See* Breweries; Liquor stores
Bellhouse Park, 213
Benny's Bagels, 16
Berry picking, 199

Bicycles. *See* Cycling
Bird sanctuaries, 119, 122, 196
Bishop's restaurant, 54
Blackcomb Mountain, 167, 221, 228
Bloedel Conservatory, 104
Blue Horizon hotel, 26
Boating: canoeing, 85, 150–52, 220, 227; with children, 199; cruising, 152–53, 155, 216, 220; emergencies, 12; instruction, 163–64; kayaking, 96, 150–51, 212, 216, 220; marine forecast, 12; rentals, 85, 151–52; river rafting, 162–63, 228; sailing, 163–64; tours, 87–88, 95–96; windsurfing, 173
La Bodega restaurant, 60–61
Bookstores, 179–82, 204
Botanical gardens. *See* Gardens
Bowen Island, 36, 74, 77
Brandywine Falls Provincial Park, 227
Bread Garden restaurant, 16
Breweries, 86, 99, 227
Bridges connecting Vancouver, 3
Bridges Restaurant and pub, 47, 86, 145
Britannia, mv, 87–88
B.C. Ferries Corp., 74–77, 208, 209
B.C. Place stadium, 8, 130–31, 162
B.C. Rail, 73, 87–89, 223–24
B.C. Transit: buses/SeaBus/SkyTrain, 67–69; lost and found, 14
Buchan Hotel, 28
Buddhist temple, 29, 131
Buildings, ten best, 97
Buntzen Lake, 121, 151
Burnaby, 7, 37, 130, 202
Burnaby Village Museum, 130, 202
Burrard Inlet, 3, 7, 153, 156, 200
Bus depot, 71
Buses, 67–69, 71, 76, 86, 153, 224. *See also* SeaBus; SkyTrain

Cabs, 72
Café Fleuri, 40
Calendar of events, 99–100
Camera stores, 187
Camping, 36–38, 150, 212, 216, 227
Canada Place, 20, 70, 100, 154, 202
Canadian Pacific Railway, 7, 127
The Cannery restaurant, 46
Canoeing. *See under* Boating
Canyon Court Motel, 31
Capers restaurants, 40–41
Capilano fish hatchery, 115
Capilano River Regional Park, 115–16, 121
Capilano suspension bridge, 115
Carpets, Oriental, 178–79
Carr, Emily, 132
Cars: auto clubs, 13; emergency, 13; on ferries, 75; parades, 100; parking, 72; racing, 100, 150; rentals, 71–72, 223; road conditions, 13; towing, 13. *See also*

Limousine Service; Taxis
Centennial Seawalk, 159
Chartwell restaurant, 44
Cheese stores, 190
Chez Thierry restaurant, 56
Children, 30, 85, 86, 109–10, 196–206
Children's Festival, Vancouver, 100, 203
Chinatown: map, 90–91; restaurants, 63, 93;
    shopping, 177, 198; sights, 89–93, 102–3
Chinese: Cultural Centre, 90–91; festivals, 99;
    food stores, 89, 93, 191; garden, 82, 91,
    102–3; people 8, 89; restaurants, 50–53, 93
Chiyoda restaurant, 60
Christmas events, 100, 112
Churches and synagogues, 15
City hall, 6, 7
Classical music, 140–41
Cleveland Dam, 115
Climate, 9–10
Climbing: indoor walls, 160, 200; outdoors,
    160, 228
Clothing stores: children's, 104–5; men's,
    182–84; outdoor, 186; secondhand, 184;
    women's, 182–83
Cloverdale Rodeo, 160
Clubs, 146–48. *See also* Bars; Lounges
Coach lines, 71, 224
Coal Harbour, 3, 7
Coffee: bars, 49; stores, 190
Comedy: clubs, 144; festival, 100
Communities, 5, 13, 154–55, 176–77
Consignment stores, 170, 184, 205
Consulates, 14
Coquitlam, 5, 38
Crafts: galleries, 83–85, 134; museum,
    128–29; supplies, 85, 86
Le Crocodile restaurant, 56
Cruising. *See under* Boating
Currency exchanges, 14
Customs regulations, 14
Cycling, 153–55, 199, 212, 216, 220, 227
Cypress Bowl Provincial Park, 120–21, 168–69

Dance: clubs, 146–47; companies, 141–42
Day trips, 82–93, 197–201. *See also*
    Sightseeing; Tours
Deadman's Island, 108
Deep Cove, 151, 152, 199
Deer Lake, 151, 199
Deighton, John ("Gassy Jack"), 7, 96
Delany's on Denman Coffee House, 49
Delicatessens, 60, 190–91
Delta Pacific Resort & Conference Centre, 30
Delta Vancouver Airport Hotel & Marina,
    29–30
Dentists, 12
Dionisio Point Provincial Park, 213
Discos. *See* Nightclubs
Discovery, HMCS, 108
Doctors, 12
Downtown: accommodation, 20–26; buses,
    67; map, 66; restaurants, 63; shopping,
    176–77
Dragon Boat Festival, 100
Drugstores, 16

Dundarave Concession, 47
Duty-free shops, 15, 79

East Indian: food stores, 191; people, 8;
    restaurants, 55–56
Ecco Il Pane bakery/restaurant, 43
Emergency phone numbers, 12
Emily Carr College of Art and Design, 85, 133
Endowment Lands. *See* Pacific Spirit Regional
    Park
English Bay, 2, 99, 108, 150, 171
English Bay Inn, 27
Eskimo art, 134
Ethnic: food stores, 191–92; groups, 8–9;
    restaurants, 50–63
Events, calendar of, 99–100
Executive Inn, 24
Expo 86, 3, 8

False Creek, 3, 82, 150, 151, 161
Ferries, 74–77, 208, 209; maps, 75, 208. *See
    also* Aquabus Ferries; Granville Island
    Ferries; Harbour Ferries; SeaBus
Festivals 99–100, 202, 203. *See also* Calendar
    of events
Film Festival, Vancouver International, 100
Film processing, 187
Fire department, 12
Firehall Arts Centre, 137
Fireworks, 93
First Thursday, 124
Fish hatchery, Capilano, 115
Fish House restaurant, 42, 109
Fishing: industry, 10; sport, 155–58, 216
Fish stores, 192
Flight and Transportation, Canadian
    Museum of, 131–32
Flying Wedge pizza, 46
Folk Music Festival, Vancouver International,
    100
Food stores, 189–94
Football, 7, 162
Ford Centre for the Performing Arts, 3, 8,
    137–38
Foreign visitors, 14
Forest: industry, 10; walks, 82, 105, 120–21
Four Seasons Hotel, 21
Fraser, Simon, 5–6, 114
Fraser River: bridges, 3–5; fishing, 158; gold
    rush, 6; rafting, 162; walks, 114, 155
French: people, 8; restaurants, 56
Fringe Festival, 100
Furniture stores, 184–86, 205–6

Galiano, Dionisio Alcala, 6
Galiano Bluffs Park, 213
Galiano Island, 209–14; accommodation,
    209–11; recreation, 212–13; restaurants,
    211–12
Galleries. *See* Art galleries
Gallery Café, 44
Gardens: Bloedel Conservatory, 104; Dr Sun
    Yat-sen Classical Chinese, 82, 91, 102–3;
    Nitobe, 112–13; Queen Elizabeth Park, 104;
    UBC Botanical, 113–14; VanDusen Botanical,

100, 111–12, 201
Garibaldi Provincial Park, 227
Gassy Jack (John Deighton), 7, 96
Gastown: bus, 69; history, 7, 96–98;
   restaurant, 45; shopping 2, 177; tours,
   96–98; Gastown Grand Prix, 100
Le Gavroche restaurant, 56
Gay clubs, 147–48
Gem Museum, Sri Lanken, 131
General Motors Place, 3, 8, 162
George V pub, 24
Georgia, Hotel, 23–24
Il Giardino di Umberto restaurant, 57–58
Glacier flight, 88
Gladys restaurant, 41
Go-karts, 201
Gold rush, 6
Golf, 158–59, 213, 227–28; museum, 131
Goods and Services Tax, 15, 69
La Grande Résidence hotel, 31–32
Grand King Seafood Restaurant, 52–53
Granville Island: bars, 86; boating near, 86;
   children's activities, 197–98; events, 86;
   ferries, 86; galleries, 83–85; getting to,
   86–87; jogging route, 161; Kids Only
   Market, 86, 197; maps, 82, 84; public
   market, 76, 83, 192–93; restaurants, 64, 86;
   sailing schools, 164; shopping, 85–86;
   sights, 82–86; theatres, 85
Granville Island Brewery, 86, 99
Granville Island Ferries, 86
Granville Island Public Market, 83
Le Grec restaurant, 57
Greek: food stores, 192; people, 9; restaurants,
   57
Greyhound buses, 71
Grouse Mountain, 116–17, 167–68, 199
GST, 15, 79
Gulf Islands: 208–20; air tours, 208; diving,
   165–66; ferries, 77, 208; Gulf Islands Bed
   and Breakfast Registry, 208; history 208;
   map, 208

Hamburger Mary's restaurant, 16
Harbour, Vancouver: boating, 153; cycling,
   154; diving, 164–65; industries, 10; map,
   98; tours, 99
Harbour Air, 93–94
Harbour Ferries, 86
Hastings Mill Museum, 131
Heart Smart restaurants, 42
Helicopters: heli-skiing, 228; Vancouver
   tours, 117; to Victoria, 80; to Whistler, 224
Hemlock Valley, 169
Highways, 3, 5, 13
Hiking, 160, 228; Belcarra Regional Park, 121;
   Blackcomb Mountain, 228; Buntzen Lake,
   121; Capilano River Regional Park, 115,
   121; Cypress Bowl 120–21; Grouse
   Mountain, 117; Lighthouse Park, 117–18,
   121; Lynn Headwaters, 120; Montague
   Harbour Provincial Park, 212; Mount
   Maxwell, 221; Mount Parke, 216; Mount
   Seymour Provincial Park, 119, 120; Pacific
   Spirit Regional Park, 114–15, 120; Whistler

Mountain, 228. *See also* Parks; Forest Walks
Historical walking tours, 96–97
History of Vancouver, 5–9
Hockey, 3, 7, 162
Holiday Inn Express, 31
Holidays, public, 14
Hon's Wun Tun House restaurant, 52
Horse: carriage tours, 98; racing, 160; riding,
   220, 228; shows, 196
Horseshoe Bay: buses, 69; ferries, 77; fishing,
   158; transportation routes, 3–5
Hospitals, 12
Hostel, Vancouver, 32
Hotel Georgia, 23–24
Hotels, 20–38; maps, 66, 68
Hotel Vancouver, 7, 23
Howe Sound, 87–88, 152; map, 152
Hudson's Bay Company, 6, 7, 109
Hyack Festival, 100
Hyatt Regency Hotel, 145

Ice cream stores, 192–93
Imax Theatre, 202. *See also* Omnimax Theatre
Indian. *See* East Indian; Native Indian
Indian Arm, 151
Indonesian food stores, 191
Industries, 10
In-line skating, 99, 160–61; rentals, 161
Inuit art, 134
Isadora's Co-operative Restaurant, 41, 86, 204
Italian: food stores, 192; people, 9;
   restaurants, 57–59

Japanese: food stores, 191–92; garden,
   112–13; people, 9; restaurants, 44, 59–60
Japanese Deli House, 44
Japantown, 9, 191–92; map, 90–91
Jazz: clubs, 144; festival, 100
Jewish: food stores, 192; people, 8;
   restaurants, 60
Jogging routes, 161
Johnson, Pauline, 108, 109, 110
Johnson House bed and breakfast, 33

Kaplan's Deli, 60
Kayaking. *See under* Boating
Kenya Court Guest House, 29
Kids Only Market, 86, 197
Kids Traffic School, 109–10, 198
Kingston Hotel, 25
Kirin Mandarin Restaurant, 51
Kitchenware, 186
Kitsilano: 2, accommodation, 29, 35; beaches,
   93, 154–55, 161, 171, 172, 199; cycling,
   154–55; map, 125; museums, 125–28;
   restaurants, 64; shopping, 176
Kitsilano B & B, 35
Kitsilano Beach, 93, 154–55, 161, 171, 172,
   199
Kitsilano Pool, 171
Kosher food stores, 192

Legal services, 12
Library, 3, 8, 92
Lighthouse Park, 117–18, 121, 200

Lighthouse Park Bed and Breakfast, 34–35
Lighthouses, 117, 213, 217
Liliget Feast House restaurant, 63
Limousine Service, 72
The Lions (mountains), 110–11
Lions Gate Bridge, 3, 7, 109
Lions Gate Travelodge, 31
Liquor stores, 16
Little Folks Festival, 202
Little Mountain, 104
Locarno Beach Bed and Breakfast, 33–34
Logger sports shows, 116
Lonsdale Quay Hotel, 30
Lonsdale Quay Public Market, 30, 69
Lost and found, 14
Lost Lagoon, 104, 161, 198
Lounges, 22, 23, 25, 29, 86, 144–45. *See also*
  Bars; Clubs
Lumbermen's Arch, 109
Lynn Canyon Bed and Breakfast, 34
Lynn Canyon Park, 200
Lynn Headwaters Regional Park, 120

Magazines, 18, 179–82
Malinee's Thai Food, 61
Manning Park, 170
Maplewood Children's Farm, 196
Marathon, Vancouver International, 100
Marine: emergencies, 12; forecast, 152
Marineview Coffeeshop, 45–46
Maritime Museum, 126, 201
Markets. *See* Granville Island Public Market;
  Lonsdale Quay Public Market; New
  Westminster Public Market
Mayne Island, 214–17; accommodation,
  214–15; recreation, 216–17; restaurants,
  215–16
Mazes, 112, 201
Metric conversion, 14
Metropolitan Hotel, 20
Mexican: food stores, 192; restaurant, 60
Middle Eastern food stores, 192
Mining industry, 10
Montague Harbour Provincial Park, 212, 213
Motor vehicles. *See* Buses; Cars
Mountain biking, 227
Mountaineering, 160, 228
Mount Baker, 169
Mount Maxwell, 221
Mount Parke, 216
Mount Seymour Provincial Park, 118–19, 168
Movies, 129, 201, 202. *See also* Film Festival
Museums, 82, 123–34, 227. *See also* under
  individual names
Music: children's, 202; classical, 138, 140–41;
  festivals, 100; folk, 100; jazz, 100, 144;
  rhythm and blues, 144; rock, 146–47;
  stores, 187–88

The Naam restaurant, 16, 46
Nanaimo-to-Vancouver bathtub race, 100
Narvaez, Jose Maria, 5
Nat Bailey Stadium, 162, 201
Native Indian: art at airport, 77–80;
  bookstores, 180; galleries, 134; history, 5;

people, 9; restaurant, 63. *See also*
  Anthropology, UBC Museum of; Totem poles
Neighbourhoods. *See* Communities
New Diamond Restaurant, 53
Newspapers, 18
Newton Wave Pool, 200
New Westminster, 7, 13, 70, 71, 100
New Westminster Public Market, 70, 71
Night clubs, 146–48; tour, 147
Nine O'Clock Gun, 108
Noor Mahal restaurant, 55
North Shore. *See* North Vancouver; West
  Vancouver
North Vancouver: accommodation, 30–31;
  buses and SeaBus, 69–70; fishing, 158;
  getting to, 3, 5; information, 13; parks,
  115–19; restaurants, 64
Nude beach, 103–4
Nyala Ethiopian Restaurant, 56

Observatory, Gordon Southam, 128
O'Doul's Hotel, 25–26
Old English Bed and Breakfast Registry, 34
Old Spaghetti Factory, 204
Omnimax Theatre, 129. *See also* Imax Theatre
Opera, 141
Orpheum Theatre, 138–39
Outdoor: clothing, 173, 186; equipment, 186;
  restaurants, 47–48; swimming pools,
  171–72; tennis courts, 172–73. *See also*
  Gardens; Hiking; Parks; Sports/Recreation

Pacific Coach Lines, 71, 95
Pacific National Exhibition, 95
Pacific Palisades Hotel, 25
Pacific Space Centre, 127–28
Pacific Spirit Regional Park, 114–15
Paddle Wheeler Neighbourhood Pub, 71
Pan Pacific Hotel, 20
Park Royal Hotel, 30–31
Parks: Ambleside, 159, 161, 200; Bellhouse,
  213; Brandywine Falls, 227; Buntzen Lake,
  121, 151; Capilano River, 115–16, 121;
  Cates, 165; Cypress Bowl, 120–21, 168–69;
  Dionisio Point, 213; Dr Sun Yat-sen, 103;
  Galiano Bluffs, 213; Garibaldi, 227; George
  C. Reifel Migratory Bird Sanctuary, 119,
  122; Grouse Mountain, 116–17, 167–68,
  199, 200; Lighthouse, 117–18, 121, 165,
  200; Lynn Canyon, 200; Lynn Headwaters,
  120; Manning, 170; Montague Harbour,
  212, 213; Mount Maxwell, 221; Mount
  Parke, 216; Mount Seymour, 118–19, 168;
  Pacific Spirit, 114–15; Queen Elizabeth, 104,
  199; Richmond Nature, 196; Ruckle,
  220–21; Vanier, 125–28; Whytecliff, 165.
  See also Beaches; Gardens; Stanley Park;
  Water parks
Periodicals, 18
Pharmacies, 16
Phnom-Penh restaurant, 62
Pho Hoang restaurant, 62
Photo: developing, 187; galleries, 134; supply
  stores, 187
Piccolo Mondo restaurant, 58

Pink Pearl restaurant, 50–51
Planetarium, H.R. MacMillan, 127–28
Playgrounds, 85, 197, 198, 199, 200
Playland, 201
Plays. *See* Theatre
Polar Bear Swim Club, 99
Police: emergency phone number, 12; lost and found, 14; museum, 131
Population of Vancouver, 8–9
Port Moody, 5, 38
Port of Vancouver. *See* Harbour, Vancouver
Post office, 15
Presentation House, 139
Public transit, 67–71
Pubs, 24, 71, 94, 145–46. *See also* Clubs; Lounges

Queen Elizabeth Park, 104, 199
Queen Elizabeth Theatre and Playhouse, 139
Quick Shuttle bus, 71

Radio stations, 17
Radisson President Hotel & Suites, 29
Rafting, river and whitewater, 162–63, 228
Railways. *See* Amtrak; B.C. Rail; Canadian Pacific Railway; Rocky Mountaineer Railtours; Royal Hudson steam train; VIA Rail
RainCity Grill, 54
Raintree Restaurant, 62
Raku Kushiyaki restaurant, 54
Rape Relief, 14
Recorded music, 187–88
Recording studio, 201
Reifel, George C., Migratory Bird Sanctuary, 119, 122, 196, 199
Restaurant Des Gitanes, 71
Rhythm and blues clubs, 144
Richmond, 5, 29–30, 37, 196, 199, 201
Richmond Nature Park, 196
River Run Cottages, 36
Riviera Motor Inn, 26
Road condition information, 13, 223
Road service, emergency, 13
Roberts Bank, 10
Robson Square, 44, 132–33
Robson St, 2, 82: accommodation, 25; shopping, 176
Rock music, 187–88; clubs, 146–47
Rocky Mountaineer Railtours, 73–74
Rodeos, 160
Rosellen Suites, 27
Rowing, 150–52
Royal Canadian Mounted Police, 12
Royal Hudson steam train, 82, 87–89, 199
Rubina Tandoori restaurant, 42, 55
Ruckle Provincial Park, 220–21
Rugs, Oriental, 178–79

Sailing. *See under* Boating
St Roch, 126, 201–2
Salmon: fishing, 155–58, 216; as food, 192, 194; hatchery, 115
Salmon House restaurant, 48
Saltspring Island, 217–21; accommodation,

218–20; recreation, 220; restaurants, 220
Savary Island Pie Company restaurant, 43
Sawasdee Thai Restaurant, 61
Science World, 129–30, 201
Scuba diving, 164–65, 213, 220
SeaBus, 8, 67, 69–70
Sea Festival, 100
Seafood, 194; restaurants, 42, 45–46; stores, 192
Sea lions, 94, 100
Seaside Reflections, 36
Seasons in the Park restaurant, 48–49
Seattle, 71, 73
Sea Village, 85
Seawall, Stanley Park, 108–10, 153–54, 160–61
Settebello restaurant, 48
Seymour Demonstration Forest, 99
Shakespeare festival (Bard on the Beach), 100, 137
Shaughnessy, 154
Shijo Japanese Restaurant, 59–60
Shoe stores: children's, 204; men's and women's, 188
Shopping centres, 177–78
Sightseeing, 82–100. *See also* Parks; Tours
Simon Fraser University: Art Gallery, 133; history, 7; tours, 99
Simpatico Ristorante, 57, 202
Siwash Rock, 108
Skagit River, 158
Skating, 166
Skiing: with children, 116, 200; cross-country, 169–70; downhill, 116, 166–69, 228; instruction, 116–17; map, 167; rentals, 170
SkyTrain, 67, 70–71
Snow Goose Festival, 100
Soccer, 8, 162
Sophie's Cosmic Café, 204
South Granville, 177
Southlands, 155
Souvenir stores, 188–89
Splashdown Park, 200
Sports Hall of Fame and Museum, B.C., 130–31
Squamish, 87–88
Stadiums: 3, 8, 130–31, 162,
Stanley Park: accommodation near, 26–29; "Around the Park" bus, 69, 110; beaches, 109–10; Children's Farm Yard, 110, 197; cycling, 153; getting to, 105; history of, 5, 7, 104–5; jogging in, 108–10; Kids Traffic School, 109–10, 198; Lost Lagoon, 104, 109; map, 106–7; miniature train, 110, 198; pitch and putt, 109, 159, 198; playground, 109–10, 198; pool, 171, 198; restaurants, 42, 48, 109, 110; seawall, 108–10,; Siwash Rock, 109; tennis, 109, 172; Theatre Under the Stars, 110; totem poles, 108, 198; trees, 105; Vancouver Aquarium, 111, 196–97; walks, 108–10, 120
Starbucks espresso bars, 49
Steam clock, 45, 98
Stern-Wheeler boat, 96, 200
Steveston, 95, 100
Sugar refinery, Rogers, 99

Sunset Inn, 27
Sunshine Coast: buses to, 71; ferries, 77;
    fishing, 158
Sun Yat-sen Garden, Dr, 82, 91, 102–3
Surrey, 5, 37–38
Sushi, 59
Sutton Place Hotel, 21
Swimming, 171–72, 199, 200
Sylvia Hotel, 28–29
Symphony of Fire, 93
Synagogue, Beth Israel, 15
Szechuan Chongqing restaurant, 51

Take-out food, gourmet, 190–91
Taxes, 15, 79
Taxis, 72
Teahouse Restaurant, 48, 109
Telephone area codes, 12
Television stations, 17–18
Temple, Buddhist, 29, 131
Tennis, 85, 172–73, 213, 220, 216, 228
Terra Breads bakery/restaurant, 43–44
Thai: food stores, 191; restaurants, 61
Theatre, 85, 100, 136–40
Theatresports, 140
Theatre Under the Stars, 110, 139
Tojo's restaurant, 59
The Tomahawk restaurant, 41, 204
Tony's Neighbourhood Deli, 44–45
Topanga Café, 60, 204
Totem poles, 108, 124, 125, 198
Tourists: information, 13; RCMP alert, 12
Tours: by air, 93–94; by boat, 87–88, 95–96;
    by bus, 95; on foot, 82–87, 88, 89–93,
    96–98, 99; horse and carriage, 98;
    nightclub, 147; special interest, 99; by taxi,
    99; by train, 87–89
Towing companies, 13
Town and Country Bed and Breakfast
    Registry, 33
Toy stores, 206
Traffic regulations, 12–13
Trailer parks, 36–38
Trains, 7, 72–74, 82, 87–89, 127, 199, 223–24
Transportation, 66–80. *See also* Airport; Buses;
    Cars; Ferries; Helicopters; Highways; Public
    transit; Trains
Transportation museum, 131–32
Travel: accessories, 178; bookstores, 181;
    information, 13
Trees, 105, 120–21
TRIUMF, 91
Tsawwassen, 5, 37, 74–75, 77
24-hour services, 16
2400 Motel, 30

Universities. *See* Simon Fraser University;
    University of British Columbia
University of British Columbia:
    accommodation, 32; Anthropology,
    Museum of, 124–25; Aquatic Centre, 172;
    art gallery, 133; Bookstore, 181; Botanical
    Garden, 113–14; with children, 200; cycling
    in, 155; Endowment Lands, 114–15; golf,
    158–59; history, 7; Nitobe Garden, 112–13;

tennis courts, 173; tours, 99

Vancouver, Capt George, 5, 8
Vancouver Art Gallery, 132–33
Vancouver East Cultural Centre, 139–40
Vancouver Museum, 127
Vancouver Symphony Orchestra, 138, 141
Vanier Park, 125–28
Vassilis Taverna, 57
Veterinarians, 12
VIA Rail, 72
Victoria: by airplane, 80; by bus and ferry, 71,
    76; by car and ferry, 74–75
Vij's Restaurant, 55–56
Villa del Lupo restaurant, 58

Walking tours, 82–87, 88, 89–93, 96–98, 99.
    See also Hiking
Wall Centre Garden Hotel, 21
Walter Gage Residence, 32
Waterfront Centre Hotel, 22
Waterfront Theatre, 140
Water parks, 85, 197–98, 200
Water St Café, 45
Weather, 9–10
Wedgewood Hotel, 23
West End, 2, 7; accommodation, 26;
    restaurants, 64
West End Guest House, 27
West Vancouver: accommodation, 30–31;
    getting to, 3, 5 67–69; parks and recreation,
    117–18, 159, 161, 200; restaurants, 64
Westin Bayshore Hotel, 26–27
Whales, 76, 111
Wheat Pool, Alberta, 99
Whistler, 221–23; accommodation, 224–25;
    map, 222; recreation, 226–28; restaurants,
    225–26; skiing, 166–67, 169–70;
    transportation to, 223–24
White Rock, 13, 37
William Tell restaurant, 54–55
Windsurfing, 173
Wine: B.C., 61; liquor stores, 16; festival, 100
Women in View Festival, 99
Won More Szechuan restaurants, 51–52
Writers Festival, Vancouver, 100

Yaletown, 176–77, 184
YWCA Hotel, 24–25